*Word's*
**OUT**

# Word's
# *OUT*

*Gay Men's English*

William L. Leap

 University of Minnesota Press

Minneapolis

London

Published by the University of Minnesota Press
111 Third Avenue South, Suite 290, Minneapolis, MN 55401-2520
Book design by Will H. Powers
Typesetting by Stanton Publication Services, Inc.
Graffiti by the University Avenue Gang, St. Paul
Printed in the United States of America on acid-free paper
**Second printing 1997**
LIBRARY OF CONGRESS CATALOGING-IN-PUBLICATION DATA

Leap, William.
     Word's out : gay men's English / William L. Leap.
        p.     cm.
     Includes bibliographical references (p.     ) and index.
     ISBN 0-8166-2252-3 (hardcover). — ISBN 0-8166-2253-1 (pbk.)
        1. Gay men—United States—Language (New words, slang, etc.)
     2. English language—Social aspects—United States.    3. English
     language—United States—Slang.    4. Americanisms.    I. Title.
PE3727.G39L43    1996
427'.973'086642—dc20                                            95-35967

The University of Minnesota is an
equal-opportunity educator and employer.

# Contents

# *Examples*

# Acknowledgments

When I started writing this book, lesbian–gay language research was not a visible theme in anthropology, sociolinguistics, or gender studies. I am happy to report that these conditions have changed. I want to thank Ellen Lewin, Esther Newton, Glorianne Leck, Birch Moonwomon, Kira Hall, Anna Livia Braun, Martin Manalansan, Norris Lang, Ralph Bolton, Doug Feldman, Michael Clatts, David Bergman, and Gil Herdt for the enthusiasm (and criticism) they have given to this project, especially when others were less supportive of the endeavor.

Colleagues at The American University (Washington, D.C.)—particularly Brett Williams, Elizabeth Sheehan, Lesley Gill, Geoff Burkhart, Ruth Morgan, Mindy Michels, Alan Hersker, Christian Mendenhall, and Greg Lewis—have supported my study of gay language–culture themes by listening to oral summaries of new ideas, reading drafts of papers and book chapters, and providing new references and new research data. I am fortunate to work in an academic environment that treats lesbian–gay studies so positively.

Ellen Lewin, Ralph Bolton, and Gil Herdt made helpful comments on the prospectus for this book. Gil gave the almost-final manuscript a very close read and suggested a series of helpful adjustments, most of which I incorporated into the final text. Janaki Bakhle, my editor at the University of Minnesota Press, nurtured this project unselfishly for several years, and I have benefited immeasurably from her sound advice and guidance. Jeff Moen and others at the University of Minnesota Press smoothed over many a wrinkle during the production process, as did the copy editor, Kathy Delfosse.

And thank you, Angui, for your usual "everything."

# INTRODUCTION

## Studying Gay Men's English

My purpose in writing this book is to explore some of the ways in which gay men in the United States use English in everyday life and to demonstrate that Gay English is an important and valuable component of gay experience in those contexts. I am interested in the stereotypic varieties of Gay English: for example, the catty, bitchy dialogue associated with Matt Crowley's *Boys in the Band*; the self-absorbed linguistic play during "cruising"; and the code words that confirm gay identity during informal conversations between strangers in public places. But I am also interested in gay men's use of English when they have a quiet evening at home with close friends or interact with colleagues and friends, gay and straight, on the job, at a restaurant, or in a shopping mall.

Luce Irigaray has noted that to speak as a woman is to speak from a certain place and to a certain audience (1985: 135, 136). I will show here that to speak (English) as a gay man also involves notions of action, place, and audience. The politics of speaking are different, of course. Men, including gay men, have access to opportunities in U.S. society in ways that are not available to women, and gay men's constructions of texts reflect that privilege. But privilege—as well as a (not always implicit) sexism—does not make Gay English any the less real (or any the less important) for the men who use it. Acquiring Gay English is central to gay socialization and to the "coming out" process. Gay English fluency provides a range of formats for cooperative conversation between gay friends, and it lessens the risks inherent in self-disclosure during conversations with strangers.

### Defining the Subject Matter

Precise definitions are problematic for any project in lesbian and gay studies, and as will become the case here, terminology often becomes the underlying concern of the whole enterprise. So at this point, let me simply say that Gay English, in the sense in which I use this label, refers to a distinctive, gendered approach (actually, an aggregate of approaches) to oral, written, and signed text making.[1] Gay English texts may include a specialized vocabulary or may be rich in male homoerotic content, but fluency in Gay English involves more than a personal familiarity with those words and phrases. Similarly, while the speakers (or writers or signers) of Gay English are, in the main, gay or gay-identified men, other people also talk (or write or sign) Gay English — or claim the ability to recognize Gay English whenever they encounter it.

If Gay English cannot be defined in terms of topic or gender category, what is the cornerstone of its definition? Initially, I hoped to answer that question with a list of structural features, in the same way that others have used such features to highlight unique properties of grammar and discourse in other varieties of American English (Smitherman 1977; Baugh 1983; Lakoff 1975). And to some extent, I have been successful in developing such an inventory (see chapters 3 and 4). Isolating and classifying linguistic features soon proved to be disruptive to my research interest, however, because the significance of these features lies in their connections to other forms of social practice — in this case, to the social practices that define and delimit gay experience in U.S. society — and cannot be assessed in isolation.

Frank Browning (1993) characterizes gay experience in terms of a "culture of desire." Judith Butler (1990) writes about connections between gay gender and performativity. Eve Sedgwick (1993) places shame at the center of queer experience. All three observations offer useful ways of describing the importance of Gay English discourse in gay men's lives: that is, Gay English as a language of desire, as a format for performative display, and as a release from shame. In this book, I add at least two other descriptions to this list: Gay English as cooperative discourse and Gay English as a language of risk, both of which also position gay language squarely within gay practice.

Cooperative discourse and language of risk are not necessarily unique to Gay English discourse. But desire, shame, or performance are not exclusively gay provinces, either. The fact that these features are shared does not lessen their significance for gay experience, and the purpose of this inquiry is to account for that significance. Besides, definitions do not need to claim uniqueness or exclusivity as much as they need to establish a sense of the terrain within which subsequent inquiry will proceed. Defining Gay English as an aggregate of distinct, gendered approaches to text making that are closely connected to other forms of social practice in gay experience certainly meets that goal, if only by raising additional questions about approaches to text making, about connections between language and social practices, and about the content of those social practices themselves.

### Establishing a Point of View

My goal throughout this project has been to present an informative, well documented, and balanced description of Gay English as I have come to understand it through my research. But it has been difficult for me to remain entirely objective about these interests. Gay English is a part of my own linguistic repertoire, learning Gay English was an important part of my life "inside the closet" (academically and socially), and maintaining Gay English fluency has been even more important for my life as an openly gay man. I have observed uses of language similar to those described in this book while entertaining friends in my own apartment, while attending dinner parties in other homes, while teaching and being part of committee meetings on my university campus, and during my visits to bars, restaurants, and other gay locales. I have watched as others have participated and reacted to Gay English text making in these settings, and I have also observed my own involvement in such text making and my reactions to those texts.

Such personal associations with the subject matter unavoidably reach deeply into data gathering and analysis and color the process of interpretation and representation that translates research findings into books like this one. Accordingly, while I have drawn (and heavily so, at times) on the writings of colleagues in linguistics, anthropology, and gender studies throughout this research, I have framed much of this discussion in terms of my own observations, discoveries, and frustrations.

### Discovering the Research Topic

Although I have been surrounded by Gay English for most of my adult life and I have used it in personal conversation and for other purposes on a daily basis, Gay English has only been a focus for my scholarly research since 1988. Prior to that time, my linguistic interests centered around American Indian languages, bilingual education programs for American Indian schools and communities, and the unique varieties of English spoken by American Indians and Alaska Natives living in reservation, rural, and urban settings. By working in Indian country, I learned at firsthand about the relationships between language, social context, and historical tradition, relationships that became central themes in my writing, in my teaching, and in other components of my professional career.

The realities of the AIDS pandemic prompted my shift from American Indian studies into gay research. People were living with AIDS, people were dying, people were doing what they could to help their friends, people were indifferent to their own HIV status, and people were struggling to develop a language that could convey thoughts and feelings in the face of uncertainty, hope, and fear.

I wondered how people could talk about HIV concerns when the tone of the conversations was so nonneutral and when there was no agreement even about appropriate terminology or styles of references for such discussions. (Indeed, during the first years of the pandemic, there was not even consensus regarding the correct way to label this phenomenon.) So I began studying the linguistic features relevant to face-to-face discourse on AIDS. I found regularities in that discourse that cut across specific conversations, some of which I describe in chapter 8. More important, I found indications that gay men were using their "language of AIDS" in a way that was somewhat different from the way other speakers of English spoke about AIDS, and these contrasts prompted me to wonder whether the distinguishing features of these conversations were also present when gay men talked about other, less menacing themes.

The development of a general education program at my university gave me a new teaching assignment, a survey course entitled Sex, Gender, and Culture. Assembling materials for discussion of language and gender prompted additional questions about Gay English. I found ample treatment of women's languages in the scholarly journals and popular press, but I found many fewer sources focusing directly on language-and-gender issues directly relevant to lesbians and gay men. These papers mainly discussed gay-oriented vocabulary. They said almost nothing about other components of language-related knowledge and skill, things comparable to the turn taking, narrative style, cohesion, and avoidance of interruptions now documented for "women's English." Yet these were the very issues that I wanted to discuss—for lesbians, gay men, heterosexual women, and heterosexual men—when I talked with my students about language and gender.

My first efforts to explore gay language themes on my own were quite modest. I asked colleagues in anthropology and linguistics, students, and friends outside of academe to share their thoughts on gay language and its place within the arenas of gay experience known to them. I found, to my delight, that the men with whom I talked were very interested in discussing these themes and had many language-centered anecdotes (either from their own experience or from the experiences of others) that they were eager to share. Comments from those conversations gave me some new ways to look at communication patterns in gay bars, in restaurants, and in other settings where language was a critical component of gay interaction. I quickly realized that I could find moments of Gay English discourse at the supermarket, in department stores, on airplanes, in health club locker rooms—in almost any setting where I took the time to look for it.

At first, studying Gay English was something I did in my spare time or when I wanted a break from Indian language and Indian English research or from other, more traditionally academic tasks. But in fall 1989, I received a telephone call from a former student, working at a health club in the D.C. suburbs, who told me that men were having sex with other men in the club locker room, that some clients had complained about the impropriety of that action, and that most of the complaints had come from gay clients (her term), and not from straight clients (also her term). Why, I wondered, were gay men objecting to cosexual erotics in this setting? To answer that question, and to address the many issues connected to it, I began a detailed analysis of men's interpersonal communication in health club settings, focusing on how a gay-centered knowledge of English affects the process and content of communication between gay men and between gays and straights in those domains. I found recurring patterns in gay men's uses of English that, as was the case for the "language of AIDS," conflicted in interesting ways with the patterns attested in the English of heterosexual men. But working systematically within specific sites also helped me identify areas of diversity within both gay and straight English; among other things, this discovery forced me to use categories like "gay" and "straight" more cautiously when writing up my research findings.

I reported on all of this research at several academic conferences and in public lectures, and the positive responses that these presentations received encouraged me to focus my plans for a sabbatical leave during the 1991–1992 academic year exclusively around a Gay English research agenda. Much of the material discussed in this volume grows out of research activities during that sabbatical year, although the work I have done since that time and my reading of the ever growing body of theory in lesbian and gay studies have helped me recast and enrich earlier statements of findings.

Also influential in the preparation of this manuscript has been the support that this work has received from colleagues in anthropology, linguistics, and gender studies. Indeed, I have been pleased to discover that other scholars are trying to apply lesbian and gay perspectives to linguistic research and to carve out new areas of interest within "language and gender" studies. Many of these scholars came together for a one-day conference on Lavender Languages and Linguistics that was held on the campus of the American University during the April 1992 march on Washington, D.C., for Lesbian, Gay, and Bisexual equal rights and liberation. They have continued to meet for follow-up discussions since then, and they return to the Lavender Language conferences now held annually on our campus.

Particularly gratifying has been the number of younger scholars who have become interested in these questions, and who hope to make lesbian and gay language research a central theme in their own career development. Talking to all of these people about my ideas and hearing how they are pursuing similar themes has helped me reposition many of my initial thoughts about Gay English. These conversations also assure me that—unlike the case in earlier times—heterosexual discourse is no longer the only voice that defines and rewards "appropriate" linguistic research inside and outside of academe.

### Assumptions about Language

My studies of Gay English build directly on my twenty-plus years of work with American Indian languages and specifically on my work with the American Indian English used in reservation schools and other tribal and community settings. My earliest attempts to account for these language varieties used word and sentence structures as a basis for interpreting reference and meaning. But as I became more familiar with the intricacies of these codes and listened more closely to Indian English conversations and narratives in schools, homes, council meetings, and other speech settings, I realized that such accounts required a broader database than syntactic structure alone. It was helpful, for example, to explore the contexts of language use, the linguistic backgrounds of both speaker and hearer, their socioeconomic statuses, their tribal affiliations and enrollment statuses, and the topic and function of the speech event. It was also helpful to consider how speaker and listener assumptions about appropriate speech affected language choice and how such choices influenced details of word and sentence structure.

The results of this inquiry led to a study of Indian English centering around two separate but interconnected themes.[2] First, there was Indian English grammar, that is, the speakers' knowledge of form (syntax), reference (semantics), and context-marking strategies (pragmatics) specific to particular Indian English codes. Second, there was Indian English discourse, the speakers' construction and interpretation of oral or written messages, as guided by their linguistic knowledge and knowledge from other social and cultural sources.

This distinction between grammar and discourse has become quite helpful to my Gay English research, and I use it to focus discussions of linguistic structure and usage in each of the following chapters. In addition, again as I did in my Indian English research, I have found it helpful to distinguish discourse (that is, a generalized use of language by an aggregate of speakers) from the texts that particular speakers construct within specific settings and for particular purposes.

Text making may be a completely idiosyncratic activity, but more commonly text making builds on the rules of grammar and discourse processes that are shared by a group of speakers—persons that linguists refer to as members of the same speech community. In other words, text making is a form of social practice, and as such it may coincide with or disrupt other social practices that are also relevant to the particular site.

Texts are products of social practice, but they never provide "all there is to say" on any topic or theme. Instead, texts contain comments that speakers consider to be appropriate to the discussion of the topic at hand, given what has already been said on that topic in the speech setting and the assumptions underlying the discourse of which this text is a part. As M. A. K. Halliday explains, "Text represents choice. A text is 'what is meant,' selected from the total set of options that constitute what can be meant. In other words, text can be defined as actualized meaning potential" (1978: 109).

Halliday's reference to choice has important implications for the analysis of Gay English texts. Choice implies intentionality—that is, speakers expect that the texts they construct will convey intended messages, and they organize the details of text construction in terms of those expectations. Listeners are also guided by sets of intentions, and whether they interpret text messages along the same lines as speakers or in entirely different terms depends on other negotiations (and, at times, contestation) surrounding the text-making process.

Text-as-choice also affirms that meaning is not inherent in text but is instead a product of situated, social action that must be studied accordingly.

Text-as-choice also underscores the need to examine the form of the text as well as the multiple interpretations assumed by its content. Features such as the sequence of topics in a narrative or a conversation, the syntax of specific sentences or paragraphs, the use of turn taking and interruptions, and the placement of pauses display the participants' attempts to coconstruct meaning during each segment of the speech event and provide other insights into the social practices that occurred within the setting.[3]

### Assumptions about Gender

Gender studies is a relatively new addition to my research agenda. Prior to my work with Gay English, I had paid very little attention to language–gender themes in any speech setting. This is an embarrassing admission, but I am not the only researcher in my generation who has been negligent in this regard. As Sherry Ortner and Harriet Whitehead have observed, most of us have simply assumed that "male and female are predominantly natural objects rather than cultural constructions" (1981: 1) and that we "know" in some sense "what men and women are" before we begin our research.

Particularly important in anthropological discussions of gender (as in studies of gender in other academic fields) has been the idea that genders are socially constructed categories that give cultural representation to the biological differences between female and male. Language figures prominently in such representations for at least three reasons: First, gender categories are labeled categories, and gender may be marked in other areas of grammatical structure. Second, gender is one of the social variables governing linguistic diversity within speech communities. And third, what people can and cannot say about gender is always strictly regulated by rules of linguistic discourse.

Language-oriented perspectives on gender also draw attention to the variability associated with meanings of female and male in all societies. The close ties between systems of gender and systems of opportunity, privilege, and power in human societies help explain the conditions of variability and the linguistic features that women and men use to describe it in each case.

Opportunity, privilege, and power are themselves socially constructed and can be modified, in varying degrees, through social practice. Other social variables—such as age, ethnicity, race, kinship ties, occupation, and ritual obligations—mediate ties between gender and power and ensure that genders have multiple representations across social groups and across the life course of the individual.

Not addressed in these claims about gender and power are questions about erotic interests and practices and more general notions of desire. Language-oriented research offers useful perspectives on these concerns, as I will discuss in the following chapters.

### Studying the English of Certain Gay Men

During my studies of American Indian languages and American Indian English, I developed an inventory of skills in language-oriented data gathering and analysis, and most of these skills proved to be equally valuable for Gay English research.[4] Particularly important were verbatim note-taking techniques (especially when conversations needed to be transcribed discreetly in public places), interviewing on culturally sensitive subjects (particularly when an interview concerned issues that respondents may never have put into words before), managing focus-group discussions, and conducting context-specific observations of speech situations in which I was also a participant.

From a technical point of view, Gay English research did not force me to confront any data-gathering problems that my previous research experiences had not prepared me to resolve. However, studying Gay English did present some unfamiliar questions in other areas.

I had never had a problem identifying "the speakers" of American Indian languages or related Indian English codes. Tribal enrollment requirements, residence on the reservation, family and clan membership, allegiance to social, political, or ceremonial responsibilities, and other factors provided the criteria that distinguished members of American Indian communities from those not considered to be part of the community structure. And although fluency in American Indian English was never defined very precisely, I only had to listen to a person's English to determine if he or she should be included in the research sample.

As I have already suggested, however, *speakers of Gay English* is itself a diverse and fluid social category, and even though those speakers may share familiarity with forms of gay practice and the linguistic representations that those forms command, they may have little else in common. Age, gender, ethnicity, national origin, occupation, residence pattern, and the like, the variables that structure the conditions of social and linguistic diversity for speakers of other varieties of English, are also relevant here. To make my project workable, I needed to specify the segments within this inclusive grouping with which I intended to work.

I decided to concentrate exclusively on the English of gay men and not to include the English of lesbians in this project. This decision did not, and does not, reflect my disinterest in Lesbian English research; in fact, there are several issues related to that code that I find quite intriguing.

Particularly important here is the idea that, because language as such is heavily permeated with patriarchal values and frames of reference, "lesbian language" simply cannot exist (e.g., Hoagland 1988: 13-20; and also Spender [1980] 1987: esp. 1-6, who applies this argument to "women's language" as a whole). Other lesbian scholars present different perspectives on this question (such as Diana Fuss's [1989: 55-72] critique of Irigaray's *parler femme*) or offer explicit strategies for undermining patriarchal discourse and restoring women's control over voice (e.g., Penelope 1990: 211 ff.). At issue here are the same questions about language, gender, and power that were orienting my studies of Gay English, and reviewing lesbian scholarship on this theme made me eager to develop a gay critique of these themes.[5] But before I could do that, I had to become more familiar with the politics of language relevant to Gay English grammar and discourse, and that required a research focus that centered on Gay English text making—or, in effect, working within my own speech community, in speech settings and with language skills that were already accessible to me.

Nothing like that had been possible when I studied Indian languages and Indian English. In fact, anger over ancestral language loss, distrust of non-Indians, and other factors had restricted my involvement in Indian language conversations, even in reservation or community settings where I felt quite at home. Moreover, since I was always an outsider and had no legitimate reason to claim space within the speech community, each time I returned to one of the reservations I was forced to justify my research activities to Indian friends and to opponents.[6]

Studying Gay English—and concentrating specifically on the English of gay men—gave me the chance to do fieldwork in much less alienating domains. Certainly, there were always some gay men who objected to my work, questioned my research findings, or challenged my right to pursue these issues in the first place. But those reactions were coming from members of my own speech community, so I could respond to those reactions as a community member rather than as an outsider. If anything, "outsider" was now a status reserved for heterosexual skeptics, and I was the one imposing the category, not the one suffering under its weight.

Studying Gay English in terms of my own speech community did impose some limits on this project. For example, the primary participants in this project were likely to come from one of two groups:

1. gay men from my own age bracket and ethnic or social background (Euro-American men, over forty and under sixty [to word the issue discreetly], employed in middle-level management, academic, or social service jobs); and
2. gay college students (typically eighteen-to-twenty-five-year-old men from Euro-American, African American, and Latin American backgrounds).

For a time, working primarily with persons from these two categories seemed somewhat arbitrary, especially given the range of persons associated with the label "gay" in U.S. society and the need for gay scholars to affirm the polyvocal quality of gay voice, not erase it. My studies of gay language socialization (chapter 8 reviews some of these findings) convinced me that gay men in these two categories occupy quite different places in gay cultural history; that discovery made these restrictions somewhat easier to justify.

Deciding to work within accessible sites and with accessible persons also helped me resolve some problems in the selection of research sites. Initially, I planned to work only in two locales: gay bars (specifically, a cocktail lounge in the Dupont Circle area frequented by gay men in the "over forty" category) and gay churches (specifically, the weekly mass and social hour of a predominantly gay Roman Catholic congregation, whose meetings also occur in the Dupont Circle area). By choosing only two sites, I hoped to become familiar with the dynamics of communication in its settings through frequent visits and informal on-site interviewing, then to begin describing and recording specific forms of verbal interaction relevant to particular activities that occurred there. This was the game plan guiding John Read's (1980) study of a gay bar in Seattle, Washington, Edward Delph's (1978) exploration of the rules of silence in gay interpersonal communication, and Joseph Goodwin's (1989) assessment of the functions of folklore in middle-American gay life.

Once fieldwork began in earnest, I found that I did not need to restrict myself so rigidly. Washington, D.C. has a large gay community, and it is difficult to find an arena in this city where some form of gay presence is not visible, even if "gay presence" is restricted solely in terms of my two targeted categories. In effect, I could observe Gay English text making in any location where gay men were present, whether they were interacting with other gay men or with persons in mixed-gender settings. Pursuing a data-gathering plan that drew widely on local opportunities for speaking seemed to be the wiser course of action under these circumstances, and the mixture of speaking domains discussed in this book suggests the scope that this inquiry ultimately assumed.

I realized, of course, that Washington, D.C.'s gay community is not typical of gay communities found elsewhere in the United States, and the data for my study of Gay English could not be drawn exclusively from speech settings found within the D.C. area. To remedy this situation, I decided to integrate Gay English–related research tasks into my plans for professional and personal travel. For example, I asked friends in other cities to take me to what they considered to be more interesting sites and facilities within their gay communities. And when I was alone, I used my own intuition (what my younger gay friends term "gaydar") to locate potentially productive research locales.

Recent studies on gay culture and collections of gay men's life-story narratives also helped me place my D.C.-based research data into broader perspective, and so did short stories and novels describing gay life in urban and rural settings.[7] Indeed, contemporary gay fiction contains some of the best

ethnographic data on gay men's culture in America, and it certainly offers
wonderful insights into Gay English.

### An Overview of This Book

This book, a first-person scholarly narrative, is a summary of research findings and a blueprint for the work I hope to do for the next few years. I begin
the discussion (chapter 1) with some questions about authenticity in Gay
English discourse, in effect asking what features a text must contain in order
to be considered a Gay English text.

The next two chapters look closely at the cooperative nature of Gay English discourse. Chapter 2 explains why cooperative text making is important
to gay experience; chapter 3 describes some of the strategies that gay men
build into their text making to ensure that discourse is suitably cooperative.

Chapter 4 shifts focus from gay-friendly conversations to conversations
that occur outside of gay-centered speech settings. Here, using Gay English
involves certain risks, and Gay English texts have to address those risks in
certain ways. Chapter 5 balances risk taking against another set of considerations, equally relevant to gay men's daily experiences: the creation of gay
"space" in the midst of places that are not otherwise likely to be responsive
or sympathetic to gay men's concerns. Chapter 6 continues this discussion
by describing the complex set of negotiations surrounding male-homo-
erotic discourse in a health club locker room; contrasts between Gay English and other men's English in this setting underscore the difficulties that
researchers face when they confuse gender with erotic practice.

Chapter 7 shifts focus and explores the ways in which the acquisition of
Gay English contributes to a young person's socialization into gay culture
and acceptance of a gay identity. Chapter 8 looks at another issue relevant
to contemporary gay experience: the AIDS pandemic and the effects that HIV
illnesses are having on our lives.

The conclusion returns to the initial discussion of authenticity, recasting
the concerns raised in chapter 1 in terms of recent claims about performativity and other concerns about the language that queer theory inspires.

# 1

## Can There Be Gay Discourse without Gay Language?

On a Friday evening in June, I was standing in a Dupont Circle bookstore–sidewalk café, near the center of what some people describe as Washington, D.C.'s "gay ghetto."[1] This bookstore-café does not claim to be a "gay business," though gay men are always a prominent part of the clientele. The place was crowded, as it always is on weekends, especially in the summertime. I was with friends that evening, standing in the foyer of the café waiting for a table, and I was listening to a forty-two-year-old man as he inquired about seating in the café for a mixed-gender group of five. A man in his midtwenties was acting as the café's maitre d' that evening. Example 1.1 displays my transcription of their conversation.

I had noticed speaker A and his party when they first entered the bookstore, and I watched as he and his friends browsed through the book collections on their way to the café. The maitre d' was away from the podium at that time and returned to his station just before speaker A approached the café foyer. I cannot say if these men had exchanged eye contact or pursued other forms of nonverbal communication prior to the start of their spoken conversation; however, given the layout of the bookstore, the maitre d's initial absence from his work station, and speaker A's active participation in conversation with the rest of his party, I consider such preluding unlikely.

My first reaction to this exchange was to consider it as an instance of serious cruising. That is, the two men considered each other to be potential sex partners and were using this conversation to negotiate an erotic liaison or, at least, to begin arrangements to that end. A cruising subtext helps account for the overtly sexual references that the speakers included at the end of the conversation, comments that would have been inappropriate had this simply been a business exchange: for example, A's reference to dessert drinks (dessert often provides a prelude to other activities) in line 13 and B's paraphrase of Mae West's classic expression, "Why don't ya' come up and see me sometime," in lines 14-15.

---

**Example 1.1** But you people are more fun. (Source: WLL field notes; setting: bookstore-café in Dupont Circle, Washington, D.C.)

1    A: Table for five—how long do we wait?
2    B: Table for five. [*Pauses, consults list*] About one hour.
3    A: One hour. [*Consults with group*] Nope, can't do it. That
4       is too long.
5    B: Try the Mocha House. They might not be too crowded
6       tonight.          ⤷ popular meeting place for gay men
7    A: Yeah, OK, we can go there. But you people are more
8       fun.
9    B: Well, I don't know about that. [*While he says this, moves*
10      *head to side, drops voice level, gives trace of smile*]
11   A: Yeah, you're right. [*Establishes direct eye contact*
12      *with maitre d'*] Maybe the Mocha House is more fun,
13      but I still like your dessert drinks here.
14   B: [*Not breaking eye contact*] Well, you'll just have to
15      come back and try us again sometime.

---

Examined more carefully, however, erotic references and other cruising strategies become only one of several components within the design of this conversation. First, there is the opening exchange (lines 1-4), which could occur in an exchange between customer and service personnel in any restaurant setting, whatever the participants' gender or erotic interests. Then, there are the two episodes within the body of the text—the maitre d's recommendation of an alternative café (lines 5-6) and speaker A's indications of preferences for the present site (lines 7-8 and 11-13). Both of these episodes appear to be gender-neutral at first reading but are actually quite rich in gay-centered, gendered messages. Let us look more closely at the linguistic details in both episodes.

The maitre d's suggestion of an alternative café (lines 5-6) appears to be an effective form of customer relations—particularly so, given that the maitre d' had no other way to respond promptly to speaker A's request. But the Mocha House is located more than four blocks from the bookstore-café, and to get there, speaker A and his party would have had to pass several other cafés and coffee houses. So why did the maitre d' favor this site over other, more conveniently located facilities? And what did the maitre d's reference to the Mocha House add to this conversation?

For one thing, the Mocha House is located just around the corner from a street filled with gay-oriented businesses, and it is immediately adjacent to two of D.C.'s publicly identified gay–lesbian restaurants. Moreover, the Mocha House itself is a popular meeting place for gay men, especially during the summer months when the management opens the outside café. If speaker A were gay and familiar with the D.C. area, he would certainly recognize the maitre d's reference to an explicitly gay locale. This, in turn, would prompt him to listen for other gay-related messages in the maitre d's verbal and nonverbal language and allow him to infer—without the maitre d' addressing the issue explicitly—that the maitre d' himself is a gay man.

But besides being a gay-friendly environment, the Mocha House is also popular with heterosexual customers, who enjoy the good coffee and the opportunity for out-of-doors conversation. So although mentioning the Mocha House could establish a foundation for gay-centered exchange, it did not necessarily obligate the listener to think about the conversation—or about the maitre d' himself—in gay-specific terms.

Statements like the one in lines 5-6 are very common in Gay English conversations, especially when the speakers know very little about each other's personal backgrounds and interests. And how other participants respond to such statements helps determine how speakers will construct gendered messages in the next segment of the conversation.

Speaker A's response appears to disregard the reference to a gay-centered locale that the maitre d' offers in the preceding two lines. He notes that he prefers to have refreshments in the bookstore-café, not at the Mocha House, and by doing so, he appears to reject the clues to gay interest that can be inferred from the maitre d's comment.

At the same time, speaker A explains his preferences for the present locale by suggesting that the bookstore-café (that is, "you people," a personalizing of the site that he repeats with "your" in line 13) is "more fun" (lines 7-8). He says nothing more about the meaning of this term and he does not explain how it applies to the bookstore-café environment.

The maitre d', in turn, builds directly on the ambiguity in speaker A's reply and not on its rejection of gay message: "Well, I don't know about that," adding a sideways movement of his head and a drop in voice level that usually express skepticism in English conversations (lines 9-10). But the maitre d' also introduced a faint trace of smile into his package of nonverbal cues, and that prompted me (as third-party observer) to wonder whether the maitre d' was also inviting further discussion of this theme.

Speaker A responded directly to that invitation by withdrawing the "more fun" label from the bookstore-café and shifting it to the Mocha House. Then he added (line 13), "but I still like your dessert drinks here," which identified a point of contrast between the Mocha House and the bookstore-café (the Mocha House has no liquor license, whereas the book-store-café offers an assortment of beers, cocktails, and after-dinner specialty drinks) and suggested that the bookstore-café offers speaker A something that the Mocha House, even if it is more fun, is unable to provide. What that "something" might be, speaker A left unstated, but he punctuated his comment by fixing his gaze directly on the maitre d'.

This combination of verbal and nonverbal statements was much more forceful than any of the other statements in the text and provided the basis for the more elaborate and somewhat more gay-explicit version of "please come again" that the maitre d' used as his closing remark (lines 14-15).

There was nothing explicitly gay in either of these men's verbal state-ments or in their use of nonverbal communication. The exchange did, how-ever, contain features of text design and text construction that show up in other instances of gay-centered conversations and narratives, two of which—principles of cooperative discourse and language-based risk tak-ing—are especially important to the themes of this volume.

But are these features of text design and text construction really proper-ties of a specifically "gay language," or are they merely linguistic reflections of more inclusive properties of gay-centered social discourse?

If, for example, cooperative discourse, language of risk, and other fea-tures of text design are part of the grammatical skills—a gay-specific knowl-edge of language—that enable gay men to participate, as gay men, in situ-ated social exchange, then Gay English is substantially different from the English used by heterosexuals, lesbians, or men who acknowledge same-sex desire but are not familiar with other forms of gay cultural practice. Accord-ingly, fluency in Gay English depends on the speaker's acquisition of spe-cific forms of linguistic skill and on conscious efforts at skills maintenance and renewal.

If, on the other hand, features like cooperative discourse and language of risk are not necessarily language skills specific to Gay English at all but are representations of an interplay of power and social process informing gay experience across a variety of sites, then Gay English can still be a vi-able component of gay culture, but the contributions of Gay English to the integrity and authority of gay culture are somewhat less important. The uniqueness of Gay English (if in fact this is a unique variety of English at all) in this case derives from sources external to linguistic knowledge—

personal identity, speech context, content or topic of discussion — and gay language is a specialized vocabulary (or, at best, an inventory of idiom and metaphor). Accordingly, there is no need for researchers to take the details of linguistic form into account when exploring gay culture or gay communication. Moreover, the absence of a uniquely gay English suggests that gay resistance to heterosexual oppression is not a linguistically dependent form of social action; *any* variety of English can be a suitable format for such resistance, and any speaker of any variety of English can participate knowledgeably and with authority in its construction.

Certainly, debates over the "place" of language "at the site" of social experience and over the connections between language and social discourse are not restricted to studies of gay men's culture(s). The same issues regularly emerge in discussions of lesbian languages and of the contradictory status that such codes occupy in lesbian experience (Hoagland 1988; Penelope 1992: esp. 78-131), and they continue to be relevant to efforts to describe women-centered language skills (Lakoff 1975; Irigaray 1985: 135, 136; Belenky 1986; Tannen 1990, 1994). Unfortunately, the connections between language and social experience have not been addressed in previous studies of gay men's strategies for text making, verbal imagery, or verbal rhetoric (cf. the papers in Chesebro 1981, and Ringer 1994; Dynes 1985; Rogers 1972; and other descriptions of the gay lexicon). Delph (1978), Goodwin (1989), Read (1980), Warren (1974), and other gay ethnographers have taken the opposite tactic: They acknowledge the importance of language and other forms of communication in gay men's experience, but they pay only minimal attention to the rules of grammar and text construction on which such usage depends. Understandably, the designation "Gay English" is itself a relatively recent addition to the gay studies literature — and not a widely accepted category, at that.

### On Authenticity in Gay English Text

I propose to demonstrate the linguistic uniqueness of Gay English grammar and discourse by exploring *authenticity* in Gay English text making. That is, following Gilbert Herdt and Andrew Boxer (1991; 1993: 243-54), I want to show how Gay English speakers use language to distinguish between "what is genuine as opposed to spurious (fake) in gay men's world views and relationships" and to construct opportunities for social action that are "optimal, valuable, and life cherishing" (Herdt and Boxer 1993: 3).[2] And by doing so, I hope to show how themes of genuineness and value are as viable to Gay English grammar and discourse as are the themes of oppression, alienation, and same-sex desire that are more commonly associated with gay men's lives.

Let us consider examples 1.2 and 1.3 in this regard. These texts suggest the contrasts in text form and text content that recur throughout my Gay English database, and analyzing them together draws attention to several of the benefits and problems that grow out of text interpretation that focuses on Gay English authenticity.

---

**Example 1.2** "Gay insulting" at the dinner table. (Source: Murray 1979: 216-17; scene: during an after-dinner conversation. A and B are "recognized masters at producing exotic insults in quick repartee" [Murray 1979: 216] and have both been invited in hopes that they will demonstrate their talents. As this passage opens, the anticipated exchange has already begun.)

1     A: We can't afford to lose another sofa, Chapped Cheeks.
2     B: Your ass is so stretched you should put in a draw-string.
3     A: Word is you've had your dirt shute mack-tacked.
4     B: And you've wall-papered your womb.
5     A: Where do you find tricks who'll rim your colostomy?
6     B: You douche with Janitor in a Drum.
7     A: Slam your clam.
8     B: Slam it, cram it, ram it, oooo but don't jam it. [*Demonstrating*]
9     A: Cross your legs, you're showing your hemorrhoids.
10    B: You need to strap yours forward so you'll have a basket.
11    A: Better than back-combing my pubies, like you do. Preparation
12       H is a great lubricant.
13    B: This girl's hung like an animal—a tsetse fly.
14    A: Four bull dogs couldn't chew off this monster.
15    B: I don't think even a bulldog would want that in his mouth.
16       Besides, I've seen chubbier tits.
17    A: Peeking under the door in the washroom again?
         [*And the exchange continues*]

---

Example 1.2 comes from Steve Murray's article "The Art of Gay Insulting" (1979); example 1.3 is one of many texts that I have collected and analyzed during my own research. Both of these texts emerged in the context of all-gay dinner parties, that is, dinner parties in gay men's homes where all of the invited guests were gay. And in both cases, all participants in the text making—actors and audience—already knew each other prior to the beginning of the exchange.

Example 1.2, as Murray describes it, is part of a ritualized drama ("gay insulting," which Murray likens to instances of "playin' the dozens" in urban African American discourse). Both of the speakers in this example are experts at "insulting" and were invited to this party in hopes that they would engage in such an exchange for the entertainment of the other guests. As a review of this dialogue shows, the guests were certainly not to be disappointed in that regard.

Two characteristics are apparent: One is the persistent use of sexual and erotic reference, comments that suggest (on first reading at least) that gay experience is based in a shared "culture of desire." And another characteristic

---

**Example 1.3** What color is the brown water pitcher? (Source: WLL field notes; setting: an at-home dinner party, two hosts and six guests. Dinner has ended. One host [A] is washing dishes in the kitchen while other guests continue to chat in the dining room. A guest [B] moves into the kitchen to get some water.)

| 1 | B: | Can I get a glass of water? [*Moves toward sink where A* |
| 2 | | *is washing dishes*] |
| 3 | A: | There is ice water in the fridge. |
| 4 | B: | OK. Thanks. [*Opens refrigerator door, looks inside*] |
| 5 | A: | [*Notices pause in action*] In the brown pitcher. |
| 6 | B: | [*Continues to look; raises head toward A*] I don't see |
| 7 | | a brown pitcher in here. |
| 8 | A: | Sure. It's brown, and round, and on the top shelf. |
| 9 | B: | [*Looks inside again*] Nope. |
| 10 | A: | [*Stops washing dishes, dries hands, moves to fridge,* |
| 11 | | *removes pitcher, pours water*] |
| 12 | B: | That pitcher is not brown, it is tan. [*Pause; A remains* |
| 13 | | *silent*] It is light tan. |
| 14 | A: | It is brown to me. [*Slight smile*] |
| 15 | B: | No, you said brown; so I looked for something dark |
| 16 | | chocolate. |

---

is the persistence of woman-related imagery and metaphor, so much so that the progress of the entertainment appears to depend on the participants' willingness to create gay-centered text references at women's expense.

Example 1.3, on the other hand, contains no evidence of misogynist ritual. Rather, this was a spontaneous conversation between two friends, a guest at a sit-down dinner for eight and one of the hosts. The conversation took place after the meal had ended, while one host was washing dishes and the other and guests were in the living room enjoying spirited chitchat. The exchange began with a familiar guest-to-host request (a glass of water), shifted in a miscued discussion about the location of the water pitcher in the refrigerator, and ended with a debate over the correct way to identify the color of the water pitcher. As in example 1.2, strains of conflict contribute to text making here, but deliberately crafted insults were not exchanged directly at any point in this conversation.

It seemed tempting, when I began the analysis of these texts, to summarize these contrasts by arguing that example 1.2 (given its misogynist tone) is much less "optimal, valuable, and life cherishing" than is example 1.3, and hence that example 1.3 is a more "authentically gay" text. A more detailed review of this material, combined with discussions of their significance with other gay men, swiftly provided different ways to interpret these data.

For instance, example 1.2 does have a certain statistical authenticity, given that speakers A and B may resemble familiar stereotypes for some readers of this essay (the phrase "a bunch of bitchy queens" may already have come to mind, though that also associates negative value to women's behavior). The style of conversation may also be familiar to some readers, even though they recognize that they cannot construct text in similar terms themselves.

It is also possible that the woman-centered imagery in the text may not be an attack on women or action at women's expense so much as an attempt to depict the uniqueness of gay men's gender identity by reworking female imagery rather than recasting images associated with heterosexual males. Viewing such usage as a form of resistance does not excuse the misogyny, but it does help me account for it somewhat more easily.

Example 1.3 raises somewhat different problems in interpretation. Unlike example 1.2, with its familiar, gay-associated bitchy style, example 1.3 does not appear to be "gay" (in any essential sense) at all. My partner reminds me, for example, that this is a conversation that his parents could have standing in their kitchen in Puerto Rico. And Nora Ephron (1983: 20-21) provides interestingly similar dialogue (in an exchange centering around the question "Where's the butter?") to explain why "Jewish princes are made not born" (1983: 20).

Hence, example 1.3 may be authentic in some evaluative sense, but the distinctiveness of the text detail and the close connections to gay experience are anything but self-evident.

To move beyond these contrasts and conflicting interpretations, I decided to orient my analysis around a situated, actor-centered analysis of text construction.

To begin with, think of both of these texts as instances of cooperative discourse, instances in which a primary emphasis on mutually negotiated maintenance of text prompts speakers to curtail their use of divisive, disruptive, or agonistic commentary. Hence, while example 1.2 is certainly competitive, neither speaker tries to subjugate his opponent completely or to vanquish him from the text-making scene. Instead, both speakers work creatively and cooperatively to prolong the exchange and see how many different references each speaker can supply before the exchange, by mutual consent, comes to an end.

Example 1.3 shows similar concerns with cooperation and mutuality. There is also evidence of friction in this exchange, and the evidence becomes more apparent as the conversation progresses. Still, neither party allows disagreement to disrupt their communication. Hence, for example, speaker A introduces silence and nonverbal action at a strategic point in the conversation (lines 10-11) when prolonging the "yes it is—no it isn't" debate would have erupted into more serious consequences.

Speaker B shows similar concerns with text maintenance in his response to this comment. And by shifting discussion from "location of the pitcher" to "location of color" (lines 12-13), speaker B focuses the final segment of the conversation around a comical parody of the initial dispute, and ultimately (lines 15-16) he introduces an exaggerated parody of the parody. Speaker A supports speaker B in the resulting minstrelsy; in fact, speaker A ends up playing the "straight man" to speaker B's comic relief, further assuring that any lingering threat of disruption is dispelled.

Example 1.2 also contains ample instances of parody, minstrelsy, and exaggeration—consider lines 1, 5, 8, 11-12, and 16-17. Admittedly, the content of the wordplay unfolds at women's expense and alternative frames of reference could have been employed (such as example 1.3's exaggeration of the widely held belief that gay men are instinctively skilled at color recognition and other forms of interior design). Still, it is important not to lose sight of the process of wordplay evidenced here or of the speakers' uses of other components of grammatical skill. In effect, speakers in both examples are using Gay English to rework "verbal dueling" into something with special message and appeal to gay men and are thereby grounding the location of text making even more securely within gay experience. The text-making strategies may differ in these examples, but the consequences of text making—the transformation of place into space—are very much the same.

I want to mention one more area of similarity that these texts share. Not all instances of gay men's use of language will occur in private, protected, and gay-positive domains or in settings that (although ostensibly gender neutral) can easily be recast into gay space, through a judicious use of imagery and metaphor, without serious threat of controversy. In fact, much of gay discourse—in both its linguistic and social forms—unfolds in public domains, in settings in which the interlocutors' sexuality and erotic interests are not necessarily constructed in similar ways and in which gender itself may become a point of contestation and conflict.

Given such realities, Gay English grammar has to provide speakers with the language skills that will enable the maintenance of self, and assurances of safety, in nongay as well as gay environments. Fluency in the "language of the closet" is one viable option, under these circumstances; learning how to code gay messages within seemingly gender-neutral references (and how to identify and decipher messages that others have packaged in neutral terms) is another such option. Direct confrontation with oppressive heterosexuality is a third option, one that is becoming an increasingly popular gay discourse strategy in recent years.

Whatever the gay man's strategy of choice in any setting, all three options require the acquisition of specific linguistic skills, and all three require some opportunities for rehearsal. I want to suggest that both learning and rehearsal are taking place in the speech events displayed in examples 1.2 and 1.3. Each of these examples, while socially productive in their specific domain, show gay men using opportunities for gay-centered language development in safe havens for experimentation with these skills.

At issue here are the types of language skills that all of us, as gay people, may be called upon to employ—or may hope we will be able to employ—when confronted by homophobic or heterosexist discourse in the workplace, in the classroom, on the street corner, while visiting with family and friends, or while on vacation. I suggest that the audience fascination (and tolerance) with the give-and-take in example 1.2 can be explained, at least in part, by recasting this exchange as an instance of gay language socialization.

### Implications

My comparison of these two examples has identified text-making strategies that enable cooperative discourse between gay participants; that use imagery and metaphor to transform "neutral" place into gay space and draw on other grammatical strategies to ground text production in gay terrain; and that provide opportunities for rehearsal, so that participants will be able to transfer language skills from gay-positive to less-positive speech domains.

I suggest that any such text making speaks to authenticity in gay experience because it enables such seemingly ordinary, mundane, and offensive events in gay experience to become "optimal, valuable, and life cherishing," and to become opportunities for genuine rather than spurious social exchange.[3]

I use Herdt and Boxer's paraphrase of Sapir, but I do not intend to tie gay authenticity exclusively to those points of value. More relevant to my interests here are the transformation of experience that both instances of gay text making allowed and the affirmation of gay presence and gay distinctiveness that grows out of text making when conducted in such terms.

I realize that this is a somewhat different conclusion about language, gender, and authenticity than that reached by feminist scholars probing authenticity in women's voice. For example, Irigaray's discussion of what it means to "speak as woman" (1985) associates parler femme with uses of language when "women [are]-among-themselves," not when women are in "dominant language domains." Indeed, she explains, parler femme is appealing to women precisely because it provides an alternative to dominant language discourse and thereby offers women a means of placing themselves "at-distance-from" each time they construct discourse within such domains.

Alternativeness and separatism may provide the cornerstone for authenticity in parler femme. But gay language, as I have just explained, is ultimately constructed *in relation to*, not *at distance from*, socially dominant discourse. The fact that gay men are men, and therefore are aligned with dominant language interests even when we try to sabotage or conceal those alignments, helps account for this point of contrast. How Gay English speakers balance *in relation to* against authenticity in Gay English texts or whether *in relation to* is a form of authenticity itself remain issues for discussion in subsequent chapters.

# 2

---

## *Gay English as Cooperative Discourse*

---

The first time I really *listened* to Gay English was in Albuquerque, New Mexico, in 1969. I was sitting in a movie theater watching the film version of Matt Crowley's play *Boys in the Band*. I had already learned a few things about the folklore surrounding gay speech from high school locker-room conversations and joke telling, late night college dormitory conversations, and my few gay encounters while in graduate school. But before I saw this film, I had not been party to any type of sustained conversation (however artificially constructed) between gay men.

I was enchanted by the scenario displayed in that narrative—chic rooftop apartments in Manhattan, summers on Fire Island, a close circle of gay friends, meeting regularly for cocktails and clever conversation. I was also struck both by the creativeness of these men's verbal exchange and by the viciousness that colored its tone, and I was painfully aware that my own linguistic skills (whatever the setting) could never measure up to those standards of performance. Then I noticed that Hank, the recently divorced schoolteacher, was not very skilled in this regard, either. Perhaps teachers were somehow exempt from gay wordplay, I decided, so maybe it was a good thing that I, too, wanted to become a college professor.

Since that summer, I have been part of many conversations that duplicated the form and the flavor of Crowley's script; the dispute about the brown water pitcher in example 1.3 is one example, and I will introduce others. But I have also heard other "gay conversations" organized in terms of entirely different blueprints, such as those in examples 2.1 and 2.2.

Compared to example 1.3 (and certainly to Murray's transcription of after-dinner conversation in example 1.2), these conversations are less acidic in tone, and the turn taking and other forms of negotiation that they contain are much less competitive. Still, each of these conversations reflects its own version of "gay style." Some of the differences between them may be due to the differences in speech setting (example 2.1 occurred between strangers in the public area of a department store, whereas example 2.2 occurred among

---

**Example 2.1** Sweatshirts. (Setting: in the men's department at a large, suburban department store in the Washington, D.C. suburbs. On display on a large table are Champion sweatshirts in various colors, some of which are on sale. S [an African American man in his thirties] is folding sweatshirts and putting the display back in order as C approaches the table and begins looking through the merchandise. S sees C approach, turns, smiles, and the dialogue begins. [I was standing next to the table, looking through a rack of sale shirts, close enough to hear the conversation without intruding physically into the exchange.])

1    S: Can I help you find something?
2    C: No thanks, I am just looking.
3      [*Pause. S continues to fold and arrange the merchandise.*
4      *C continues to browse; both look discreetly at*
5      *each other; ten seconds pass*]
6    C: What are you asking for these? [*Points to one set of*
7      *grey sweatshirts*]
8    C: Oh. I'm afraid they're not on sale today. But that col-
9      ored shirt would look nice on you. [*Points to a pile*
10     *of lavender sweatshirts, which are on sale*]
11    C: Yeah, I know. I own a few of them already. [*Grins*]
12    S: [*Grins back; no verbal comment*]
13    C: Thanks for your help. [*C walks off*]

---

friends and in the privacy of a gay apartment), but setting cannot be the only factor shaping conversational form. Examples 1.2 and 1.3—very different from example 2.2 and different in some ways from each other—also took place among friends and in private homes.

Given how little we know about Gay English grammar and discourse, it is tempting to center my discussion of these conversations by listing and describing specific features of text form. But in order to account for the authenticity of these texts, the analysis needs to focus on the *significance of* textual features—that is, the contributions that these features make, individually and in conjunction with other components of the text, to the speakers' construction and exchange of meaning within this setting.

What Joseph Goodwin has termed the "double subjectivity of interpretation" (1989: 12) speaks directly to these interests. Goodwin noticed, through his studies of language and folklore in gay bar settings, that the messages people send are not always the messages people receive and that

---

**Example 2.2** The Irish come to America. (Setting: after dinner in a gay couple's apartment. S1 and S3 are the hosts; S2 is one of the guests; two other persons are also present, S2's partner and S4, but neither says anything during this exchange.)

| | |
|---|---|
| 1 | S1: Is it 9:00 yet? |
| 2 | S2: 9:00? |
| 3 | S1: I am going to watch *The Irish Come to America* on HBO |
| 4 | at 9:00. |
| 5 | S3: [*Preoccupied*] So many little bugs, there are so many |
| 6 | little bugs. |
| 7 | S1: Thank you for sharing that with us. |
| 8 | S2: What movie? |
| 9 | S1: The Irish movie. Big film. Made no money. With Tom |
| 10 | Cruise. |
| 11 | S3: Robert looks like Tom Cruise, don't you think? |
| 12 | S2: [*Said to S1 and S3, jointly*] I can't keep up with conversations |
| 13 | in your house. |

---

any number of contextual and interpersonal details may contribute to such interference during context-centered meaning exchange. Under such circumstances, meaning has to be "doubly subjective," he argued, "relying on both the sender and the receiver for parts of its content" (1989: 12). Listing and classifying jokes, vocabulary, life stories, and other types of gay bar-related language use, as he does throughout the volume, allowed him to identify the content relevant to mutually supportive message exchange in these settings. It also helped him understand how the confusion (his term) that often emerges in such cases can be "put to good advantage by groups [like gay men—WLL] seeking private means of interaction" (1989: 12), particularly in public settings.

"Double subjectivity" influences the organization of conversations in all of the examples discussed in chapter 1. Throughout the exchange of "gay insults" in example 1.2, both speakers were confronted with statements having more to do with contextualized politics than with the real-world references that the comments purported to describe. To participate effectively in this dialogue, each speaker had to assess the intended message of his opponent's preceding comment, then construct a comment that extended, exaggerated, and moved beyond his sense of the opponent's intentions.

The audience (which now includes the researcher and the reader) was also a party to double subjectivity in this case. The audience was expected to interpret the messages implicit in both speakers' use of metaphor while keeping track of the interpersonal politics being displayed and negotiated throughout the dialogue as a whole. Granted, those persons present at the dinner party (and for whose benefit this exchange was originally staged, as Murray observes [1979: 216]) could use their knowledge of speaker background to decipher some components of the text's coconstructed meaning. But they did not need biography to interpret comments like "You douche with Janitor in a Drum" (Example 1.2, line 6), "Cross your legs, you're showing your hemorrhoids" (line 9), or "I don't think even a bulldog would want that in his mouth" (line 15); more relevant here was an awareness of the contested themes of gender and power that permeate gay experience, an appreciation for the sense of theatrical performance underlying text making in this specific setting, and a willingness to interpret these statements in terms of context-specific references.

While the dialogue in the "dispute" over the brown water pitcher (example 1.3) may appear to have become acrimonious *(angry/bitter)* on initial reading (as it certainly did when I observed it), the participants were not involved in the kind of detailed verbal dueling that example 1.2 displayed. Instead, one speaker (the guest) was seeking services, and the other speaker (the host) was trying to provide them. And although the exchange began with a misunderstanding that continued to grow as the speakers tried to identify the source of the confusion (to use Goodwin's term), the speakers were willing to defuse the conflict rather than let the disagreement get completely out of hand.

Viewed strictly from the point of view of context, the conversation between salesman and customer in example 2.1 really did not need to occur. The customer declined the salesman's offer of help at the beginning of the dialogue (lines 1-2), since he appeared interested in browsing through the sweatshirt collection on his own. But even though his follow-up statement (line 6) retains the businesslike tone of his opening remarks, the salesman seems to have located a personal message in the statement, and addressed both messages in sequence in his reply: "Oh. I'm afraid they're not on sale today" (which speaks to the customer's question about cost) and "But that colored [lavender] shirt would look nice on you" (which, while equally service-oriented, also speaks to more gay-explicit interests). I am not certain if the customer intended line 6 to move the dialogue in both directions. But ↳*"what are you asking for these?"*

a double-subjective analysis of statement content could easily have led him to that conclusion, and once the salesman responded, the customer continued to develop the conversation along the same lines.

All the participants in example 2.2 had to be actively and personally involved in the exchange in order to maintain coherence in text construction. The omission of some areas of text content and the implicit, coded presentation of other content in other areas may make it difficult for an outsider to understand what the speakers are trying to accomplish here. And without being able to assume shared subjectivity, the participants themselves might also have lost focus.

### The Cooperative Nature of Gay English Discourse

All of these examples confirm Goodwin's claims about the importance of double subjectivity in gay men's communication. But, as they also suggest, double subjectivity is not controlled by a single participant within the speech event. Texts are coconstructed phenomena; multiple text makers share responsibilities for text design and for the situated significance of its message.

Thus, it is helpful to study Gay English conversations and narratives as instances of *cooperative discourse*.[1] Intentionality and coherence, properties of text design that I discussed in the introduction, are additional forms of cooperative process, as are carefully negotiated styles of turn taking, the use of descriptive imagery and metaphor, inference strategies, and a range of additional techniques ensuring listener- as well as speaker-involvement in each exchange.

Rather than discussing these features as abstract categories, let me turn to a specific instance of Gay English as cooperative discourse—a conversation that occurred during a Sunday afternoon brunch in fall 1991—and describe the construction of that text, and its meanings, in some detail.

#### Gay English at a Sunday Brunch

The setting for this exchange was a private home in the D.C. suburbs. The participants included the host and fourteen guests, all gay men with college degrees and professional, white-collar jobs in the D.C. area. All were of Euro-American background. They ranged in age from twenty-five to forty-eight, with most guests in their midthirties. While not all of them were "out" to friends, family, and coworkers, all had been actively involved in gay life for several years.

The host and eight of the guests were members of the same choral group; the other guests were all friends of the host, and (except for my partner and I, the only couple attending the event) they had not otherwise been introduced prior to this event.

We arrived (ten minutes fashionably late) to find the singers grouped inside a circle of chairs, chatting away and laughing loudly. Other guests milled around the living room, circulated through the house, and wandered into the kitchen to try and help the host with last-minute preparations. Not being members of the chorus, we joined the other guests in these migrations, but we learned that, without introductions, other third-party mediation, or name tags, attempts at conversation were difficult.

We found that several of us were familiar with the Pennsylvania State University (though for rather varied reasons), and for a while we exchanged stories about our visits to State College and the surrounding area. Once the meal began, those of us not in the choral group filled plates from the dining room buffet, returned to the living room, and sat by ourselves or next to another outsider, eating, talking occasionally, but mostly listening from a distance to the choral group's continuing flow of (to us, incomprehensible) references to people, events, and performances.

The social dynamic began to change once the meal ended and people began enjoying coffee, tea, and more drinks. No one said anything, nor did the host do anything, to formally orchestrate the change (at least, not that I observed), but slowly the boundary between the choral group and the "outsiders" began to disappear. The seating patterns changed so that individuals were more likely to be facing each other rather than staring at people's backs. And the conversational pattern shifted as well.

Example 2.3 presents my on-the-spot transcription of the opening lines of this exchange. I used an ink pen and wrote in shorthand on some paper napkins, a verbatim note-taking technique that I developed during my Indian-language research in the Southwest; after we left the party, my partner added his marginal comments to those notes and amplified my records in other ways.[2]

I noticed several things when I began to review my transcription. First, the speakers explored a wide range of topics during this exchange. These topics included Miss Louisiana's choice of beauty pageant costume, more appropriate costume choices, David Duke, Duke's politics, costuming oneself like David Duke, gay bed linen, gay Klan attire, and voter responses to the 1992 presidential campaign—all within the space of a twenty-one-line text segment.

Second, the shifts between topics occur almost as frequently as the speaker–listener turn taking shifts. In part, this is the result of a particular rule of adjacency pairing that has not been associated with structured verbal play reported for speakers of other English codes. Under this rule, speakers are obligated to use a segment of the reference presented in the preceding speaker's comment as the core of the statement he constructs when re-

---

**Example 2.3**  Sunday brunch.

| | |
|---|---|
| 1 | S1: Did you see the costume on Miss Louisiana? Imagine—she |
| 2 | dressed up like a crawfish! |
| 3 | S2: Well, the contestants were supposed to wear something typical |
| 4 | of their home state. |
| 5 | S3: And it's difficult to walk out on stage dressed like a bayou. |
| 6 | S4: I wouldn't mind being by-you, that's for sure. |
| 7 | S5: Maybe she should have dressed up like a Creole princess. |
| 8 | S6: Or like David Duke. |
| 9 | S2: Now there is a roadkill for you—all over the pavement. |
| 10 | S3: But his face is so cute— and the way he wears his hair! |
| 11 | S1: Yeah, but what comes out his mouth isn't so cute. All that |
| 12 | trash makes him ugly. |
| 13 | S5: She could have worn a David Duke costume. |
| 14 | S2: I have a triangle-shaped hat. Maybe I could have gone |
| 15 | dressed as David Duke. |
| 16 | S1: Pointed at the top of your head? |
| 17 | S2: And a white sheet to match. [*Pause*] Ralph Lauren. |
| 18 | S7: 200 thread count. |
| 19 | S8: 200 thread count Ralph Lauren. |
| 20 | S2: And embroidered eye holes. |
| 21 | S4: Do you really think anyone will take that man seriously? |

---

sponding to that comment; in the remainder of the statement, the speaker must introduce new information and move the conversation in a new direction, thereby setting the stage for the next speaker's construction of commentary under the same rule.[3]

Hence in lines 1-2, speaker S1 refers to Miss Louisiana's choice of costume in the recently televised Miss America pageant, and speaker S2 responds (lines 3-4) by overlapping S1's reference to the crawfish costume with his new comment about pageant rules. Speaker S3 incorporates compliance with pageant rules (from S2's statement) within his reference to an alternative, if less functional costume imagery (line 5), and speaker S4 (line 6) makes a pun on the key word from S3's suggestion ("bayou"), thereby diverting the meaning of that statement into an entirely different domain.

S4's comment is of interest to this discussion for several reasons. What he said replied directly to information presented in the preceding speaker's statement and used one segment of that comment as the focus for introducing new information into the exchange. At the same time, S4 used personal feelings as the focus for the required new information rather than more neutral references (TV pageantry, costuming), which could be shared by the group as a whole. The equation of "bayou" and "by-you" is clever, but somehow it stands apart from the linguistic imagery displayed in the other participants' statements. Like the preceding comments, line 6 is rich in gay subtext, but it is explicitly gay and has none of the subtlety of reference that other speakers' statements contain.

All of these properties explain the next speaker's (S5) reaction to S4's comment. S5 returns to the discussion of costuming difficulties presented by S3 (the old information), and introduces (as new information) another, more feasible costume idea. Speaker S6 starts with S5's reference to more feasible costume (old information) and matches it with a reference to David Duke (his new information). And the exchange continues, new information built on old information as required by the adjacency rule, almost as if S4's statement had never occurred.

At the same time, although other speakers bypassed his statement, they did nothing to exclude S4 himself from participation in the conversation, nor did they make him the target of any other form of negative sanction. S4 was free to rejoin the turn taking activity any time he wished, and when he did (line 21), other speakers used his statement to shift group discussion from one topic (gay Klan attire) to another (David Duke's presence in the 1992 presidential campaign) and responded to it in other, positive ways. This, too, is a dimension of cooperative discourse that I do not find reported for other English codes—particularly so, in instances where each speaker's status within the speech community is as closely tied to verbal skill as is the case in Gay English domains.

S5's reaction to S4's comment (line 6) suggests that participants were following certain agreed-upon rules when selecting topics to explore in this exchange. Where possible, for example, speaker comments were to appeal directly to shared knowledge and experience, particularly knowledge and experience building on gay-centered cultural themes. Hence the references to pageantry, television programming, male beauty, and fashion that permeate the portion of the dialogue being examined here. Similarly, the repeated references to costume and "dress up" (lines 2, 5, 7, 13, and 14) are closely tied to the notions of image building and exaggerated disguise widely attested in U.S. gay life inside as well as outside of gay "ghettos." And likewise, an extended discussion (lines 17-20) pokes fun at gay men's stereotypic interests in top-of-the-line consumer goods by describing how a gay man might solve his wardrobe needs once he became a member of the Ku Klux Klan. The image being constructed in these lines is so improbable as to be believable, a union of themes that speakers of Gay English frequently employ, regardless of setting or discourse theme.

There were few restrictions on the topics that could be introduced into this conversation, judging by speaker reactions to others' statements. Definitely to be avoided, however, were topics that were relevant or interesting only to a portion of the participants. Just as there were reactions to S4's extremely personalized statement (line 6), so were there reactions to speaker S2's use of the term "roadkill" to describe David Duke (line 9). Several participants looked puzzled when they heard the term, prompting another participant to explain (in an aside not recorded in example 2.3) that S2 had attended a chorus costume party dressed like a country highway, with stuffed animals carefully flattened and strategically placed across his chest and back to suggest the outcome of encounters between wildlife and diesel trucks.

Also to be avoided were statements that contained direct attacks on any individual within the group. The avoidance of sanction against S4 fell under this category, and so did speaker S2's rapid diffusing of speaker S1's attempt at sarcasm (lines 16-17).

Given such restrictions on topic selection, it is not surprising that the participant structure underlying this exchange was highly inclusive and speaker friendly. Over half of the persons present at the brunch participated actively, as speakers, in the conversation, and those who did not speak helped create an attentive, supportive, and receptive environment within which the speakers could play out these exchanges. Moreover, according to my observations (and those of my partner, who later reported having the same reaction to this event), there was no penalty for silence in this setting. Any member of the group who wanted to speak had ample opportunities to do so. Hence, while speakers S1, S2, and S3 were highly visible participants throughout the exchange being examined here, their "presence" did not prevent speakers S7 and S8, who had remained silent during opening statements (lines 1-16) from elaborating on speaker S2's reference to Ralph Lauren sheets (lines 18-20), comments that resulted in coconstructed references to gay bed linen and the gay Klan attire that conclude this segment.

### Gay English and the Queering of the Klan

Why do I consider this conversation to be cooperative discourse? In what ways did its being cooperative overlap with the gay-centered focus and the authenticity of this exchange?

Again, a useful entry point for answering these questions is the notion of intentionality, and specifically the evidence of intentional text making that is evidenced within the text. It may seem difficult to comment on this issue, given that so many speakers were involved in the exchange and so many instances of language use have to be assessed in that regard. The scope of that involvement is itself powerful evidence of the shared intentions that helped to organize and regulate this exchange.

This was, after all, *not* an in-group conversation; all but two of the comments (line 6 and line 16) appealed broadly to participant knowledge of gay culture and "style." Since many of the participants had met each other for the first time that afternoon and speakers had not had opportunities to interact widely with other guests before the meal, speakers did not necessarily have firsthand evidence of coparticipant knowledge in this area. They could infer such knowledge, of course, from the gay-centered social setting, from other contextual factors, and from the expectations that they may have brought, as individual gay men, into the speech event. But it was only by participating in this conversation and making certain that opportunities for participation were open to others that speakers were able to confirm the validity of these expectations.

Gay culture, writ large, is an underlying content theme in this text. And issues of gay sexuality and erotics, certainly part of that cultural inventory, also show up in this text, though much less frequently and in a more subdued fashion than the literature's emphasis on Gay English vocabulary might imply. These speakers' comments could have been more explicitly sexual in reference; gay men frequently use such statements in their conversations with other gay men while in private, comfortable, gay-controlled social domains. So the absence of erotic comments in this exchange cannot be disregarded and joins the inclusive nature of the turn taking as evidence of a gay-related intentionality permeating the cooperative nature of text design in this case.

The cooperative nature of this text is also reflected in the speakers' use of metaphoric imagery—specifically, the attention given to gay Klan attire that concludes this segment of the dialogue (lines 17-20).

Two themes—*dressing up* and *special costumes*—provide the basis for this construction. Neither of these themes is uniquely gay, but both are closely connected to gay experience. They contribute to the day-to-day strategies for disguise and concealment found in every gay man's cultural wardrobe. They also contribute to the flamboyant, exaggerated masquerade associated with drag, cross-dressing and gender-fuck—activities that promote the "subversion of phallogocentric identities and desires [by] confronting heterosexist essentialism with the artifices of gender and the errant play of desire" (Tyler 1991: 32). Carol-Anne Tyler focuses these comments specifically on male impersonation. (Presumably the actors here are females, though a good argument could be made that male impersonation is also central to some forms of gay men's day-to-day disguise.) Hence, "once masculinity is seen as a put-on, mere style," (a message, by the way, that is displayed both by female-to-male and some gay-to-straight impersonators), "its phallic imposture is exposed as such and so delegitimized" (Tyler 1991: 32).

Few groups symbolize Tyler's notion of phallogocentric identity as explicitly as does the Ku Klux Klan. For a gay man actually to put on Klan attire and adopt other forms of Klan identity—either in jest or as a serious (if self-hating) endorsement of their homophobic agenda—constitutes a marvelous subversion of that identity, since such action contradicts the allegiance of heterosexist essentialism that is the cornerstone of the Klan's charter.

It is equally subversive, I submit, for a group of gay men to fantasize about such action, even when the fantasy unfolds in the safety of an all-gay household. Especially when the language of this fantasy (for example, David Duke's boyish good looks, 200 thread count Ralph Lauren bedsheets) draws so heavily on metaphoric connections to gay culture.

The construction of these references in this setting depended heavily on the listener's inferencing skills and on other components of cooperative discourse that have been explored in this chapter. No one person controlled the production of these statements, and it is not clear whether the first speaker to suggest this reference (S5, line 13) expected that others would embellish the comment so dramatically. The fact is, other speakers did respond to line 13 by contributing elements to a chain of metaphoric references (David Duke's costume = Klan costume = Klan robes = bed linen = gay bed linen = gay Klan robes = gay Klansmen) that gradually recast the somberness (otherwise) implicit in the initial reference with increasingly visible, gay-centered satire and minstrelsy.

"Queering" is now one of the popular terms for such acts of subversion.[4] Richard Mohr defines queering as "gay men's appropriation for themselves and representation to others of men's worlds and death's dominion" (1992: 6). Broadening that description (since gay men are not the only persons who participate in queer discourse and being gay is in no sense a prerequisite for such participation), I can describe queering as the appropriation for ourselves of objects, activities, and identities found in everyday experience and the representation to others of those objects, activities, and identities as queered appropriations. Queering is about the construction of imagery and the reconstruction of images along lines that maximize the visibility of lesbian/gay/bisexual/transgenderal content and form; whether the object, activity, or identity already has such content and form to begin with is irrelevant to this process. In some cases—as in the gay Klan example here—the absence of such references at the beginning of the process makes the resulting subversion of the ordinary all the more appealing.

It seems to me, whether one accepts Mohr's definition, my definition or another, that queering may become the ultimate form of cooperative discourse in gay English. By "ultimate," I do not mean the "best" or the "highest"; queering is a relatively new text-making strategy in Gay English (as I explain in chapter 5), and practitioners (listeners as well as speakers) are still negotiating evaluative privilege in that regard. I do mean, however, that queering an object, activity, or an identity draws on the same notions of intentionality, coherence, turn taking, and metaphoric process that are regularly found in Gay English usage and give Gay English its cooperative and gay-centered characteristics. Perhaps speakers of Gay English are really queering English each time they speak, listen, read, or write in this code, and if so, queering offers another way of specifying authenticity in Gay English text.

# 3

---

*Ensuring Cooperative Discourse:*
*Exaggeration, Turn Taking,*
*Pauses, and Terminals*

---

Cooperative discourse may be a desirable goal in Gay English text making, but other components in the speech event may compete with and even undermine speaker efforts in this area. Speakers use self-parody and mutual teasing to offset such distractions; this is what happened in example 1.3, where guest and host began to make fun of their initial disagreement over color terminology. Speakers can also ensure cooperative discourse through other text-making strategies, and I examine several of those strategies in this chapter.

### Initiating Cooperation Exchange: Exaggeration and Metaphor

Gay English speakers regularly include in their text making features like exaggerated language, gay-oriented metaphor and innuendo, and references to prominent gay characters and events in gay history. Adding these features allows speakers to draw attention to the presence of gay message within text content without having to become explicit about the content of that message. A gay man can say a lot to a listener about loneliness and fondness for a new companion by noting: "It's nice to wake up in the morning next to a hairy chest"; he can introduce a cautiously explicit reference to gay identity into a business conversation by suggesting that the client send his materials to "PO Box XXX, Cooper Station — that's Cooper, like in Gary Cooper."

Such comments depend on the listener's willingness to interpret the speaker's statement in terms of its gay associations, rather than in a more conventional frame of reference. If such comments are carefully placed, speakers can use them to invite listeners to shift away from a more neutral discourse style and to begin a cooperative, gay-centered coconstruction of text. This is exactly what happened during a midafternoon airplane flight from Washington, D.C., to Chicago, several years ago, when a flight attendant and a coach-class passenger had the conversation shown in example 3.1.

---

**Example 3.1** Vodka and tonic. (FA: flight attendant; P: passenger)

1    FA: Get you a cocktail?
2    P:   Sure. [*Pause*] A vodka and tonic.
3    FA: OK. [*Begins to mix the drink*] That's my drink, too.
4    P:   Yeah? I think it's the only drink that's safe before six.
5    FA: [*Pause*] Huh? [*Stops mixing the drink*] I thought you
6         said "safe before sex." [*Pause*]
7    P:   Oh-h. [*Giggles*]
8    FA: Well, I guess it's that, too. [*FA hands P the drink; P*
9         *hands the attendant a five-dollar bill*] Here, I'll sell
10        you two for five dollars.
11   P:   Fine. [*P watches while FA mixes a second drink, hands*
12        *it to P, then pushes the cart to his next station*]

---

Both the flight attendant and the passenger were in their midthirties, and both were white, middle-class Americans. The passenger was seated in the front of the coach cabin, on the right side of the aisle, with no other passenger seated on his row.[1] Prior to departure, the flight attendant had been busy in the back of the airplane, and there had been no communication between him and the passenger before this conversation began. Shortly after the plane "reached a comfortable cruising altitude," the flight attendant and a female colleague began pushing the drink cart through the aisle to dispense refreshments.

I have examined this exchange in some detail in Leap 1993, and I do not want to repeat that commentary here. Let me note, however, that while there is nothing explicitly gay about either speaker's use of language in this conversation, there are displays of implicitly gay meaning at three points in the dialogue: "vodka and tonic," in the passenger's first response to the flight attendant (line 2); "safe before sex," in the flight attendant's comical restatement of the passenger's preceding comment, "safe before six" (line 6); and "I'll sell you two for five dollars," the flight attendant's closing comment (lines 9-10). The placement is not arbitrary, it seems to me. Each of these comments occurs at a critical point in the conversation, and each frames the style of presentation for the segment of the exchange that follows.

P's comment in line 2, for example, may not have intentionally been a gay reference. But asking for a vodka and tonic (a popular drink among middle-class gay men in the northeastern United States, especially on vacation) gave FA the opening he needed to shift from "commercial" to "personal" discussion. FA's comment in lines 9-10, on the other hand, returned the discussion to a business format, and his "special deal" (two for five dollars) helped to diffuse any discomfort about the exchange that P "might have" retained.

With regard to FA's comment about safe sex in lines 5-6, friends (gay and straight) who are familiar with the airline business, including several flight attendants, have told me that they are surprised that FA was so brazen, aggressive, and outrageous (these are three friends' descriptors) during the conversation. My reply to their comments is simply to point out the invitation that he had received. P's comment (line 2) was suitably ambiguous, and FA's reply ("That's my drink, too"—line 3) was equally so. FA's reply was also personal, and P responded with a comment matching that tone ("I think it's the only drink that's safe before six"—line 4).

This five-line exchange, with line 2 as its anchor, was not explicitly gay in content, but it established both speakers' willingness to construct a cooperative text—cooperative in the sense of maintaining the same balanced negotiation of meaning that led to the queering of the Klan during Sunday brunch in example 2.3 and prevented example 1.3's debate over the water pitcher from getting out of hand. While FA's reference to safe sex in line 6 may have been brazen, aggressive, or outrageous, it was also an entirely reasonable statement at that point in the exchange. In fact, it is a highly cooperative construction, and it invited P's next comment to be the same.

As the dialogue shows (P giggled—line 7), P did not respond in kind.[2] Given P's noncommittal response, FA had to close the conversation in the only fashion he could, by a noncommittal reply (line 8) and a return to business format (lines 9-10). Of course, the drink in question in the two-for-one exchange was still vodka and tonic, so the gay message that initiated the exchange was preserved, even if FA's attempts at cooperative discourse were not entirely successful.

### On (Gay) Metaphor

Before going on to the other texts discussed in this chapter, which contain instances of strategically placed exaggeration, I do want to comment briefly on two of the sources from which gay men derive their exaggerated comments: films and Broadway plays that have gay-centered messages, and anecdotes from the life stories of famous entertainers and other persons with recognized gay appeal.

For me, items in the first category include *The Wizard of Oz, Boys in the*

*Band, Annie, A Chorus Line,* and *La Cage aux folles,* and persons in the second category include Bette Davis, Joan Crawford, Tallulah Bankhead, Jackie Kennedy, and Madonna. Other speakers of Gay English will follow different criteria when constructing their version of this list; speaker age, ethnic background, and class can be particularly influential in that regard. But however they are identified, a strategic introduction of material from any of these sources—such as the three comments attributed to the late, great Tallulah Bankhead, displayed in example 3.2—can rapidly shift a conversation from initial ambiguity into a gay-friendly, cooperative mode.[3]

---

**Example 3.2**  Classic quotations from Tallulah Bankhead.

- *I adore your gown, but your purse is on fire.*
  Ms. Bankhead's comment to a richly bedecked Anglican priest as he passed her pew during the solemn procession at a Christmas Eve midnight mass.
- *All I have to say is, "Fuck Betty Crocker."*
  Her reaction when, after she had worked for some time to prepare a late supper for a few close friends, items on the stove overheated, pots caught fire, and the oven exploded (apparently, the servants, not the diva, did the cooking in Ms. Bankhead's home).
- *How would I know? He's never sucked my cock.*
  Her response when a nosy companion asked if a mutual friend was really homosexually inclined.

---

Statements do not have to be exaggerated in order to encourage a cooperative exchange between speakers and listeners in Gay English conversations. Speakers can also make effective use of metaphoric references—statements whose word content and imagery are likely to suggest to the listener additional associations between sentence reference and gay point of view.

Example 3.3 lists five statements, collected during my field work, that contain different types of metaphoric constructions. I have included two items (items 2 and 4) with erotic references because Gay English metaphors are frequently tied to sexual practices and their meanings. The remaining examples show how Gay English speakers can also construct metaphoric reference out of nonerotic reference sources.

Item 1 is a comment made by a guest (a thirty-five-year-old gay man, of Italian American background) attending a Fourth of July party in our apartment, when he went out on the balcony to enjoy the view of the city. My partner had placed citronella candles on the balcony table to keep away the summertime insects. The odor from the candles was more potent than either of us had expected, and the odor also surprised our guest, as the wording of his comments suggests.

---

**Example 3.3** Gay metaphor: Imagery and innuendo.

1  It smells so butch, why'd they have to give it a name ending in "nella"? Why not just call it "citron"?
2  Like, sex today is so-o-o-o boring. It's like eating a Twinkie without peeling off the cellophane wrapper.
3  We sit in the same pew at church.
4  You like fingerin' my ass? You're gonna love fuckin' my ass—right? So now kiss my ass.
5  Send it to PO Box XXX, Cooper Station—that's Cooper, like in Gary Cooper.

---

"Butch" is a familiar reference from the gay lexicon; used by itself, the word has positive, complementary and desirable associations and suggests comparisons with Castro street clones, the Marlboro Man, or any man who wears Levis and flannel shirts to perfection. Combining "butch" with a reference to odor reworks familiar associations of masculinized power to confirm the potency of the candles' fragrance. Whether the speaker considered this fragrance (or any butch odor, for that matter) to be desirable is another matter, part of the ambiguity of the reference and part of what makes it such an effective descriptor in this setting.

The statement also had its intended effect. Our guest made the comment, I burst into laughter, and the candle was extinguished, without anyone feeling embarrassed by our mistake in judgment.

I heard item 2 during one of my focus group sessions with gay male college students. Participants in this session were talking about safe-sex issues and outlining objections to safe-sex practices. Most of the students were harshly critical of those who disregarded the rules (one participant's term for the widely circulated safe-sex guidelines under discussion in the group). Another participant, a college junior, was reacting silently but with increasing hostility to the others' commentary, and at one point he interrupted the conversation and blurted out the statement in item 2: "Like, sex today is so-o-o-o boring. It's like eating a twinkie without peeling off the cellophane wrapper."

Consider the multiple meanings that the term "Twinkie" introduced into the text making: a sweet pastry that is fun to eat, a forbidden food (Twinkies are not recommended for the diet conscious), a penis-shaped object that squirts white cream once the mouth is applied, a delicious treat that can be enjoyed only once, and a code term for a young, attractive gay man. So, besides suggesting connections between food and sex, the speaker's use of the Twinkie metaphor also introduced more subtle linkages between temptation and power, and between desire and danger, into the discussion.

The speaker intended this comment as an objection to what he considered to be overly self-righteous posturing about safe-sex practices. He told me later that at least two of the other participants regularly avoided safe-sex practices, as he knew from his own erotic experiences with each of them. But to say that he did not agree with the discussion, to speak in favor of condom avoidance in the time of AIDS, could have had disastrous consequences within the group setting and (I suspect) for his social life. So (he explained), rather than be disruptive, he decided to be comical and to make his point by drawing an analogy with which he hoped the other participants could relate.

Item 3 contains the type of statement that Gay English speakers often use when they are in a public (particularly a heterosexually dominated) speech setting but want to confirm the gay identity of some third party. There is nothing explicitly gay in the comment or in the imagery that conveys it. If anything, the resurgence of connections between right-wing, conservative politics and religious orthodoxy that emerged in the United States during the 1980s makes church attendance something hostile to lesbian and gay interests and suggests that references to church will carry similar implications.[4]

In order for metaphors to be effective within any text, speakers and listeners have to agree that the intended meaning of the statement is not necessarily the literal meaning. Here, the hostility between church and gay makes it unlikely that the speaker actually attends church with the person under discussion, and it implies that the speaker's comment refers to common interests in some other area. Unavoidably, the inferencing required to make associations like this creates cooperative ties between speakers and listeners, even when speakers or listeners do not intend those ties to emerge.

Item 4 is a text segment from a Joey Stefano film. The particulars of scene and plotline are not important, since Stefano's films consistently revolve around the same general theme: the transformation of the insatiable and arrogant "bottom" (Stefano's character in the opening segment of the film) into the insatiable and cooperative "bottom" (Stefano's character in the final segment of the film). Indeed, the idea of "taming Joey Stefano" is the inducement that attracts both the characters in the film and the persons who are viewing it into the text making.

Stefano's character addresses comments like the one in item 4 to other characters and to the audience. And just as his statements invite his sex partner in the film to initiate further action, they also invite the viewers to imagine themselves as his sex partner, as someone who could under other circumstances actually assume that role. The pronoun "you," repeated in each statement, establishes this equation between actor and viewer, and (when his eyes are not half-closed in a dreamily erotic self-absorption), Stefano's gaze drifts languidly between actor and audience, further underscoring this equation and the prospect of cooperative opportunity that it invites.

I heard item 5 during a telephone conversation with an administrative assistant at a textbook supply company in a large northeastern city. He used this reference to make certain that I had the correct spelling of the post office branch to which I should send my follow-up correspondence. But the sudden reference to Gary Cooper added a second layer of meaning to his comment. I did not find his introduction of gay meaning to be out of place in the discussion, and hearing it prompted me to listen more closely for other signals that might more explicitly confirm a gay identity. I expect that I may have introduced one or two comments on my own, to that end— initiating a type of cooperative exchange different from that which had occurred in the earlier segments of the conversation.

### Negotiating Cooperation: Turn Taking and Format Tying

Turn-taking strategies regulate cooperative exchange in all conversational settings, but turn taking can be especially valuable for Gay English text making—both in amicable settings (like the Sunday brunch in example 2.3) and in instances where unresolved antagonism and conflict are threatening to disrupt the exchange.

#### Everybody Loves Little Kiwi

Ethan Mordden's short story "The Precarious Ontology of the Buddy System" (1987b) contains several instances in which Gay English speakers use turn taking to diffuse antagonism and conflict, one of which is displayed in example 3.4. The story is part of a series of narratives (see also Mordden 1986, 1988) that chronicle gay men's lives in Manhattan in the years between Stonewall and the onset of the AIDS pandemic. An unnamed narrator provides the point of view for this description. He reports in each story on what he sees, what he hears, and what others around are doing, but he reveals little about himself. And while he never gives his name, several clues in the text suggest that he could be the author's alter ego, and I refer to the narrator as EM in the following discussion.

---

**Example 3.4** Everybody Loves Little Kiwi. (Source: Mordden 1987b: 51)

1    I've told Dennis Savage to call first. I've lectured him on
2    the rudeness of prowling into my fridge uninvited. I've warned
3    him that Little Kiwi's charm is lost on me. And all he says
4    is: "Have you noticed how lamplight picks up the tones in his
5    hair?"
6        "How old is that kid, anyway?" I once asked him.
7        "Old enough to love."
8        "He has the interests of a child of eight."
9        "He voted in the last election."
10       "For whom? The Velveteen Rabbit?"
11       "Everybody adores him. They dress up for him and bake a
12    pie. Look at you." I keep house in jeans and a sweatshirt.
13    "And what do you give us to eat? BLTs!"
14       Actually, I give Dennis Savage BLTs. Little Kiwi subsists
15    on grilled-cheese sandwiches and sliced tomato.
16       "Everyone wants Little Kiwi," says Dennis Savage. You
17    should know this. Except no one can have him but me."
18       "Oh, yeah?"
19    Dennis Savage chuckles. "I dare you."
20       How satisfying it would be to outfox Dennis Savage, though
21    on the other hand his relationship is too fascinating to
22    menace . . .

---

The setting for the conversation in example 3.4 is EM's apartment in "the east fifties" in midtown Manhattan. EM's neighbors Dennis Savage and Dennis's new boyfriend "Little Kiwi" have dropped in unexpectedly. And even though EM has objected to such interruptions on previous occasions (he is trying, with limited success, to write the all-American gay novel), both guests proceed to make themselves at home at EM's expense.

Some other details of background: EM and Dennis Savage knew each other in prep school and recently reestablished their friendship after meeting unexpectedly during the first intermission of a performance of the opera *Tales of Hoffmann*. Dennis helped EM secure an apartment in his building, which is how they became neighbors and (quite quickly) confidants.

Dennis met Little Kiwi in the standing-room-only section of a Broadway theater during a performance of *The Best Little Whorehouse in Texas.* Dennis and EM are in their thirties; Little Kiwi is barely out of his teens and often acts that way. EM describes him as "very young, very silly, and very uneducated" (1987b: 50).

Finally, some points of method: Because the number of actors here is somewhat smaller than in the Sunday brunch example and because the conversation centers around an "argument," the turn-taking strategies displayed in example 3.4 are structured somewhat differently from those in example 2.3. In example 2.3, participants regularly used information already established within the conversation as their base for bringing new ideas into the discussion and pushing the conversation into additional reference domains. In example 3.4, however, speakers were more concerned with restating or refuting information already established in the text, and they brought new ideas into the discussion only when those ideas strengthened positions they had already adopted and explained. In other words, the speakers in example 3.4 work to maintain the initial focus of the dialogue, not to broaden, expand, or move beyond it.

Marjorie Goodwin (1990: 177) uses the phrase "format tying" to identify this type of topic-preserving turn taking. She also describes a second turn-taking strategy—"scene transformation"—relevant to text design in example 3.4. Scene transformation allows speakers to preserve continuity in the text-making process by, for example, bringing new participants into the conversation, shifting the discussion toward new persons or themes, or reorganizing the content of the conversation in other ways.

A close reading of example 3.4 will show how format tying, scene transformation, and other text-making strategies help speakers maintain cooperative discourse throughout this exchange.

The conversation in example 3.4 opens (lines 1-5) with EM complaining about his neighbors' unannounced visits to his apartment. The comments suggest how irritated EM has become by these interruptions. They also set up the opposition between EM and Dennis Savage that surfaces repeatedly throughout this text. Note particularly EM's reference in line 2 to the "rudeness of prowling" versus Dennis Savage's reference in lines 4-5 to "how lamplight picks up the tones in his hair." The verbs in these statements ("prowl," "pick up") have different meanings, though both can be used to describe actions during the earliest stages of erotic encounter. The presence of these references here suggests EM's disapproval of the relationship between Dennis Savage and Little Kiwi and anticipates the tone of the format tying that will structure the discussion of that relationship in the remainder of this passage.

Line 6 establishes age as a point of contention. According to mainstream stereotype, age is one of the primary concerns of gay discourse. In this case, the reference to age is considerably more specific in its focus: Line 6 implies that Little Kiwi is underage, which makes Dennis Savage a child molester, not a complimentary name in most gay circles. Dennis Savage recasts EM's reference to age in line 7, validating his infatuation with Little Kiwi: "Old enough" not only means that he is over the age of consent but that there is no immoral undertone to Dennis Savage's passion. EM reworks line 7's "old enough" reference to suggest (line 8) that Little Kiwi is behaviorally immature, whatever his age or legal status. Dennis Savage reworks line 8 to provide additional evidence of Little Kiwi's chronological and legal maturity, using as his focus an activity (voting) associated with responsible behavior in U.S. society.

EM's reply (line 10) links line 9's reference to voting with a symbol of the immature, underage behavior (the Velveteen Rabbit) that he has already indexed in lines 6 and 8. At this point (lines 11-13), Dennis Savage draws on another format-tying strategy—scene transformation—to broaden the force of authority in the dialogue and to shift the dialogue's focus away from Little Kiwi. Now, instead of merely offering his own thoughts on Little Kiwi's behavior, Dennis Savage suggests that (an unspecified) everyone considers Little Kiwi to be socially acceptable and that others are much more responsive and polite to Little Kiwi than is EM: They "dress up for him and bake a pie," whereas EM wears sweatshirts and jeans and serves BLTs. In other words, EM, not Little Kiwi, is the socially immature member of this group.

Understandably, EM is not willing to accept a refocusing of the dialogue in these terms. In lines 14-15, he reworks line 13's food reference to suggest that Little Kiwi has special food requirements: He subsists on grilled cheese sandwiches, not BLTs. Note the distinctive verb describing his food consumption. The comment continues the reference to Little Kiwi's child-like behavior begun in lines 6, 8, and 10. But unlike those remarks, this comment is directed to the reader, not to Dennis Savage. By upstaging Dennis Savage's remark in this way, EM attempts to gain reader support for the position he is presenting in this debate, and in the process, he counters Dennis Savage's use of scene transformation by attempting a scene transformation of his own.

Dennis Savage reacts to EM's comments in three ways. First (lines 16-17), he modifies his scene transformation to make sure that EM is now fully included within the scene: "Everyone wants Little Kiwi . . . You should know this." Second, repositioning EM within the argument allows Dennis

Savage to reassert the position he has maintained throughout this exchange: He finds Little Kiwi quite acceptable, and other people's evaluations (EM's in particular) don't matter. Third, Dennis Savage's reassertion of this position now contains a mixture of erotics and power—"no one can have him but me"—that is different in tone from the more delicately worded references to lamplight and age that characterized his earlier comments. In fact, it carries the implication that EM harbors a (yet to be explicitly stated) erotic interest in Little Kiwi and that this interest has made him resentful of Dennis Savage's relationship.

EM's reply (line 18) is unlike any statement he has made so far in this exchange. He does not recast or rework Dennis Savage's comment, nor does he repeat ideas that he himself established earlier in the dialogue. In effect, his statement—"Oh, yeah?"—contains nothing for Dennis Savage to build on; it does, however, address EM's obligation to be cooperative in this setting and allows the responsibility for follow-up to revert back to Dennis Savage.

It is important that Dennis Savage treats line 18 not as a hedge (that is, as a deliberate attempt to avoid responsibilities in turn taking) but as a legitimate contribution to the conversation. He uses the erotic and power implications presented in his previous comment (line 17) as the foundation for making an inference here. His response (line 19)—"I dare you"—directly challenges EM's still unstated desire for Little Kiwi and his equally unstated interests in acting on that desire.

The focus of the reference here is between EM and Dennis Savage, another instance of scene transformation in this text. Little Kiwi may be the object of desire in this setting, and he certainly has been the topic under discussion until this point. But this passage ends with the relationship between EM and Dennis Savage becoming the centerpiece in this dialogue; hence Dennis Savage's person-to-person comment: "I [Dennis Savage] dare you [EM]." And hence EM's response, which notes that he (EM) would find it satisfying to outfox Dennis Savage and then refers to his (EM's) fascination with Dennis Savage's relationship but makes no mention of Little Kiwi at all.

Example 3.4 shows how a Gay English conversation filled with statements of competition and conflict can still develop into an affirmation (or, importantly, a reaffirmation) of speaker-to-speaker solidarity. The passage also shows how Gay English principles of cooperative discourse play key roles in that development.

For one thing, individual statements aside, it is not clear that either speaker actually intended this to be or to become an occasion for seriously divisive argument. There were expressions of conflict here, to be sure, but while some components of the conflict will ultimately be resolved (for example, Little Kiwi ultimately demonstrates his own suitability as a life partner for Dennis Savage—see Mordden 1988: 235-71), other components remain unaddressed (such as Little Kiwi's disruption of EM and Dennis Savage's best friends/confidants/buddies relationship) even at the conclusion of the exchange. Both participants come out of the dialogue reminded of the ground rules underlying their status as best friends/confidants/buddies. In fact, I could argue that participation in the exchange was a kind of practical reminder of the significance of those rules and the obligations they impose.

Certainly, for all of the competitiveness displayed in the turn-taking strategy, both participants made certain that their comments did not extend too far beyond implicitly agreed upon boundaries. For example, Dennis Savage never directly accused EM of actual erotic indiscretion or of harboring any serious intentions in that regard, and EM never linked Little Kiwi to any explicitly inappropriate social behavior. If anything, the more somber the issues under discussion became, the more likely either one or both speakers were to romanticize or satirize that phase of the dialogue, or to draw freely on stereotypes of gay behavior or other sources to exaggerate the references they were exploring and to thereby diffuse their significance.

Note how both parties pull away from the dialogue just at the point (lines 16-18) when the conflict implicit in the exchange unavoidably moves closer to the surface. EM's use of "Oh, yeah?" (line 18) in place of a more content-specific format tie is especially important in that regard. But equally so is Dennis Savage's response: "I dare you" (line 19). Rather than using this as an occasion to vanquish his opponent, Dennis Savage uses the line to repersonalize the commentary and shift the dialogue back to the good friends/confidants/buddies posture (another example of scene transformation), something that both speakers ultimately decided to maintain, initial disagreements notwithstanding.

### What Color Is the Brown Water Pitcher? Revisited

But, some readers may now be saying, this passage is fiction. Why treat the dialogue as if it were a real conversation? Why analyze its contents in terms of the feelings and motivations of its fictional characters? I can answer several ways. First, I find all of Mordden's writing to be superb ethnography and suspect that there is more real-life experience contained in his narratives than his status as an "author of gay fiction" implies. (I also think this is true for many other writers of gay fiction, as I noted in the introduction.)

Second, the use of language displayed in this example parallels quite closely the seemingly acrimonious text making that occurs in real-life Gay English speech events and suggests the strategies that gay men use to diffuse and resolve conflicts in such settings.

Consider, from this point of view, the "brown pitcher" dispute that I discussed briefly in chapter 1 (example 1.3). I suggested in chapter 1 that, contrary to initial impressions, the speakers actively grounded this exchange in a mutual commitment to cooperative discourse and that this was not really a disagreement at all. Now, drawing on my analysis of example 3.4, I want to offer a more detailed analysis of the linguistics of this "dispute."

The conversation in example 1.3 occurred during an at-home dinner party involving two hosts and six guests, all gay men. The men had known each other for some time and had been guests in each other's homes. The atmosphere at the party had been cordial throughout the evening, and once dinner ended, cordial conversation continued in the living room over after-dinner drinks.

After the drinks were served, one of the hosts, A, returned to the kitchen and started washing the dishes. He was already well into his task when one of the guests, B, went to the kitchen to get some water.

I was seated in the living room but was close enough to the kitchen to hear the conversation and to observe the participants as it unfolded. Once again, pen-and-paper-napkin note-taking skills helped me record a largely verbatim account of the exchange.

I am going to give this conversation the same type of close reading as I gave to Mordden's text because I want to draw some parallels between the fictionalized argument over Little Kiwi and the events that took place in this real-life exchange.

The conversation began (lines 1-2) when B made a request for service: "Can I get a glass of water?" While it is unlikely that A would say no to such a request, B did not go into the refrigerator uninvited (remember how EM disliked having people prowling in his refrigerator—example 3.4); and by wording his request politely and deferentially, B underscored his status as guest in A's home and his unwillingness to take his hosts' hospitality for granted.

Both B's statement and its underlying meaning placed an obligation on the host to provide services, and A acknowledged receipt of the request but indicated that he was not willing to satisfy the terms of the request himself: "There is ice water in the fridge" (line 3). If B wanted water, B could get it himself.

The tone of line 3 was curious when I heard it. But remember: A was washing dishes while his partner was busy entertaining the guests in the living room. A's self-imposed exile into the kitchen may have contributed to the tension and anger in this line, but so may B's intrusion into what had become, by default, A's personal space.

When I reviewed my notes later that evening, B's behavior reminded me of the Les Nessman character from the original television program, *WKRP in Cincinnati*. Nessman felt he deserved a private office, but management assigned him to a workspace shared with other members of the WKRP staff. So he created his own "office" inside that room by placing strips of masking tape on the floor and requiring people to "knock" before crossing that boundary. He would ignore anyone who approached his desk without going through this pantomime.

A, it seemed to me, was responding to B in a similar way, for similar reasons. Checking with the other host later that evening, I learned that A often "went into a snit" (his partner's wording) if A volunteered to wash the dishes at a dinner party but found that no one would help him.

Perhaps B was aware of this component of A's behavior; he had been to dinner at their home before. Or perhaps he sensed the underlying irritation and decided to move carefully around it. For whatever reason, as line 4 suggests, B accepted A's statement from line 3 at face value and took appropriate action himself.

As it turned out, A was not so distant from B's activity, after all. While he continued to wash the dinner dishes, he noticed that B was searching the refrigerator for the ice water, but did not seem to be able to find it; he offered his follow-up suggestion ("In the brown pitcher"—line 5) before being asked. He did not otherwise interrupt his routine, however.

At this point (lines 6-7), B's tone began to change, and with it, the turn taking of the preceding lines shifted into format tying. B's statement "I don't see a brown pitcher in here" recast the meaning of A's comment (line 5) and thereby challenged A's statement (line 3) and the deference-to-host that preceded it. There is an underlying chain of inference presented here: I asked politely, you've not gotten the water for me, you've asked me to get it myself, you've told me where to look, I did, but it isn't there. The inference chain points to a single message—you are not a good host—which is not especially complimentary under the circumstances.

A responded to B's comment by reshaping B's statement into its positive counterpart ("Sure. It's brown, and round, and on the top shelf"—line 8), and by providing more information about the location of the pitcher, he attempted to meet his obligations as host and, thereby, refocused the point of the inference chain as well.

B's one-word reply—"Nope"—is similar in form to EM's "Oh, yeah?" (line 18) of example 3.4. In both examples, the construction allows the speaker to meet his obligations in turn taking but provides no information out of which the other speaker can construct a reply. (I will discuss the use of such *terminals* later in this chapter.) The responsibility for the next statement was entirely A's. And his response: silence. He said nothing; instead (lines 11-12), he interrupted the dishwashing, crossed the room to the refrigerator, pulled out the pitcher, and poured a glass of ice water for B.

A met the obligation of host that was at issue in B's opening comment (line 1). B could have accepted the water, said "thank you," and returned to the living room, which would have left unresolved some of the other issues that had emerged in the dialogue and the tension that had also emerged.

Instead of dropping the dispute over color terminology, B decided to continue it. His response—"That pitcher is not brown, it is tan" (line 12) — restated and intensified his earlier comment (lines 6-7), which recast A's initial reference to color (line 5) and first identified B's problem with that reference. By doing this, B also continued to press his implied charge that A was not a good host.

But B's inclusion of the additional color references in this line did something else. It linked B's comment here and A's comment in line 5 to a stereotype about gay men commonly repeated in U.S. society (and reinforced in scientific writing by some academics): Gay men are supposed to be experts in color description, regularly incorporating references to fuchsia, puce, chartreuse, and mauve into their dialogues and their daily lives. Most gay men recognize this as a shallow generalization, as stereotypes usually are; but that does not prevent gay men from using those stereotypes—as points of satire, minstrelsy, or exaggeration—when such references are required in text making.

Satire, minstrelsy, and exaggeration are not solitary vices, however. To make such references, the speaker has to have an audience that is familiar with the code and the culture surrounding it and is willing to participate, as an audience, in those terms. Presenting A with satire directly invokes assumptions of cooperative discourse and, in effect, invites A to become a co-participant rather than an antagonist in the conversation.

Note, then, A's response to B's lines 12-13: "It is brown to me." The comment restates A's earlier assertions of color (lines 5 and 8), but its significance lies in other areas. With this statement,

- A has now shifted away from the more specialized forms of format tying that both speakers used during the middle portion of the exchange, and he has returned to the more conventional turn-taking alternation used during the opening statements.
- A has also recast the form of his color labeling. The pitcher is no longer brown; now the pitcher "is brown to me"—a personalized reference to color that admits that others might view color in different terms.
- And by repeating his color reference in the face of B's counterassertions, A showed a willingness to join B in this minstrelsy. Hence his punctuation of line 14 with a slight smile.

In effect, the speakers transformed an exchange that was bordering on conflict and hostility into something more explicitly cooperative. Rather than competing, A and B overlapped their statements so that their reference making was directed toward a common goal: the coconstruction of the color of the water pitcher in the refrigerator. That two gay men would invest time in such an activity, or take time to disagree over the label, is itself a wonderful parody of gay excessiveness. B's closing line—"You said brown, so I looked for something dark chocolate" (lines 15-16)—implies that B was willing to extend the parody but that he knew it was not necessary to do so: The threat of conflict present earlier in the dialogue has now been diffused.

### Maintaining Continuity: Pause, Silence, and Transition

Besides threats of conflict, another type of problem regularly occurs during Gay English text making: speakers may not be sure what to say in a given setting, or may have nothing to say at all. As in most varieties of English, silence becomes an uncomfortable discourse strategy for Gay English speakers, and silence can certainly disrupt speaker efforts at cooperative text making.

#### Cooperative Silence: How Philip Met Eliot

David Leavitt describes such a situation in *The Lost Language of Cranes*, when Philip, one of the central characters in the story, first meets Eliot, who becomes Philip's significant other for a short period of time. This exchange takes place at a cocktail party in the apartment of Philip's good friend Sally, someone who had been instrumental in easing his transition into gay life while they both were in college. One reason she invited him to the party was to meet her new friend Eliot, whom she is certain Philip will like. He does, and his excitement, eagerness, and nervousness spill over into his use of language throughout the opening exchange (example 3.5).

The conversation begins with a widely used strategy in cocktail party dis-

course, gay and straight: ask about his or her job. Eliot's question (line 1—
worded as a statement, not a direct request for information) prompts seven
lines of commentary from Philip. When he completes his comment, he
pauses, giving Eliot the opportunity to respond; however, he does not ask
Eliot for any information.

---

**Example 3.5** How Philip met Eliot. (Source: Leavitt 1986: 37-38)

| | |
|---|---|
| 1 | "Sally tells me you work in publishing," Eliot said. A |
| 2 | slight shifting of the knees. Eyes unwavering. Philip was |
| 3 | relying completely on peripheral vision to make out the tuft |
| 4 | of hair emerging from his collar, the clean, close-cropped |
| 5 | fingernails, all the tiny erotic details. |
| 6 | "Well, actually I work for what's called a packaging company," |
| 7 | Philip said. "We're in the romance field. What I do |
| 8 | is edit and rewrite those terrible novels—all about desert |
| 9 | islands, pirate ships, cruise ships. The line's called |
| 10 | Wavecrest Books. Right now, for instance, I'm working on |
| 11 | *Tides of Flame*, which is all about how hardy and tempestuous |
| 12 | Sylvia falls in love with evil Captain Dick Tolliver." |
| 13 | Eliot laughed and Philip was relieved. |
| 14 | "Are you living uptown, too?" Eliot asked. |
| 15 | "More uptown than this—105th Street, off Amsterdam. How |
| 16 | about you?" |
| 17 | "I live in the East Village." |
| 18 | "How's the rent down there?" |
| 19 | "Mine isn't bad. I was lucky." |
| 20 | "Do you have a lease, or is it a sublet?" |
| 21 | "Oh no, it's my lease." |
| 22 | "That's great." |
| 23 | "Uh huh." |
| 24 | Then there was nothing else to say. They stood there not |
| 25 | looking away. Philip was studying Eliot's eyes. . . . A minute |
| 26 | passed without a word and still they stared. Every now |
| 27 | and then Philip let out a snort of breath, almost a laugh |
| 28 | and his smile widened a little, and Eliot smiled too and |
| 29 | let out a thin stream of smoke. |
| 30 | "So what do you do?" Philip asked finally, mostly |
| 31 | because there was no one else there to interrupt, no Sally, |
| 32 | no dinner bell. |

---

Eliot responds with another standard cocktail party question: Where do you live (line 14). Philip replies and builds the reply into a question (lines 15-16), which begins a five-line exchange about apartments, rents, and leases—topics within which residents of Manhattan can easily find common ground. Notice that Philip now takes the lead in asking questions—lines 15-16, 18, 20. Eliot's responses are brief, one-line statements (lines 17, 19, and 21) that reveal little information about Eliot's life and contain suggestions for topics that will elicit more productive discussion. He responds in the same fashion—"Uh huh" (line 23)—to Philip's content-neutral statement, "That's great" (line 22).

There are traces of cooperative discourse in the exchange, but other factors are actively creating barriers in that regard; clearly, this conversation is not getting off the ground. Persons familiar with the novel (or the film) will recognize how Eliot's conduct in this passage anticipates his behavior throughout his brief relationship with Philip. Eliot is intensively independent and self-absorbed. He shares little of himself with others and tends to be verbal only during the segments of the text when he can be the speaker-in-control. Even then, he assumes that others will do the "work" necessary to maintain social interaction; his priorities lie elsewhere.

Philip's use of language responds directly—but positively—to Eliot's display of "attitude" by intensifying his efforts to cooperate with the intent of the text making. He responds in detail when asked about his job, to give Eliot lots of ideas on which to base his turn taking. When Eliot uses none of them, shifting instead to another "standard question," Philip repositions his use of language as well—brief comments designed to solicit comments on similar themes from his coparticipant. Eliot does not respond to those overtures, either.

Philip does not want to walk away from the conversation; he wants the exchange to continue. (Leavitt's description [1986: 36-37] of the first moments of their meeting has already made this clear.) But what can he do to keep the conversation alive?

Here is what he does: He recognizes that there is nothing else to say (line 24), so he stops speaking and lets eye contact take over the textual space that would otherwise be occupied by words. He stares at Eliot's eyes, and Eliot returns the gaze. Philip smiles. Eliot smiles. Philip breathes. Eliot breathes, a response highlighted and punctuated by his cigarette smoke, which signals Eliot's now-active participation in the nonverbal turn taking.

Importantly, even though communication is continuing, the absence of words begins to make Philip nervous. And because no outside source seems likely to intervene (lines 31-32), he tries again to construct verbal exchange, this time relying on the cocktail party standard that Eliot employed at the beginning of the conversation: "So what do you do?" (line 30). Philip's wording of this familiar ploy is quite different from Eliot's, however. Philip structures the statement so that Eliot has no choice but to respond; moreover, by focusing the question directly on Eliot's actions, Philip allows Eliot to set the direction for this next segment of the conversation—a strategy that (as Leavitt's narrative shows, pp. 38 ff.) turns out to be satisfactory and productive for both parties.

Shifting from spoken language to silence (as in lines 24-30) is one of the strategies that gay men regularly employ when they want to maintain cooperative discourse but need time to rethink the strategies they will use to address that goal. Gay communication is not disrupted during this segment of text making; gaze, physical contact, and other nonverbal media continue to express speaker commitments to cooperation quite explicitly here, as Leavitt's example suggests. Moreover—and this is very different from Delph's (1978) claims about the restrictions on gay men's verbal communication in erotic settings—the shift to silence does not preempt a return to spoken language. It does, however, reinforce messages already presented in verbal terms and prompts speakers to assume that an additional round of verbal exchange is about to follow.

   The transitional messages implicit in gay men's use of silence helps explain why, after shifting to silence, Philip maintains silence for only a brief period before moving on to another scene-saving strategy. Of course, such shifts from speech to silence, then from silence back to speech, regularly occur in other English conversational settings. In those settings, the absence of spoken language often becomes problematic, since speakers of English generally consider "having nothing to say" as evidence of defective social skills. This point of view may contribute to Philip's shift from silence to speech in line 30, but under the rules of Gay English text making, it is not the only factor contributing to that shift.

### Cooperative Silence: Buying Sweatshirts

The conversation in example 2.1 also shows how a judicious use of silence gives speakers the chance to rethink and renegotiate the direction of a Gay English conversation. As I explained when looking briefly at this text in chapter 2, the speakers in this case were a customer shopping in the men's section of a suburban D.C. department store and a salesman working there. On prominent display in the men's section that day was a tableful of Champion sweatshirts in various colors; some of the sweatshirts were on sale, according to a sign attached to the table. The salesman, S, an African American gay man in his thirties, was folding sweatshirts and putting the display back in order as the customer, C, a Euro-American gay man in his midforties) approached the table and began browsing through the merchandise. When S saw C approach the table, he turned, smiled, and began the conversation displayed in example 2.1.

I was standing next to the table, looking through a rack of sale shirts, close enough to hear the conversation without feeling intrusive. I noticed the brief opening exchange and the period of silence that followed; my curiosity over the next segment of the dialogue prompted careful note taking as the exchange continued.

The opening of this conversation involved mechanical, predictable dialogue between salesman and customer. The remainder of the exchange was decidedly gay-positive. It was limited in detail, perhaps, by the public setting in which the dialogue occurred and by other factors (chapter 4 continues this discussion of Gay English as a *language of risk*), but it was filled with gay-related message and meaning, all the same.

Note, for example, C's choice of pronoun in his opening statement (line 6): He asked, "What are you asking for these?" rather than "How much are these?" The "you" personalized the question and gave S the leeway to construct a response in equally personal terms. He did so (line 8), and once again, pronoun choice ("I'm afraid . . .") expressed a personal point of view. That statement laid the groundwork for the intimacy expressed in his next comment ("But that colored shirt would look nice on you" — lines 8-9). The reference was ambiguous, since there are several reasons why a lavender shirt might look nice on someone. In other circumstances, such ambiguity could indicate the speaker's disinterest in terminating the conversation. This was not C's interpretation, however. Instead of taking lines 8-9 as an opportunity to back away from the exchange, C replied with a similarly ambiguous comment of his own (line 11): "Yeah, I know. I own a few of them already." This could be a comment about wardrobe or a more explicit confirmation of gender preference implied in the preceding line. The grin that punctuated the comment and S's reply (line 13, also a grin) made the second interpretation a more likely reading for the comment and made C's final statement much less formulaic than it might otherwise seem.

Bridging the two segments of the text was a thirty-second period of silence. Coming immediately after C's seemingly terse response to S's initial question, the shift to silence here might appear to indicate that communication had come to an end. While conversation ceased, nonverbal messages continued to be exchanged, and once the conversation resumed, it built directly on the personalized sentiments implicit in those nonverbal messages—just as was the case during the follow-up to Philip and Eliot's mutually cooperative period of silence.

### Terminals: Marking Closure and Transition

In example 3.5, Philip preceded his shift from speech to silence with "That's great" (line 22), and Eliot's response to the comment was an equally unfocused "Uh huh" (line 23). Neither of these statements added referential content to the conversation; instead, participants used them to indicate that the discussion in the current segment of the text had come to an end and that an introduction of some new topic or a shift to some other text-saving strategy was now required.

Gay English speakers place statements that signal these two text-preserving messages at the end of text segments, and so I refer to them as "terminals." Under this definition, speaker B's "Nope" (example 1.3, line 9) and speaker C's "No thanks, I am just looking" (example 2.1, line 2) are also terminals, since these statements also marked the conclusion of one segment of these texts and preluded the refocused discussions that emerged in the next text segments.

Terminals vary considerably in their internal detail, text by text and speaker by speaker. In example 2.3, each statement in a turn-taking pair served this function. In example 2.1, the terminal was composed of a single statement, not a turn-taking pair, and the terminal itself (line 2) was quite content explicit. In example 1.3, the terminal was a single, content-specific word (line 9).

Moreover, while terminals are always associated with the conclusion of discussion within a text segment, terminals do not always result in a transition into silence. Sometimes, a carefully worded terminal prompts other speakers to change topic but to minimize the interruption of the verbal dialogue as they do so. Other times, speakers use terminals to bring discussion to a close but also to signal plans to resume the discussion at some later time.

### The Irish Come to America

The dialogue in example 2.2 took place in the home of a Washington, D.C. gay couple, who had invited three other gay friends to a potluck dinner. Two of the friends were also a couple; I was the third guest. All five of us had known each other for several years and regularly visited in each other's homes. Our familiarity allowed us to dispense with much of the patina of politeness otherwise associated with at-home Gay English discourse. It was entirely appropriate that evening, for example, for anyone who wanted a cold beer to make a pro forma request to one of the hosts, then to make his own selection from the refrigerator.

Once dinner ended, everyone moved into the living room, where the guests took seats, began leafing through magazines, and continued to chat with each other about current events, recent trips to the countryside, and one couple's newfound interest in regional wines. One of the hosts, S3, continued to listen to the conversation as he watered and pruned his extensive collection of indoor plants. The other host, S1, positioned himself in front of the television set as the dialogue began.

Immediately after lines 12-13, S3 ceased working with the plants and sat down next to the guests, while S1 turned away from the television and explained in greater detail why he wanted to watch the film, why he would recommend it to the guests, and why watching the film was not an intrusion into the social agenda of the evening. His arguments worked; the guests agreed to join S1 in viewing the film.

There are two terminals in this passage: line 7 and lines 12-13. In both cases, the comment prompted other participants to shift the discussion to broader and less antagonistic concerns.

Some background will clarify the point of line 7. S1 and S3 frequently "spar" like this in front of guests, and their close friends regularly tease them about the frequency of these exchanges, particularly in social settings in front of strangers. "Now, now, girls, no fights tonight!" is one of S2's standard remarks to that end. Line 7 could have been the overture to one of these exchanges. The wording suggests that S1 had a different intention in mind when he made this remark (something S1 later confirmed): He wanted S3 to cease his sotto voce muttering (lines 5-6); he did not expect the remark to elicit a reply. S2 also considered line 7 to be a terminal and responded appropriately with the topic shift in line 8. By doing this, he may not have prevented S3 from interpreting line 7 as an invitation to more antagonistic dialogue, but he did prevent S3 from acting on that interpretation and disrupting the fellowship of the evening.

S2, who ensured continuity in cooperative discourse in line 8, is the person who subsequently called for additional steps toward continuity. He is the source of the comment in lines 12-13. His wording of this statement reflects a familiarity with S1 and S3's self-contained dialogue and, perhaps, the beginnings of dissatisfaction with having to witness it again. Note that, whatever his intention, speakers S1 and S3 gave S2 no opportunity to elaborate on his statement. Their abrupt refocusing of their behavior in response to S2's comment (lines 12-13) shows that they considered his statement to be a terminal and that they took seriously its implications for text restructuring.

*Sleeping with a Hairy Chest*

I collected the text in example 3.6 from a friend; it was part of his description of an ongoing dialogue he was having with a gay colleague at work. His colleague was just beginning to acknowledge his emotional and erotic interests in other men, and my friend had been serving as his buddy for several months, guiding his colleague through the initial and often difficult stages of gay socialization.

He reported this conversation to me in outline, as the transcript in example 3.6 shows. Knowing about my interests in Gay English, he made a point of recording several key phrases from the conversation, which he included in that outline.

---

**Example 3.6** Sleeping next to a hairy chest.

Part I [*En route from work area to the men's room*]

1    S1: How was your weekend?
2    S2: Very eventful.
3    S1: You got some?
4    S2: I certainly did.
[*Discussion follows, not notated*]

Part II [*Open door, enter men's room*]

5    S2: One thing I want to ask: Is sucking cock without a
6        rubber safe?
[*They discuss safe sex guidelines while they finish business in the bathroom*]

Part III [*Leaving the men's room*]

7    S2: One thing's for sure: It's nice to wake up in the
8        morning next to a hairy chest.

---

S1 had been openly gay at work for as long as he had been employed at that firm. S2 was recently hired, though the two had known each other from their days when both worked for the same company in Chicago. This, S1 thinks, explained why S2 was willing to be so open and personal in what was one of the first conversations they had about gay issues.

S2 reported that he had met "someone special" at a (nongay) friend's house on Friday evening. The two had talked, gone home together, and spent the remainder of the weekend alternating between bedroom erotics, television and rental movies, snacks, and trips to the grocery store for more provisions. They ended the weekend as both parties left for work on Monday morning, after agreeing to be in touch by telephone later that morning. And sure enough, shortly before this conversation began, the new friend had called.

I wanted to hear more about the "coming out" issues underlying that story but, after reviewing S1's outline, I first wanted to know why S1 had made a point of remembering and transcribing these items and not other statements S2 had made during their conversation. He explained that he remembered lines 1 and 2 because they were the opening statements in the conversation. S1 found the guardedly provocative quality of lines 2 and 4 to be especially creative for someone so new to gay life; that is, they affirmed much without revealing anything in detail. They satisfied the cooperative obligation of the turn taking, and invited S1 to continue taking charge of the dialogue and to continue asking questions.

S1 remembered lines 5 and 6, he said, because he was pleased to hear that S2 was exploring gay erotics from the point of view of safe-sex practice, and he remembered lines 7 and 8 because they struck him as an interesting way to close the conversation. Although the reference here was not as guarded as it was in lines 2 and 4, the comment is just as provocative. S1 immediately wanted to know more about S2's reactions to his first, weekend-long gay male erotic encounter. The comment prompted S1 to confirm that he had other questions to ask, and both parties agreed that they would continue the conversation over lunch the next day—exactly the closure–transition message that I associated with this statement when I first read my friend's outlined transcript.

### A Rough Neighborhood at the Gym

I end this chapter with an example of terminal usage that I observed at the weight room at a large, coeducational health club in northwest D.C. (this health club features prominently in the ethnographic description I present in chapter 6). Both of the participants had been regular patrons at this gym for several months prior to this conversation, but (speaker S2 later told me), outside of brief hellos they had not talked to each other or spent time together until this particular evening.

Their interaction started when S1 needed someone to "spot" him during some difficult chest exercises, and when that exercise was completed, the two continued their workout together. Their last workout station was on the opposite side of the weight room from the doorway and the stairs to the front desk and to the locker rooms. Their sets completed, the two continued talking and agreed to exchange telephone numbers. After S1 put S2's num-

ber in his gym-shorts pocket, he explained that he had to leave the gym because of a previous appointment. Example 3.7 displays the turn-taking pair
that followed.

---

**Example 3.7** A rough neighborhood at the gym.

1    S1: I'll call you on Saturday. We'll get together.
2    S2: Let me walk you to the stairs. It's a rough
3         neighborhood out there.

[*That said, S2 took S1 by the arm, escorted him across the weight room floor,
and wished him good night.*]

---

# 4

## The Risk Outside: Gay English, "Suspect Gays," and Heterosexuals

In the preceding chapters, I discussed Gay English text making in instances where gay concerns were already in the foreground of the conversation. But in many settings, such foregrounding does not occur (at least, not initially): for example, when conversations occur outside of gay-centered environments, when coparticipants are strangers, or when the topics under discussion deal almost entirely with heterosexual themes. Establishing a common ground becomes a primary concern for text construction in these cases, and Gay English grammar and discourse skills give speakers several ways to address that concern.

### Conversation with Suspect Gays

Gaydar provides a starting point for many Gay English conversations under such circumstances. Michael Musto defines gaydar as "the art of spotting sisters, no matter how concealed, invisible or pretending to be straight they are." He continues:

Gaydar is an intuitive aptitude which surpasses anything in nature. A wildebeest couldn't spot another wildebeest with the same precision with which we can track down other kindred spirits, whether in a mall, on a football field, in an army barracks, or even at home. . . . There is something in the walk, the talk, the pursing of the lips, the posing of the wrist, that tips us off with great certainty, even when they're holding a live grenade or wearing a wedding ring. (1993: 120)

Several of Musto's points merit further discussion. First, while Musto writes in terms of gay male reference (for example, "the art of spotting sisters"), gaydar is not exclusively a gay man's skill, as Susie Bright's (1993) description (in an essay paired with Musto's piece) of her own use of "gay radar" (her term) readily displays. Musto's take on this topic differs somewhat from that outlined in Bright's essay, and those differences suggest more general contrasts between lesbian and gay men's text-making practices, especially where the public negotiation of erotic encounters is concerned.

Second, as is true for other elements in gay culture, gaydar does not automatically appear at some point during a person's gay career. Instead, gaydar is an acquired skill, and to use it effectively requires careful cultivation and nurturing. Gay college students use phrases like "growing up in a desert of nothing" to describe the frustrations they felt during their teenage years, knowing that there must be other gay men somewhere but not yet knowing how to identify them. (Life story narratives explored in chapter 7 describe how some individuals resolve this dilemma.)

Third, and most important, gaydar is not so much about identifying gay men at-distance but about identifying men who are, from the speaker's perspective, likely to be gay. I refer to men in this category as "suspect gays," since, once they have been identified by gaydar, confirming their "suspect gay status" usually becomes a recurring theme in the next phase in the text-making query. The speaker may, for example, initiate some form of face-to-face or behind-the-scenes negotiation to determine whether the initial assessment is valid. He may simply observe behavior at-distance, assessing what he sees against his own gay-positive criteria, or recasting those observations to conform to personal notions of fantasy and desire. Additional combinations of these strategies are also possible. The point is, instead of being a self-contained activity, gaydar provides the entry point into a much larger complex of gay identity-related social moves and queries.

Needless to say, language skills figure prominently in those efforts to elicit or confirm a suspect gay's gay identity. Often, confirmation unfolds in discreet, subtle, and almost unnoticed ways, with the suspect gay as well as the speaker contributing actively to the verbal negotiation. Let us look briefly at how two gay men have described such events.

In example 4.1, the narrator notes how the suspect gay's physical appearance was inconsistent with the narrator's expectations about a dairy farmer but coincided with the narrator's expectations regarding a (desirable) gay image; as the narrator notes, the farmer "was compact and quite cute." Apparently the dairy farmer was making a similar assessment of the narrator's suspect gay status because, according to the narrative, he was the person who first slipped something subtle into the conversation. The narrator observes, "I don't remember what it was, exactly," and that is the point: The significance of the remark lies in its gay symbolism, not in the particulars of its content, and the unexpected discovery signaled by the presence of the remark made unnecessary any additional verbal queries into gay identity.

Example 4.1 also contains an example of the strategic use of pause commonly found in Gay English cooperative discourse. Here, of course, because the conversation was between strangers, suspect gay negotiations precluded any other, more explicit forms of cooperative exchange.

---

**Example 4.1** Opera on the farm. (Source: Biemiller 1993; background: the author, a newspaper reporter, is doing a feature story on a traveling production of Aaron Copland's opera *The Tender Land*. The opera company has decided to stage each performance on the front porch of a farmhouse rather than in the artificial environment of an enclosed theater. This excerpt begins as the author leaves the airport and drives to one of these rural sites.)

So I was driving the minivan toward a dairy farm outside a town of 1,500 on a beautiful afternoon. I arrived to find that a semicircle of risers had been put up on the lawn in front of a picture-perfect farmhouse, and that the opera's director and a few staff people were sprawled across several rows each, debating how to block various scenes. There were introductions all around.

The last person I met was the dairy farmer, Lou. He didn't look at all like the pot-bellied and suspendered 55 year old I'd imagined. In fact he was compact and quite cute. It wasn't long before he slipped something subtle into the conversation that only a Gay person would have slipped in—I don't remember what it was, exactly, but I remember my surprise. While the director and the conductor discussed where to put the orchestra, I looked at Lou and he looked at me and I kind of smiled and he kind of smiled and I put two and two together: I was sitting on the front lawn of a queer dairy farmer.

---

Ben's narrative (example 4.2) suggests the same text-making sequence as displayed in example 4.1—the negotiation of suspect gay status and mutual confirmation of gay identity—followed by an elaboration of gay-centered themes. And once again, one participant's statement was able to complete the transition from suspected to confirmed gay identities. Ben recalls that segment of the exchange: "And he said, 'Well, what are you going to do this evening?' And I said: 'Well, I don't know. I may go out for a cocktail.' And he—I was living on the Hill at the time—and he said 'that's pretty tough if you don't like country and western music.'"

The reference to "country and western music" is the key sentence in this report and presumably to the original conversation. On first reading, there is nothing gay about this statement—which is why such references are so useful in negotiations of suspect gay identities. If the speaker is correct in his suspicions, the coparticipant in the conversation will read the concealed gay message (at that time, the only gay men's bar on Capitol Hill catered to

---

**Example 4.2** Country music on the Hill. (Source: Alan Hersker's interview with Ben, a gay white male in his early fifties who lives in Washington, D.C.; background: Alan and Ben are discussing how people try to conceal gay identity at the workplace and how easy it is to identify gay men in spite of those efforts.)

Ben: You sort of try to scope people out. I may not have—a new expression I read several times in the *Blade* in the last few weeks—the best gaydar around. I mean Thomas [a colleague at work—WLL] just [*Laughter, then pause*]—he picks them right away. I am not sure all of them are true.

Alan: Some of them might be wishful thinking.

Ben: You know, just sort of, you get a, well, interesting: When this guy and I first met, this friend and I, I had been there [that is, on the job—WLL] I guess six months or maybe a year and he started and it was kind of looked. We got to sort of chatting and he was friendly. Just sort of thing. I guess you maybe watch somebody just a little bit too long to see. And one night, he was walking, we both happened to be leaving and at the same time but we were all—I can't remember, he lived in Crystal City [a residential complex across the Potomac River in Arlington, Virginia—WLL] at the time so maybe he was just walking toward the metro the same way I was. And he said, "Well, what are you going to do this evening?" And I said: "Well, I don't know. I may go out for a cocktail." And he—I was living on the Hill at the time—and he said "that's pretty tough if you don't like country and western music." [*Laughter*] And I just, and we just, we both started laughing.

Alan: That's great. So after that it was . . . ?

Ben: Yeah, after that it was, it was pretty open at that point. Then we started, you know, talking about other people. And we go out to lunch, that sort of thing once in a while.

---

gay cowboy motifs) and make the appropriate connections regarding speaker identity. If the speaker has misassessed the signals and falsely identified (or fantasized) a gay identity, the careful coding of gay meaning keeps the speaker on safe ground. If the coparticipant is not gay, he is unlikely to connect musical genre, bar location, and gay gender. Consequently, he will assume that he misunderstood what the speaker said, or (and more commonly, in my experience) he will ignore the comment and shift the conversation to a new subject.

*Ignore and shift* is also the strategy that a gay man will use if he is unwilling to (or uninterested in) confirming gay identity under these circumstances. In other words, like the speaker's statement, the coparticipant's reply can be open to multiple readings; this explains why, once their gaydar is set into motion, some gay men persist in their efforts to elicit gay disclosure from a "suspect gay" even in the face of apparent disinterest. (I have more to say about the textual significance of such persistence in chapter 6.)

### We Don't Believe in Santa Claus

Rather than unfolding discreetly and centering around a judicious introduction of a single word or statement, suspect gay status is confirmed through an accumulation of conversation-based messages, packaged in a variety of formats. Such was the case in example 4.3, a conversation that took place in the men's clothing section of a department store in a suburban D.C. shopping mall.[1]

---

**Example 4.3** We don't believe in Santa Claus.

```
1    S:   May I help you?
2    C1:  [Presents items to be charged; says nothing]
3    S:   [Looks at merchandise] Was this on sale ? [C1, C2 say
4         nothing] Let me check the amount of the discount. [Leaves
5         counter, checks, returns, and begins the transaction]
6         Do you need gift boxes for these?
7    C2:  No. We don't believe in Santa Claus.
8    S:   You didn't see that movie last night? With Kate Jackson?
9         About Santa Claus and orphans. That'd make you believe in
10        Santa Claus.
11   C1:  Sounds thrilling.
12   S:   Yes, I enjoyed watching it. But my roommate fell asleep.
13   C1:  [Said to S, but half-directed at C2] Sounds like our
14        house.
15   C2:  We sit in front of the TV and I fall asleep.
16   S:   Like at our house.
17   C2:  That's why we always go to bed so early.
18   S:   Old age is not for sissies, just like Bette Davis said.
29        [Pause] Here's your purchases. I hope you'll come here
20        again.
```

---

The salesman (S in the transcript) was a Euro-American gay man in his midthirties. My partner and I were the two customers; he is C1 and I am C2 in the transcript. We were at the mall that December afternoon shopping for Christmas presents (and looking for bargains, truth be told). We shop at

---

**Example 4.4** Gay-centered messages and meanings in example 4.3.

1. S's offer to check on the customer's discount (lines 3-4)
   Such personalized service is uncommon in D.C.-area department stores and becomes a signal that the salesman may be willing to personalize the exchange in other ways.

2. C2's rejection of the Santa Claus myth (line 7)
   Santa Claus remains a primary icon of the family-oriented, heterosexual lifestyle in the United States. Also, the first person plural pronoun in this statement anticipates comments about C1 and C2's domestic arrangement presented in lines 13-17.

3. S's enthusiasm for Kate Jackson, Santa Claus, and orphans (lines 8-10)
   Introduction of this topic transposes the focus of C2's somewhat derogatory comment (line 7) into more acceptable, gay-centered imagery: a television program, starring a longtime symbol of glamorous gender style (cf. Jackson's role in *Charlie's Angels*), and describing efforts to bring Yuletide happiness to orphans (who, like some gay men, are unable to interact with parents or family members during the Christmas season).

4. S, C1, and C2's mutual confirmation of their domestic relationships (lines 12-17)
   The use of overlapping ideas—television watching, falling asleep in front of the television, sleeping together—gradually leads these strangers to this common ground. Once again, the shift in pronoun choice (S's use of "I" and "my" in line 12 becomes "our" in line 16, in response to C1 and C2's use of "we" and "our" in the intervening lines) becomes an important element in message coconstruction.

5. S's homage to Bette Davis (line 18)
   Ms. Davis's motion picture characters have provided gay men with many of their favorite one-liners, and she figures prominently in other arenas of gay culture, particularly for men who grew up in the years before Stonewall.

---

this store frequently, though neither of us remembers having interacted with this salesman before.

We had spent about fifteen minutes browsing through the assortment of sweaters, shirts, and ties on sale that weekend, and having completed our selections, we moved to the salesman's workstation to pay for them. Several other salespersons were also on the floor that afternoon, but they were already working with customers. S was folding merchandise for reshelving when we approached him. He began the dialogue presented in the transcript as soon as we reached his section of the counter.[2]

A rapid scan of this passage shows that there is nothing explicitly gay about any of the speakers' word choice, sentence construction, or sequencing of ideas. The conversation was cooperative, but no more so than might be the case while any salesperson takes care of a customer's purchases.

Although this conversation may appear to be gender-neutral, its content appeals directly to points of gay reference and to persons who can decipher such meanings when presented in code. In fact, as the inventory in example 4.4 suggests, a close reading reveals gay-centered messages and meanings encoded in every segment of this exchange.

But what is important about these coded references is not just their presence in this text but the gradual, systematic way in which the speakers introduced them into the text. Let me briefly retrace the steps in that sequence and show how the speakers coconstructed gay disclosure through their discreet though cooperative text making.

S's opening comment was appropriate to the department-store context and relatively noncommittal: "May I help you?" (line 1). C1's silence (line 2) may seem an inappropriate response, though—as explained in chapter 3, gay men often use silence to give coparticipants the chance to rethink the way they will position language in the next remark. S did precisely that. He began with another appropriate and noncommittal statement ("Was this on sale?"—line 3) and followed it with a more personalized overture ("Let me check the amount of the discount"—line 4), which answered his own question and implied that the customers might get more of a bargain from this transaction than they had initially expected.

S's next comment (line 6) was also situationally appropriate and noncommittal: "Do you need gift boxes for these?" Now the customers had a chance to offer a more personalized overture. C2 did so, with a comment that explicitly rejected Santa Claus, a key element in heterosexual, family-centered iconography. S was not put off in the least by the negative comment. In fact, he used it as a basis for his reply (lines 8-10). These comments linked C2's Santa Claus reference to motion pictures (an important cultural resource, particularly for the proponents of gay camp), Kate Jackson (the glamorous star of *Charlie's Angels* and other television sitcom classics), and orphans (who, like some gay men, have been separated from their families and have no home to return to during the Christmas holidays). In that sense, these comments recast the heterosexist Santa Claus imagery into something more relevant and sympathetic to gay interests—and invited the other participants in the speech event to choose to interpret these comments in gay terms.

C1's reply (line 11) can also be interpreted in two ways: as a reflection of his dissatisfaction with the direction the conversation was taking, or as a cautiously worded invitation for S to confirm that he intended lines 8-10 to have gay-centered meaning. S's reply provided that confirmation, but again, only if the listener was willing to give a gay reading to the word "roommate." This was exactly what C1 did (lines 13-14), when he alluded to similarities in their domestic arrangements. C2's paraphrase (line 15) of S's comment from line 12 built on C1's use of the first person plural pronoun "our" to take this suggestion one step further: C2 was specifying, though still in a cautious, tentative way, what these similarities might entail: two men in a committed domestic partnership. S's reply (line 16) confirmed the similarity, without saying anything more about the details of the relationship. C2 then acknowledged S's confirmation (line 17), and S brought the dialogue to a close.

The format-tying and other turn-taking strategies displayed in this conversation are quite different from those found at the Sunday brunch (example 2.3) and in conversations within other private, gay-controlled speech settings. At the Sunday brunch, speakers moved rapidly from one topic to another, letting turn-taking and format-tying processes provide continuity in text message. Here, the range of topics was more narrowly focused and (as in examples 4.1 and 4.2) text coherence depended on a more gradual acknowledgment of the gay messages underlying seemingly gender-neutral content cues. And here, statements of hesitation (such as lines 2, 7, and 12) that would have been devalued and disregarded during the brunch exchange (look again at the speakers' reactions to lines 6 and 16 in example 2.3) actually assisted in the speakers' presentation of gay messages.

For this conversation to work—more accurately, for it to be cooperative—all three participants had to assume the existence of a shared gay identity or, at least, had to be willing to proceed as if there was sufficient reason to act on such an assumption. I do not know the salesman's position on this issue. For our part, as my partner and I agreed during a follow-up discussion in the mall's parking lot, the salesman met several of our suspect gay criteria: He was attractive, he was tastefully dressed (all cotton, no synthetic fibers), he worked in a department store known to employ many gay men, and although not flamboyant, he was not afraid to be a little playful with strangers.

And even if the salesman turned out not to be gay (in some absolute, essential sense), his initial contributions to the conversation showed little reluctance to be a coparticipant in a conversation addressing gay themes. We assessed all of these cues, and then we acted accordingly.

In this case, the conversation worked. A little gay pleasantry, a little gay humor—and all three of us came away from the exchange happy to have found additional evidence that gay men *are*, indeed, everywhere.

### I Like San Francisco. You Ever Been There?

Not all conversations between suspect gays unfold so pleasantly. Sometimes what starts out as seemingly gay-friendly commentary turns out to be creative heterosexual humor, and sometimes what appears to be evidence of gay interest is not really interest at all.

One evening in spring 1989 I was flying from Chicago to Salt Lake City to do more fieldwork on the Northern Ute reservation. The plane had very few passengers, and most of us were assigned seats in the front third of the coach cabin. After the plane reached "a comfortable cruising altitude" (that's the second officer's wording, remember—not mine!), I moved back toward the center of the cabin where I could have three seats entirely to myself. I was swiftly followed by a man who had been seated on the aisle two rows in front of me.[3]

I sat in an aisle seat in the middle of the coach cabin, and he sat down in the aisle seat directly across from me in the same row.

He immediately said: "I have the same idea you do," which was, at best, ambiguous. If he wanted to get away from a crowded area of the plane and have a row of seats to himself, why did he move to a row where one person was already sitting? Why not move to a row all his own? This was a suspicious action, but suspicious actions can be important landmarks for defining and identifying suspect gay identity. Perhaps he intended a more coded reading of his reference to our "same idea."

So we started to exchange the sort of in-flight trivia that strangers often exchange while traveling. As the discussion unfolded, I decided to take notes, and since the cabin was dimly lit, I could do this without being too obvious about the data gathering.

"Where are you flying to?" he asked.

"Salt Lake City," I replied.

"Oh yeah, same as me. Where are you staying?"

I explained that I was driving to the Ute reservation, once I landed, and that I would eventually spend the night near Ft. Duchesne, Utah.

"I have work in Salt Lake, two days of conferences and sales." And he explained that he worked for a manufacturing company in Maine and that he often traveled to conventions to present updates on their product line. Then he said: "I'm traveling alone. I always travel alone."

I made some bland remark about being on your own in a strange city, still curious where this conversation was going. Then he added: "I live in a small town in the central part of the state. Do most of my work by computer hookup and fax. That's why I enjoy traveling: it gets me out of there. Real limited opportunities."

I couldn't resist: "What do you do for fun?"

"Nothing to do. When I get really bored, I drive to Portland [*pause*], stay with friends."

Now I was becoming intrigued with the mystery. He was giving me a cluster of signals with suspect gay subtext: over thirty and living alone (a great suspect gay giveaway!), going away from home to the city for fun, staying (pause—an important Gay English feature in its own right) with friends (a relationship not otherwise explained), and traveling alone tonight.

How could I find out if this cluster of commentary was accidental or a deliberately focused signaling? The captain's voice interrupted my thoughts, adding his welcome to those the second officer had extended earlier. He described the evening's route of flight from O'Hare, across Illinois, Iowa, and Colorado, over the Rocky Mountains, and along the Wasatch Range into Salt Lake City. After giving the estimated arrival time in Salt Lake City, he added: "And for those of you continuing on with us to San Francisco, our estimated arrival time there is . . . "

I heard nothing else: San Francisco was my cue. Gay men, whatever their individual interests, are likely to understand the gay meanings implied by a reference to San Francisco, so introducing a carefully worded reference to that city should prompt my new friend to confirm his gay sexuality.

My question was clumsy, but it was the best I could do under the circumstances: "San Francisco. I like San Francisco. You ever been there?"

"I've been there once," he replied. Then he paused and added: "with my girlfriend."

To this day, I remain uncertain about the meaning of that line. It seemed to contradict everything he had said prior to that point in our conversation (or, at least, everything I remember hearing him say). Instead of resolving my uncertainty, my San Francisco trope elicited even more ambiguities to decipher.

I did not know what to do to redirect the discussion, and frankly, was losing interest in the exchange. So I muttered something neutral, and after a few seconds of prolonged pause, I shifted my body position slightly and returned to my work.

Several minutes passed in silence. Then, after making a second opening remark (I didn't hear it well enough to record it) the man from Maine added: "Yes, I like San Francisco." By then, I was deep in my writing and was unwilling to continue talking for any reason. He sat in silence for a few more minutes, then turned out his reading lamp and went to sleep. We did not speak again, either in the air or after the plane arrived in Salt Lake City. The last I saw of him, he was boarding the shuttle bus for his hotel.

Even though I have supplied only pieces of the conversation, the narrative illustrates the confusion and the frustration that may accompany suspect gay–centered conversations. I felt both during that exchange, according to the comments that I included in my field notes (for example, "means what?" written twice in the margin, and "HE'S PISSING ME OFF!" sprawled in bold letters at the bottom of the page). Here are some of the points of confusion (and frustration) that prompted that reaction.

Why did he go out of his way to start the conversation and then repeat over and over again that he was alone? Was he simply a friendly, if somewhat unworldly, heterosexual, unaware of the gay-centered messages that a listener could read into his commentary? Or did he really want to begin a conversation that would lead to a gradual disclosure of gay themes and ultimately confirmation of gay identities?

Why the sudden reference to his girlfriend? Was this another expression of his unfamiliarity with gay discourse? Or did he suddenly realize that the conversation was beginning to convey messages that he did not wish to be conveyed, and decide to redirect the discussion toward heterosexual themes?

Or was his comment really a redirection of the text? He didn't say "girlfriend" with a "campy" or exaggerated tone of voice, but he could have meant this as a reference to a close (gay male) friend and assumed that, after my previous references, I would eagerly interpret the usage in gay terms. Or perhaps he had a girlfriend, because that is what gay men often do in small, rural towns when they want to disguise and safeguard gay identity — which further explains his earlier, unelaborated reference to staying with friends in Portland.

But even if he intended his comment about San Francisco to be gay-cooperative and to support the focus of the conversation, textual ambiguity remains. The way he presented the statement did nothing to elaborate on that focus; instead, his comment returned responsibility for elaboration to me. Recall, however, that he was the person who had initiated this exchange. Under the usual expectations governing Gay English text making, initiating the conversation places the speaker in charge of the remainder of the dialogue unless there are clear-cut signals shifting that responsibility to some other participant. From my point of view, clear-cut signals were the last things his comments were providing.

A final point: I have written these comments in terms of my own frustrations. But rereading this analysis several years after the conversation took place, I can also imagine how the coparticipant could have had the same reactions to this conversation as I did. That is, he could have been confident that he was providing explicit clues to gay identity (look again at my list of gay-centered features) and wondered why I was not being more openly disclosive. Ambiguous text readings and the responsibility for cooperative text making flow both ways in such settings.

### You Just Have to Be in the Right Place at the Right Time

I want to describe two other instances in which, rather than confirming suspect gay status, gaydar-inspired conversation produced different outcomes. In both conversations, the persons assigned to the suspect gay category proved to be disinterested in the exchange, but they expressed that disinterest quite differently, and what they said in each case had quite different effects on text construction.

The first conversation took place in the sauna of a D.C.-area health club. This club is, by design, a heterosexual facility. Membership in this health club is open to women as well as men, and women and men regularly share access to workout equipment and enrollment in aerobics classes throughout the day. But this club is also a site where men negotiate sexual encounters with other men, and where men may have sex with men if those initial negotiations prove to be successful.[4]

This particular conversation occurred in the men's sauna, which is one of the places where these male cosexual encounters often occur. I had finished my workout and was already in the sauna when the first speaker arrived, a man in his midtwenties, a graduate of a local university, and an employee at one of the federal agencies in the adjacent office building. We knew each other by sight and casual conversation in the weight room. We said hello, he sat down on the bench at right angles to where I was seated, and we said nothing more.

About two minutes later (it is difficult to estimate the passage of time accurately while in a sauna), the second speaker arrived. This was a businessman in his late forties whom I also knew by sight from previous visits to the club. He smiled at both of us and sat down on the bench across from me and at right angles to speaker one. Maybe two more minutes of silence passed. Then speaker two stood up, loosened the towel wrapped around his waist, rolled up a second towel, and placed it against the wall behind his back, draping the ends over his shoulders. He then produced a third towel (had he been sitting on them?) and used it to wipe the sweat from his forehead.

Speaker one was watching the sudden appearance of the towels with as much interest as I was—all the more so because there had been very few towels when I came into the locker room after my workout and the attendant had said that clean towels would not come out of the driers for at least forty more minutes. Indeed, speaker one had come into the sauna without a towel because none were yet available when he left the weight room floor. Certainly, forty minutes had not elapsed since I had entered the sauna. Where did speaker two get all those towels?

That is exactly the question speaker one asked him: "Where did you get all those towels?"

Speaker two replied: "Oh, I grabbed them when I came in. You just have to be in the right place at the right time."

This comment elicited silence, which didn't surprise me. Speaker two's literal reading of the intent of the question, his to-the-point response, and his tone of voice all signaled to me (and to speaker one, I later determined) a complete disinterest in talking to either of us about anything. Moreover, note the shift in pronoun reference in the reply. He began with a first person singular, speaker-specific construction, "I grabbed them . . ." Then he continued with a more generic, and much less personalized, second person construction, "You just have to be . . ." The pronoun shift allows the speaker to create distance between the event under discussion and the comment he wants to make about it. Distance, in turn, allows a more critical posture, or certainly a more self-serving one. Read literally, "You just have to be in the right place at the right time" says: "I was there, but you were not"; the comment places the person being addressed in a less fortunate position compared to the speaker's, and implies that the person being addressed is inferior to the speaker in other ways, as well.

These sentiments are not likely to inspire or encourage continuing attempts at conversation. I understood speaker one's silence, because that was the only response I would have been prompted to make had I been the one trying to initiate discussion.

Later in the evening, while speaker one and I were changing into street clothes in the locker room, I talked about this scenario with speaker one. He told me that he knew very little about speaker two and had never tried to chat with him before, but that he had noticed speaker two working out in the weight room and on the exercise machines. "His eyes are everywhere," speaker one reported. "He is always looking and watching."

"Watching whom?" I asked.

"Younger guys," he replied, "guys like me." And he grinned, inflating his chest and flexing his arms muscles slightly.                           ·

"Do you think he is gay?" I asked.

"I don't know; he could be. He is always here by himself. He spends a lot of time in the sauna after his workout. [*Pause*] And he stares a lot, in the showers."

I noticed that speaker one was now giving me a set of criteria defining suspect gay, and I wondered whether speaker one's decision to start the conversation had been influenced by those criteria. So I asked, "What did you hope to get out of that conversation—a date?"

Speaker one paused, and then replied: "Yeah, I mean, if he was interested, why not?"

"So . . . ," but before I could complete my question, speaker one continued: "Forget it, man. Too stuck up."

Was speaker two really "stuck up," or are there other conclusions to be drawn from his use of language?

For one thing, his response used a type of terminal construction not ordinarily found in Gay English conversations; more commonly, terminals place a conversation "on hold" but do not silence conversation altogether, as was the case here. Moreover, there was nothing in speaker two's statement that could cue the listener toward an appropriate follow-up remark. Such an absence of subtle invitations to continue dialogue is one of the ways through which Gay English speakers distinguish "I don't want to talk to you" from "I don't know how to talk with you." (Recall how similar cues caused my conversation with the airline passenger from rural Maine to become so ambiguous.)

Yet speaker two's apparent disinterest to engage in conversation in this (potentially homoerotic) setting has to be balanced against his reported use of gaze and other forms of male-centered erotic preluding elsewhere in the gym. These acts of communication are nonverbal and nonconversational; they take place in the public areas of the health club, not in the enclosed privacy of the sauna; and, if successful, they establish the speaker's interest in an on-site erotic follow-up when his workout is completed, which—as I explain in chapter 6—is also conducted largely in silence.

Apparently, speaker two is quite interested in male-centered communication, but he is guided by rules of gendered discourse quite different from those found in Gay English text making. Gaydar-based impressions notwithstanding, the meaning of "suspect gay" is quite different in this instance.

### Just Choose a Number between One and Four

My second example of a gaydar-inspired conversation that did not confirm the mutuality of gendered interest implied by the category "suspect" also comes from my health club research. Once again, there are two speakers in the exchange. Speaker one, S1, is a gay man in his early thirties who comes to this health club frequently and (by his own report) enjoys meeting and talking to strangers. Other gay men at the gym describe him with statements like "He is very forward," "He is quite outgoing," and "He is a little too chatty for my taste." In my observation, he has only one close friend at the gym, another gay man his own age, whom he met on the gym floor. (I described part of that encounter in example 3.7.)

Speaker two, S2, is an employee of one of the federal agencies that share the building space with this health club. He comes to the club irregularly and, as far as I have observed, always works out alone. On this particular Saturday afternoon, S2 was struggling to familiarize himself with the mechanics of some "pull-down" exercises (exercises designed to develop the triceps); however, he had not yet coordinated his arm motion with his arm position and was unable to carry out the exercise successfully.

The machine he was using was positioned in front of a wall of mirrors, so everyone on the gym floor could see his frustration and watch his disappointment.

S1 was by himself that afternoon, working with the free weights in the middle of the gym floor. The conversation began when S1 noticed S2's discomfort and walked over to the pull-down machine to help him.

I was using one of the gym's rowing machines, located some four feet from the overhead pull-down equipment. This placed me close enough to S2 to be able to overhear the conversation, and because I was facing a mirrored wall, I was able to observe the two men during their discussion. The content of the exchange interested me, so I stopped my rowing and took notes on the back of my workout schedule (the schedules come with a clipboard and pencil—very helpful for the on-site ethnographer). These notes provided the basis for the text displayed in example 4.5.

---

**Example 4.5** Just choose a number between one and four.

```
1      S1: Here, try it like this. [Walks to the pull-down equipment,
2            takes the handlebar in his hands, and demonstrates
3            the appropriate moves; S2 tries to imitate S1, but is not
4            successful]
5      S2: [Returns the bar to S1, without saying a word]
6      S1: You are afraid of the weights.
7      S2: [Turns to S1; registers surprise on his face]
8      S1: Look. Think of a number between one and four and I'll tell you
9            what you have to do.
10     S2: What? [Bewildered, and reflects this emotion in his tone
11           of voice and his facial features]
12     S1: I'll give each of your exercises a number. One is the
13           overhead pull-down. Two is the triceps pull-up. And so
14           on. Just choose a number and I'll tell you what exercise
15           to do and how much weight you need to put on the machine
16           to do it.
17     S2: No. I don't think so. [Walks off the weight room
18           floor]
```

---

S1 approached this speech event as if it were Gay English text making and, therefore, followed the rules of cooperative discourse that apply to other such text-making settings. Specifically, according to my observations, he assumed (whether due to gaydar or desire) that he and S2 shared common gender interests and that he could begin the conversation by building directly on those (assumed) shared interests; hence S1's seemingly abrupt opening comment—"Here, try it like this"—and the uninvited demonstration of correct style and form that accompanied it (lines 1-3).

It is not uncommon for people to exchange workout tips while they are on the gym floor, but in my observation, these exchanges occur only if the individuals are already positioned at adjacent workout stations or after they have agreed to alternate their use of the same equipment (to "trade off," in gym floor parlance). However, it is very unusual for one person to cross the gym floor and volunteer training services as happened here, and it is even more unusual to snatch equipment out of someone's hands when that person is in the middle of a routine.

S2 was already uncomfortable with the exercise he was trying to perform, and I saw no evidence to suggest that S1's sudden appearance made S2 any more comfortable in that regard. However, S2 did not ask S1 to leave his workout station, nor did he thank S1 for his comment and indicate that he would prefer to resolve the problem on his own. In fact, he said nothing (line 5) and simply returned the pull-down handlebar to S1, after trying to follow S1's none-too-precise instructions.

When I saw this gesture, and the silence that surrounded it, I assumed that S2 was offering to give up the machine in the face of S1's uninvited intrusion. I expected that S2's gesture would suggest to S1 that his volunteered services were not welcome and that S1, recognizing the signal, would promptly move away from the workout station and leave S2 to continue the routine on his own. But S1's next comment—"You are afraid of the weights" (line 6)—showed that he gave an entirely different reading to S2's use of silence and gesture. Instead of realizing that S2 was asking him to phase out of the text making, S1 inferred that S2 wanted him to *continue* the course of action he had already begun.

Line 6 prompted an additional silent response from S2, though the look of surprise on his face (quite visible even at distance of four feet) suggested that he was not expecting additional suggestions and certainly did not want them. So imagine his reaction to S1's follow-up comment (lines 8-9): "Look, think of a number between one and four and I'll tell you what you have to do."

I was as baffled by this comment as was S2, though rereading the text, I find it consistent with the sort of creative game playing that gay men often build into conversations with other gay men—especially when they want to ensure that unnecessary tension does not disrupt a cooperative exchange; for example, speaker B shifted the tone of the "brown pitcher" dispute (example 1.3, lines 12-13) by overextending the disagreement over the pitcher's color, and Dennis Savage finally diffused EM's hostile comments about Little Kiwi with a similarly intensified reference (example 3.4, lines 16-19). I interpret S1's statement in lines 8-9 as a similar attempt to show S2 that he recognized S2's frustration with the exercise and seriously wanted to help him resolve that problem.

S2's one-word reply (line 10), accompanied by facial gesture and tone of voice, suggests that he did not interpret lines 8-9 as an offer of kindness. Once again, however, S1 took the bewilderment in line 10 at face value, and he restated his proposal (lines 12-16), this time providing more detail to clarify what he meant by "think of a number." The wording in this comment, and its length, suggest that he expected to continue guiding S2's workout. This, however, was not what S2 wanted to hear, and he ended the exchange (lines 17-18) with the only option that remained open to him.

As was the case in the sauna room conversation described earlier, this exchange did not yield the outcome that the initial speaker intended. To understand the logic in this exchange, I have to assume that S1 entered the conversation confident that S2 would be receptive to gay-constructed discourse. The conversation showed otherwise. Rather than confirming his suspect gay status, S2 simply terminated the exchange. As an observer, I cannot tell if S2 was a gay man himself, and was unwilling to participate in a conversation dominated by the considerably more flamboyant S1, or was simply reluctant to self-identify as a gay man in a public setting. Perhaps S2 was not gay at all and was trying to find ways to extract himself from a conversation whose ground rules he did not understand. Or perhaps he interpreted the conversation as a prelude to an erotic negotiation that simply did not interest him.

So I was interested in S1's reaction to this exchange. When I asked, during a follow-up discussion, S1 replied: "Straights. What do you expect?" This comment offers a convenient way for S1 to save face in this setting, but it also suggests how misleading an initial gaydar reading may turn out to be.

### Conversations with Straights

The starting points for text making shift considerably when gay men engage in conversations with persons whom they already know to be admitted, openly declared heterosexuals. These persons are unlikely to understand the messages and meaning that gay texts contain, and they may not even recognize the gay-specific presentation of message and meaning in that discourse.

Finding ways to move across these barriers (or to remain comfortably entrenched behind them) is a recurring theme in conversations involving Gay English speakers and heterosexual speech partners. And text construction unfolds in such settings in response to each party's concerns.

What follows are some examples of these conversations and the negotiations of gay–straight linguistic distinctions that those conversations contain.

### I Knew We Should Have Eaten Downtown

David Bergman, poet, literary scholar, and gay theorist, is my source for my first example. He was giving a lecture at a university on the West Coast, and afterward he went to dinner with two friends, one gay (Michael), the other straight (Robert), both interested in contemporary gay literature. During the lecture, David had made reference to gay language. Robert had asked for an example of gay language during the question-and-answer period, but David could not think of one on the spot.

David continues the story in a letter to me:

> Then we went to dinner. I had two choices: one was a restaurant near the harbor where the food was alright but the place was saturated with Seattle atmosphere; the other was a restaurant in a neighborhood with no tourist value but served excellent food. I chose the restaurant with excellent food.
>
> We are seated by an extremely attractive waiter.
>
> Michael: Why don't you sit here [*Points to the chair facing outward*] where you can get a view.
>
> David: I'd like more than a view.
>
> Robert: I knew we should have eaten downtown. That other place has lots of atmosphere.
>
> Of course Michael and I burst out laughing. "I know, I know, I've missed something," Robert exclaimed. And I restated to Robert that I found the waiter sexually attractive.
>
> "Is that what you understood him to mean?" Robert asked Michael, who said that was exactly what he understood me to mean. "Well, I guess there is such a thing as gay language" Robert concluded.

Bergman then commented on the event as follows:

> What was especially noteworthy about the exchange was that there was no change in register in Michael's or my speech. It was said in utter casualness. Clearly gay discourse doesn't need to have extra stress or tonal changes to be marked as gay speech. The context alone can provide the occasion. What I think is going on is that specific occasions are set aside as times of possible moments of Gay American English, and semantic choices [Bergman's use of "a view" in the exchange above] is all that is necessary to signal entry into GAE. (Bergman 1993)

I agree that judiciously placed semantic choices often guide transitions from other types of conversational exchange into moments of gay discourse. In this case, the transition into gay moment also had the effect of exclusion. Michael understood the gay meaning built into David's reference to "a view," but Robert was not aware of the shift in text making that David's comment contained. Under other circumstances, Robert's confusion could have had awkward consequences, especially if the Gay English speakers had not decided to explain the coded message to their colleague.

### You Two Work Together?

My next example offers a somewhat different configuration of gay–straight dialogue. This time the conversation was between strangers, not friends, and the common theme was arrangements for language instruction, not an interest in gay discourse.

The narrative comes from one of my interviews with LL, a forty-year-old gay man in Washington D.C. We were discussing how frequently (in our experience, at least) heterosexuals misunderstand what it means to be gay and to be in a long-term, committed relationship with another man. I asked him to describe some instances where such misunderstandings had occurred. This was one of his examples:

I had to call the business office of a local adult education program, to arrange for my partner's cousin to be enrolled in their fall computer training program. [*Pause*] Actually, my partner had already started this discussion, but he didn't have time to continue it and asked me to call for him.

I got through to the counselor with whom my partner had been doing business, and I explained that I that was calling on my partner's behalf, and wanted to complete arrangements for his cousin's enrollment. I explained what I knew about the prospective student's academic background and answered other questions about his family, visa status, plans for residence here in the U.S., and so on.

As we were wrapping up the discussion, the counselor asked me for my name and address; he wanted this "for his files," he explained. I gave him the information. He paused, then he said: "You can be reached at the same telephone number where I called [he named my partner] yesterday. So you are involved in these arrangements because . . ." (and he paused again, briefly), "you two work together?"

"Yes," I replied, "that is one way of putting it."

He laughed, I laughed, but I don't understand even now what I said that was so funny.

Later in the interview, I asked LL to think again about his concluding comment: what *was* so funny about his response to the counselor's question?

LL replied:

When I first heard this guy talk, I was sure he was gay. His voice had that sound, you know, that gay sound—sort of expressive, sort of excited, sort of . . . gay. That's what I heard. But then he was so stuffy, I thought, no, he can't be gay. Back and forth, throughout the conversation, and I can't decide. Then he asks me this question— "do we work together?" and I am going, "Yeah, right, either this queen has a weird sense of humor, or this is the dumbest straight man I've come across in a l-o-o-ong time!"

I asked if, in hindsight, LL thought that the counselor was confirming his awareness of the gay relationship (if not expressing solidarity with it) by making a joke out of the obvious. If so, I suggested, this would be another instance of the exaggeration and minstrelsy that show up so frequently in conversations between gay men, and could be powerful evidence that the counselor was in fact a gay man. "No way," LL replied. "If he was going to let on that he was gay, why not be more explicit about it?" I countered: "But how could he be explicit in a work setting, talking to someone he didn't know?" And LL replied: "Gays'll find ways to work this out. It's the straights who are always at a loss for words."

### What You See Is What You Get!

In the next example, CJ, a forty-five-year-old gay man, describes a conversation that he, his partner, and another gay couple had with the female cashier in a gourmet food store. In Washington parlance, the food store is located "outside the Beltway," in a community populated primarily by retired military, Department of Defense, and CIA families. CJ knew that they were driving "to the other side of the moon" (his term) when they set out on this trip, but, as he explained, the food store is next door to a wine bar and a (reportedly) superb restaurant. These were motives enough to justify undertaking this adventure.

CJ continues:

We went into this restaurant, four of us, two couples, all gay, a gourmet restaurant with a wine bar, lots of chrome and indirect lighting, really attempting to be elegant in a subdued, suburban style. The restaurant is connected to a wine shop, selling specialty wines and gourmet food to match.

The cashier in the food store was a large woman, in her thirties, who liked to talk (we later observed) and must have considered it her job to greet customers as they came into the store, because she had something to say every time someone walked in.

When the four of us walked in, she said—she did this loudly, so that everyone in the store could hear her—"Where are the wives?" No one answered. I mean, who expected this kind of opening remark from a saleswoman in a wine store?

So we just started looking at the stock and we ignored the question. Then she asked: "You men didn't leave them at home?" One of us replied, quietly, "Something like that," but she didn't hear it.

Now other customers in the store are watching this whole thing, we are very much on the spot. She continued: "Are they out parking the cars?"

At this point, I was ready to leave, except we had driven about twenty-five miles to have dinner here and everyone was hungry. Besides, why let this person's pushiness destroy our evening, right?

So one member of the group walked up to the saleswoman and said, to her face: "Look, lady, what you see is what you get." Everyone in the store laughed—except the saleswoman, who was (thankfully) at a loss for words.

As in the interview with LL, I asked CJ to comment on the significance of this narrative, now that he had had time to think more objectively about the events. Here is what he told me:

We joked about this later in the evening, but at the time I felt very strange. Was she teasing us? Or did she really think we were four straight guys and our wives were outside in the parking lot? I mean, we were the only gay people in the store. It wasn't like shopping in Dupont Circle; no, not at all.

I, too, remain curious about the woman's response. Was she aware that these were four gay men, and trying to have a little fun—either in solidarity or in jest? Or was she truly unaware that her customers were gay men, and trying to make a joke out of an obvious, if only temporary, disruption of her heterosexually ordered universe?

But I am also struck by the cleverness of the reply that CJ offered in response to this situation—whatever the cashier's motivation. "Look, lady, what you see is what you get!" is a terminal construction, in the sense of chapter 3's discussion. Here, CJ used this terminal not to create an opportunity for participants to rethink and refocus conversational strategies but to show that he did not want any further development of the theme. According to CJ's narrative, the statement had exactly that effect. Less certain, of course, is the message the cashier wanted her silence to convey, and how she felt about being upstaged so dramatically in front of the other customers.

### Chicken Stories

My final example of gay–straight negotiations is a personal one, and it comes out of a conversation I had at the annual meeting of the Society for Applied Anthropology in spring 1992. I was talking with a group of AIDS researchers, all of whom had attended a conference on Anthropology and AIDS at the Centers for Disease Control (in Atlanta, Georgia) the previous November. I had also been invited to attend the conference but could not do so because of travel out of the country. So I stood by, silently, as other members of the group commented on the conference and the mixture of people and activities that the three-day session had contained.

Then someone introduced the phrase "chicken stories" into the conversation, and the group dissolved in laughter. Apparently (as I later learned), during one of the conference cocktail parties, someone told a joke in which chickens were the central characters. Then, someone else told a joke about chickens, then someone else did the same thing—and soon chicken stories were passing back and forth among the party-goers. People not telling stories were listening and laughing, and soon chicken stories became entrenched among the elements that defined group identity for the conference attendees.

All of that emotion flooded back across the group when people started retelling those stories the following spring. Suddenly I was an outsider, someone who did not understand a conversation that was fully accessible to everyone else. Perhaps my face, my posture, or my silence displayed this feeling, because one of the leaders of this reverie (and a chief architect of the original chicken story exchange, as it turned out) turned to me and said: "Bill, if you are going to hang around with us, you'll have to have a chicken story."

I replied, speaking loudly enough so that others around me could hear the comment: "Bob, I have plenty of chicken stories, but they're not the kind of stories you'd understand."

From the puzzled look on Bob's face, I was certain that he did not understand my meaning. The two people in the group who were more familiar with gay folklore burst into laughter. My comment had its desired effect: Chicken stories stopped being a form of in-group currency, the discussion shifted to other themes, and no one has mentioned chicken stories in my presence again.

Certainly, this was not the first time that I found myself on the outside of an in-group conversation, but being excluded in this case was difficult to overlook. I had been doing work with language and AIDS for several years prior to the time of this conversation. Bob had only recently become active in AIDS research, as had most of the other participants in that conversation. So they were the newcomers to this field, not I, and I felt they had no authority to impose conditions on my participation in their exchange.

Particularly irritating, I realized, was the fact that all but one of the participants in the group was openly heterosexual and only two people in the group (the single gay man and one of the straight women) had any familiarity with lesbian–gay concerns about AIDS or any issue of importance to our communities. So another effect of Bob's comment (Bob was not the gay man, by the way) was to impose limits on gay presence within a general discourse (AIDS research) that already excludes gay voice.

I wanted my reply to upstage this exclusion and reestablish my place within the now-polarized (that is, them versus me) group structure. To do this, I used the same turn-taking strategy (overlapping references) that structured the dialogue at the Sunday brunch (example 2.3) and in other examples explored in chapters 3 and 4: Bob's central reference—chicken stories—became my central reference, but at the same time, I recast the word "chicken" so that Bob's reference now alluded to a gay-familiar archetype,[5] not to the jokes popular at the Atlanta conference. And, by doing so, I made chicken stories something that, at least for the moment, Bob and his comrades could no longer control. Finally, while I intended my comment to meet turn-taking requirements appropriate to this setting, I also intended it to function as a terminal; I wanted the coparticipants to bring closure to this line of discussion and to shift topics.

I am not sure that most of them understood the new meaning now assigned to chicken stories, but that confusion was fine with me. I had been placed in that status several minutes earlier, when others were exchanging chicken stories so enthusiastically, and now it was someone else's turn to feel excluded. Moreover, the fact that two members of the group were able to make the transition to the new meaning of this phrase further ensured that the original in-group structure was disrupted. This was another assertion of conversational power on my part, and another way of claiming access to place—and constructing gay space—within this conversation.

### Conclusion: Gay English as a Language of Risk

Previously, researchers have described Gay English conversations in public settings in terms of two themes: *secrecy* and *silence*. Studies of secrecy (Farrell 1972; Warren 1974; J. Goodwin 1989; Dilallo and Krumholtz 1994) have highlighted gay-centered vocabulary and argot and the coded meanings that these terms convey. Studies of silence (Delph 1978; Tierney 1993) have explored the systematic erasure of gay voice in the presence of heterosexual discourse and the many forms of gay compliance with such erasure.

Secrecy and silence have been relevant to the examples explored in this chapter, particularly when speakers deliberately altered the linguistic form of the conversation to accommodate the constraints of public social context or when, faced with such constraints, speakers chose not to speak at all. But even when secrecy and silence restrict the presence of gay voice, speaker creativity is not completely extinguished and gay text making still unfolds. The content of these texts may not be as explicitly gay as are texts constructed in private settings or in public domains with more homogeneously gay participants. But the presentation of gay message—and the speakers' allegiance to gay-cooperative discourse—are still maintained.

What happens in these settings is similar to conditions that researchers in investment science regularly associate with risk taking in real estate and finance. The term "risk" has a special meaning for these researchers; risk identifies "the measurable possibility of a transaction losing or not gaining value" (Downes and Goodman 1987: 348). Under this description, risk is an unavoidable part of financial investment (Hawkins 1986: 191), but there are ways to limit the negative effects that risk may have on the rate of return. And risk taking refers to actions designed to ensure that short-term losses will not disrupt long-term financial gains.[6]

Financial risk taking is a purposeful, intentional, and goal-oriented activity. And by treating the construction of Gay English text as a form of risk taking—and Gay English itself as a language of risk—I underscore the assumptions about rational, intentional text construction that guide the analysis of Gay English throughout this volume. Moreover, describing Gay English text making in risk-related terms draws attention to features of Gay English discourse that are largely overlooked in discussions of secrecy and silence.

For one thing, secrecy and silence notwithstanding, there *is* a substantial amount of gay talk in public settings, and even when some participants ignore gay presence (as happened in the conversation with the cashier in the gourmet food store, during the telephone conversation with the school administrator, or with my fellow passenger on the late-night flight to Salt Lake City), language provides Gay English speakers with ways to refocus participant attention. Importantly, the language in question need not be flamboyant, overly dramatic, or outrageous to be effective in these settings. I deliberately avoided examples in which a speaker's Gay English usage made a confrontation with gay presence virtually unavoidable (even though such confrontations regularly occur in public domains) because more discreet, less obvious language choices have equally powerful effects on text construction, and I wanted this chapter to focus on those choices and on the linguistic skills that lead up to them. Besides, the presentation of gay message in most Gay English conversations lies somewhere between the two extremes of secrecy-and-silence and flamboyance-outrageousness, which ensures that some degree of ambiguity will recur throughout conversations between suspect gays and between gay men and heterosexuals. And that is why—as the examples in this chapter have repeatedly shown—negotiating such ambiguity, like cooperative text making, is a recurring theme in Gay English discourse.

# 5

## Claiming Gay Space:
## Bathroom Graffiti, Songs about Cities,
## and "Queer" Reference

Postmodern geographers (Cosgrove 1985; Jackson 1989) describe space as a product of interpretive process, as what de Certeau (1984: 117) describes as "a practiced place." Language is one of the practices through which people transform place into space. In this chapter, I explore these connections between place, space, and text in Gay English discourse.

### Establishing Space: Jottings on a Restroom Wall

Men's restrooms at my university, as in many public settings in the United States, are richly decorated with graffiti—brief, hand-written commentaries, usually addressing a specific sexual or political theme.[1] In some cases, the comments contain explicitly heterosexual (and often heterosexist) references; in others, comments are gay-centered, and on occasion they may be quite gay-positive. Often, these comments appear individually, as self-contained statements, though an increasingly popular format encourages writers to add their own statements to a chain of messages already unfolding on the restroom wall. "Add" does not accurately capture the action involved in these instances of text construction, however. Writers usually ensure that the content of each new statement overlaps with that of other statements surrounding it, and they may also use arrows, circles, characters, diagrams, and other nonverbal notations to connect individual statements into larger, interconnected wholes. Readers then apply their own interpretations to these texts, whether guided by these cues or by information from external sources; and readers may also add their own contributions to text detail for others to interpret.

Considered in these terms, bathroom graffiti is best described as a package of complementary and agonistic meanings, conveyed through a written conversation between several participants who themselves may represent any number of ethnic, political, and gendered interests. Previous studies (such as Moonwomon 1992) have examined bathroom graffiti (and graffiti in other locations) in terms of recurring features of content and structural form. Here, while not ignoring individual features, I want to focus more broadly on the significance of text making in such settings and to explore how the introduction of gay-oriented commentary affects the subsequent text construction as well as the text-making locale.

I started collecting samples of gay graffiti at American University's men's restrooms in fall 1993, when I returned to campus after a year of Gay English research during sabbatical leave. Of course, I had been informally observing bathroom graffiti on our campus long before I began this project. I have always been impressed by the cleverness of language that so many of these statements contained. Frequently, moreover, these comments advertised opportunities for gay erotic activity available at other sites on our campus or offered glimpses into other dimensions of campus "gay culture." This information is not generally available through the student newspaper, faculty handbooks, or other on-campus sources, and that makes informal displays like restroom graffiti an especially valuable format for information exchange.

As I learned during my sabbatical year research, gay high school and college students list graffiti-based comments about gay meeting places and other issues among the sources of information orienting them to gay culture during the earliest phases (what Troidan [1989: 50] calls the "sensitization" stage) of their coming-out process (see further discussion in chapter 7). Finding such comments assured them that other men-interested-in-men had passed through that area and were likely to return. Most respondents added that they found security in that discovery, even if they did not fully understand what that security entailed.

Information exchange and gay security are two examples of the ways in which graffiti can transform *place* (in this case, a public restroom) into a gay-positive *space*. Stated more accurately, it is the construction and interpretation of the graffiti that actually enable such an embellishment of locale. The presence of gay-oriented graffiti may also have additional outcomes, since some readers will always interpret such messages differently from others. Under such circumstances, the possibility of gay space itself becomes a site for gendered confrontation, and so may instances of graffiti themselves.

To discuss these claims in greater detail, I want to focus on the spatial consequences of one instance of gay-related men's room graffiti. The text at issue here is actually a cluster of connected statements that came to be displayed across the aluminum wall separating the stand-up urinals from the enclosed toilets in this men's room. Because I plan to describe the items within this text individually, following the order in which each item originally appeared, I am not going to display the complete text until the analysis concludes. Readers interested in scanning the complete text before they begin the analysis should consult figure 5.11.

The first of these entries appeared during the opening week of the fall 1993 semester, with additional items being added to this text until March 1994, when the spring cleanup of the building's restrooms removed almost all traces of this commentary. The men's room is near my office and across the hall from one of the classrooms where I teach. I regularly use the facilities—and scan the walls for written commentary—each day I am on campus. I noticed the first item in the text (see figure 5.1) shortly after it appeared, and once additional, gender-interesting messages became connected to it, I decided to construct a diagram of the aluminum wall, to record the statements on that diagram, and to begin an analysis of these messages. I continued the note taking and analysis process until the Building Services staff began their general housecleaning.

The text at issue here represents a particular type of restroom graffiti whose occurrence is certainly not limited to our campus. Two characteristics distinguish this category: First, the texts explore gay-related political or social concerns from a variety of gay-positive and non-gay-positive points of view. Second, the commentary emerges out of point–counterpoint exchange. These texts are composed of a series of individual entries, each written in response to entries that other writers have already positioned within the collection. I use the verb "positioned" deliberately, because—as the following analysis will suggest—the introduction of additional commentary is in no sense random or haphazard.

Let me also point out that two other types of graffiti also appeared on the walls in this bathroom during this six-month period. Some of these statements, for reasons I have explained, refer men interested in finding partners for erotic exchange to men's rooms in other campus buildings and indicate the best times during the week to visit those locales for that purpose. Additional statements include gay-centered jokes, satirical comments, and occasionally, more serious statements; references to AIDS and safe-sex activities are frequent themes under this last rubric. Texts in this category usually occur on the interior walls of the toilet stalls, and, as is the case for the referrals, these statements appear individually and do not prompt multipartied written exchange.

The opening item in the examples of graffiti that I want to discuss here

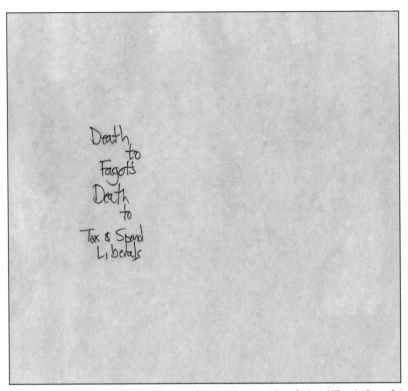

Figure 5.1. Initial Text of Graffiti: Death / to / Fagot's / Death / to / Tax & Spend / Liberals

resembles other instances of antigay scribbling found on men's room walls elsewhere on our campus. The form of the comment paraphrases the slogans shouted by participants at public rallies in totalitarian states. The statement presents a strongly focused reference to directed power and force, with gay men identified as the intended target against which power and force are to be directed. Note that the writer used the term "fagot's" (*sic*) to specify the intended target; "faggot" is usually not intended as a complimentary designation, and the image is made even more troublesome given the connection the writer makes between faggots and death. The parallel phrasing—"Death to Fagot's, Death to Tax & Spend Liberals"—comments further on the writer's less-than-progressive notions of gender politics.

Interestingly, the next writer did not choose to focus directly on writer 1's antigay sentiments. Instead, writer 2 based his comments (see example 5.2) on the recurring punctuation errors in writer 1's text, treating the presence of those errors as evidence of writer 1's deficiencies in other domains. This

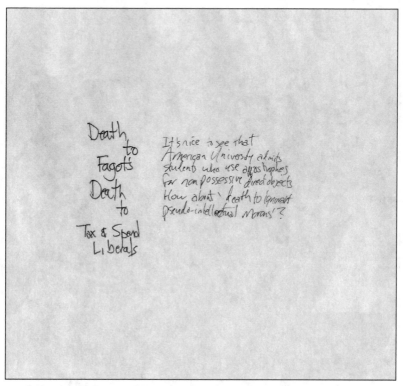

Figure 5.2. Graffiti 2: It's nice to see that / American University admits / students who use appostrophes / for non-possessive direct objects / How about 'death to ignorant / pseudo-intellectual morons'?

inference prompted the construction of the concluding image—writer 1 as an "ignorant pseudo-intellectual moron"—and the connection of that description with the death reference from statement 1. This could be a gay-positive comment, but if so, it is heavily cloaked in ad hominem rhetoric, suggesting that what is under attack here is writer 1 himself, and not his message.

Ironically, while writer 2 used mechanical errors as the basis for his attack, writer 2's text also contains mechanical errors, and this allowed the logic of writer 2's critique to be turned against his own performance. Writer 3 did this quite simply (see figure 5.3). He noted the wrong spelling of "apostrophes" in statement 2; then he encircled the error and drew a line from the circle to his two-word written comment. By physically connecting his response to the statement that he was attacking, writer 3 divided the text space into two segments: area A, the area in which writer 1 placed his open-

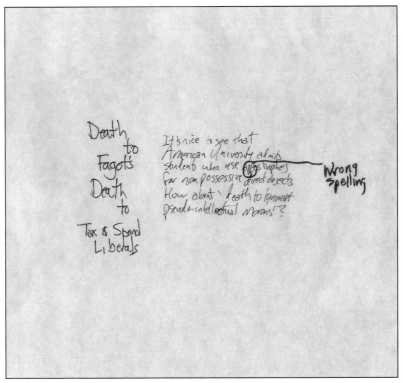

Figure 5.3. Graffiti 3: Wrong / Spelling

ing comment, and area B, the area in which writer 2 and writer 3 positioned their commentaries.

Statement 3, like statement 2, offers no attack on the antigay message in statement 1. In fact, the wording of statement 3 suggests that the writer considered statement 2, not statement 1, as the focal point for the exchange. So, apparently, did the writer of statement 4 (see figure 5.4). Granted, the hortatory tone, spelling errors, and explicit reference to a forceful silencing of points of view with which he disagrees are features also found in figure 5.1, and similarities between the handwriting in both statements suggest that they could have been authored by the same individual. But even if that were the case, the writer did not use his follow-up statement to return attention to the initial message in the text. Instead, like writer 3, the author of statement 4 chose to expand on the commentary in statement 2. Locating statement 4 in area B and connecting it with an arrow to statement 2 are other reflections of that decision.

Statement 5 (figure 5.5) introduces a less somber and much less heavy-

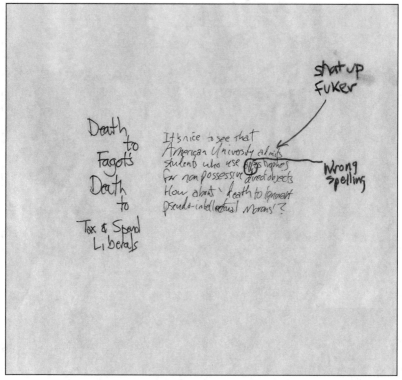

Figure 5.4. Graffiti 4: shat up / fuker

handed tone into this exchange. "Happy pills" could refer to the "don't-worry-be-happy" attitude that helps some gay men endure encounters with gay oppression, or to the chemical substances that help some gay men maintain that point of view. Happy pills could also be a paraphrase of the language that teachers use in kindergarten and elementary school class-rooms to encourage an adjustment in attitude on the part of students who are bickering, being divisive, or otherwise disrupting group harmony. Either way, this imagery does nothing to return the reader's attention to statement 1; if anything, it discourages any further consideration of statement 1's at-tack on gay voice.

Moreover, given the placement of statement 5 within area B (and at the top of that area's comments), the lighthearted suggestion that it contains now applies to all of the points of view presented in statement 2—and fur-ther discourages any serious assessment of the antigay politics unfolding in this text.

Statement 6 (figure 5.6) restores a more somber tone to this exchange.

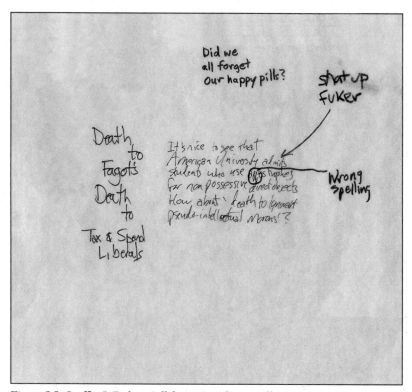

Figure 5.5. Graffiti 5: Did we / all forget / our happy pills?

Given that violence is the centerpiece of the message, statement 6 suggests parallels with messages in statement 4 and statement 1. However, statement 6 is located in the center of area B, and arrows connect it with the messages in statements 2 and 5. An additional arrow connects statement 6 with statement 4, further aligning statement 6 with the complex of messages already responding to statement 2. The antigay message in statement 1 still remains unchallenged, and the intent of that message is once again being reinforced.

This brings me to statement 7 (see figure 5.7), the first openly gay and gay-positive comment in the exchange, and the only comment so far that does not engage in ad hominem attack but speaks directly to the antigay sentiment displayed in statement 1. It is significant that writer 7 placed his statement in area A, immediately above the statement whose message it attacks. Its position on the wall establishes its connection between these messages, and so does the repetition and alternation of statement 1's vocabulary: statement 1's "fagot" is statement 7's "Mr. Faggot," with spelling

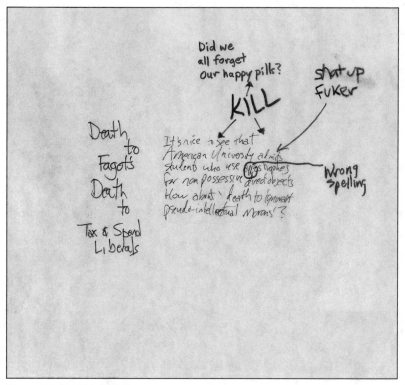

Figure 5.6. Graffiti 6: KILL

corrected, number changed from plural to singular, and respectable title "Mr." now supplied.

The "Mr." Faggot construction in figure 5.7 paraphrases a slogan on a popular gay-pride T-shirt. It also calls to mind the title of a Sidney Poitier film, *They Call Me Mr. Tibbs*, one of few Hollywood films about the experience of desegregation in the American South to be both critically acclaimed and commercially successful. One theme in this film is the recognition of personhood in the face of violent repression; the writer of statement 7 introduced similar sentiments as his response to statement 1, and in the process altered the intention of statement 1's comments quite dramatically: The recipient of intended violence, formerly described in inclusive and generalized terms ("Death to Fagot's"), is now represented in much more individualized and personalized terms ("That's Mr. Faggot").

Statement 7 alters a second feature of text construction. None of the preceding statements were addressed directly to the author of statement 1; in fact, the avoidance of such direct referencing assisted greatly in the sub-

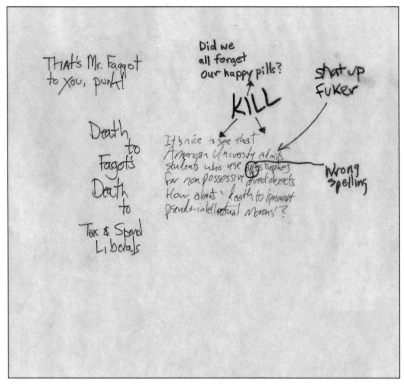

Figure 5.7. Graffiti 7: That's Mr. Faggot / to you, punk!

merging of the antigay message throughout this exchange. But the deictic markers in statement 7—the "you" pronoun and the noun-label "punk"— leave no doubt as to the specific individual toward whom this comment is directed or to the personal qualities that the writer has assigned to him. This is an "in your face" comment, the sort of statement that gay men and lesbians would like to employ (or imagine themselves employing) when confronted with "death to fagot's" sentiments. And its presence certainly brings the focus of this exchange back to the issues that initiated it.

A pause in the text-making process followed the appearance of statement 7, and the end of the fall 1993 semester, winter break, and the opening of the spring 1994 semester (a period of approximately four weeks) helps account for this pause. Once spring-semester classes began, new comments appeared on the bathroom wall. The first of these comments, statement 8 (see figure 5.8), ignores the gay-positive message in statement 7. Instead, statement 8 returns the discussion to statement 2 and paraphrases the critique of that statement previously suggested in statement 3. And

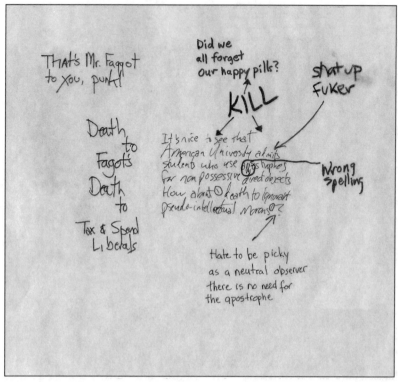

Figure 5.8. Graffiti 8: Hate to be picky / as a neutral observer / there is no need for / the apostrophe

appropriately, statement 8 is located immediately beneath statement 2, in area B.

Statement 9 (see figure 5.9), located immediately beneath statement 8, speaks directly to statement 8's complaint. No, the writer assures us, the punctuation error is not really an error at all. If anything, the author of statement 8 is at fault, for not reading statement 2 with sufficient care—a comment that writer 9 underscored by encircling the single quotation marks that begin and end the citation. Supporting the format of statement 2 may also be a way of supporting statement 2's message: if writer 2's use of grammar is correct, perhaps his critique of statement 1 and its message has validity after all. Once again, gay-positive sentiments emerge, even if (as may also have been the case in statement 2) the text form presents them indirectly.

Statement 10 (see figure 5.10) is connected to statement 8 (and hence to statements 2 and following) by an arrow, and it is also connected to state-

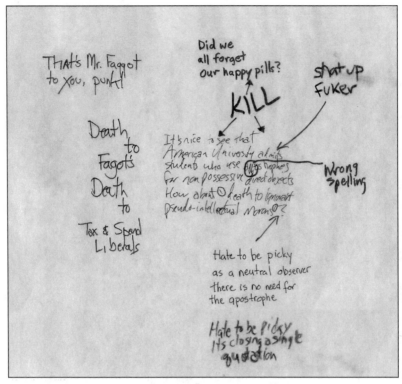

Figure 5.9. Graffiti 9: Hate to be picky / It's closing a single / quotation

ments 1 and 7 by arrows; it is located in area A. The scope of these connections makes its reference to "rednecks" somewhat puzzling. The label
might be relevant to statement 1 (though once again, this is an attack on the
writer, not an attack on the message); and it could also be relevant to statement 8 (though a redneck offering grammatical critique of another person's
written English is an interesting image). But why the connection to statement 7?

One interpretation suggests that statement 10 is a caption, not a contribution to the dialogue. It is directed to the reader, not to the other writers
and the comments that are now included in the exchange. If "rednecks" are
"what it is about," in this sense, then the "it" must refer to the exchange—
specifically, to the antigay sentiments both directly expressed and validated
through lack of objection. In sum, statement 10 supports statement 7's explicit gay critique by offering a more general, text-inclusive justification for
the point of view that statement 7 originally displayed.

Statement 11 (see figure 5.11) appeared in the bathroom within twenty-

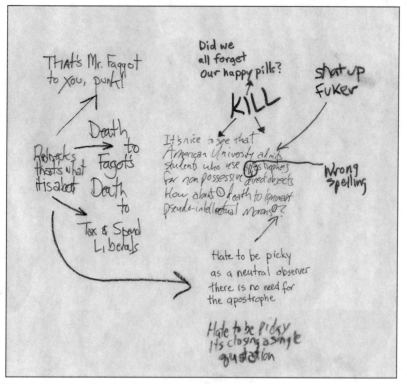

Figure 5.10. Graffiti 10: Rednecks / that's what / it is about

four hours of the appearance of statement 10. Note how the writer located the comment across the top of area A and area B, thereby letting it function like a title, caption, or headline for the whole display. How the caption connects with the other messages is open to several interpretations, however. For one thing, the passive form of the verb ("get fucked") suggests that the subject of the sentence is not the initiator but the recipient of the specified action. This statement would read somewhat differently, and considerably less violently, if "take it" rather than "get fucked" had been the writer's choice of verb. Moreover, specifying the subject as "white men" racializes this discussion of nonreciprocal power. If the race or ethnicity of the men who receive the action is relevant, then presumably so is the race or ethnicity of those who provide it, even if the specifics of race or ethnicity are not indicated directly in the text.

Another way to interpret this statement begins by pondering the implications of what it asserts. If men "like to get fucked in the ass," then what? Does that preference validate writer 1's call for death to faggots, or state-

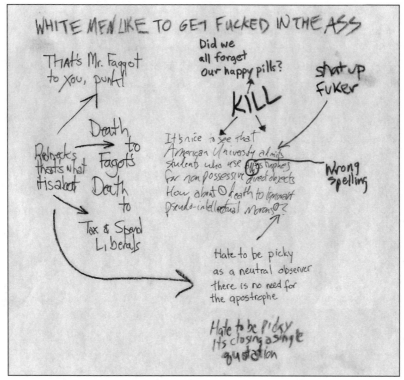

Figure 5.11. Final Text of Graffiti: WHITE MEN LIKE TO GET FUCKED IN THE ASS

ment 4's attempt to silence more supportive, pro-gay commentary? Does getting fucked in the ass actually promote faggot death? Does this statement contain a clumsily constructed reference to the AIDS pandemic?

Ordinarily, I would be able to explore these questions, as I did for other statements in this collection, by looking at the content of the subsequent responses in this exchange. Unfortunately, opportunities for writers to construct additional comments were curtailed by the campus-wide spring cleaning. When the workers washed the wall next to the urinal, they erased almost all traces of this text.

Given this description of text content, I am ready to consider how text-making practice in this case transformed a public place into a gay-specific space.

Although the passage is dominated by statements that are not necessarily gay-friendly, it does contain one explicitly gay-positive remark (statement 7:

"That's Mr. Faggot"), and the introduction of this statement certainly had a significant impact on the content and the construction of this exchange. Before statement 7 appeared, the participants either ignored the antigay tone of the initial comment (statement 1) or found no reason to attack that position in their replies. In fact, as I have explained, some writers' comments maintained and extended statement 1's position, even while participating in a debate over rules of punctuation and in a contest between conflicting attitudes.

Statement 7 disrupted the flow of this argument. Instead of disguising its concerns through an ad hominem or side-issue argument, this statement is explicitly intolerant of statement 1's homophobia and uses several lines of attack to undermine its assertions. The effects of this attack also extended over the subsequent phases of text making. Previously, new items had appeared on this area of the bathroom wall on a weekly basis; once statement 7 appeared, three weeks passed before someone introduced additional remarks into this display. School was still in session throughout this period, the men's room was still in use, and graffiti in various forms still appeared on other walls in this bathroom. So I am willing to assume that statement 7's gay-positive message affected the continuation of dialogue in this particular instance, in much the same way that a speaker's strategically placed terminal statements (see the discussion in chapter 3) allow for interruption and refocusing of dialogue during spoken Gay English conversations.

The appearance of the written terminal also prompted a refocusing of this written "conversation." Once additional statements began to appear, none of them challenged the point of view presented in statement 7. Instead, writers returned to the same strategies that had successfully distracted attention from gay debate earlier in the exchange. In effect, statement 7 receives the treatment that gay voice often receives in public conversation: Even when gay-positive comments are openly expressed, they are still likely to be ignored.

Silencing is only one of the ways in which this example displays the uses of language that Gay English speakers are likely to encounter in real-life conversations, and it foreshadows the social consequences of speaking Gay English in public domains. Moreover, the textual materials in this example suggest the range of linguistic skills that gay men need to acquire so that they can become effective participants in those conversations. Reading these texts gives Gay English speakers a chance to compare different responses to heterosexual commentary, and if they continue to visit the site and read the follow-up commentary, it allows them to trace how the wording of a particular response choice will affect the packaging of content and emotion in subsequent replies.

The spatial significance of these texts follows directly from these contributions to gay men's language socialization. If gay-related graffiti facilitates learning gay men's language and culture, then the places where graffiti occur become *spaces* for learning gay language and culture—and, thereby, become *gay spaces* in their own right. "Gay space" in this sense means something more than merely "an area where gay people congregate." Particulars of site-specific practice are always central to the transformation of place into space. In this case, these practices involved expressions of gay assertiveness and gay persistence in the face of heterosexually controlled, contested dialogue. This is not "gay space" in the sense suggested by an outdoor cruising area or a trendy, glitterati dance club; but gay space—like gay culture—does not need an erotic foundation to be a viable, authentic construction.

### Representing Space: "Home" and "City" in Popular Music

Royce, a twenty-nine-year-old white male, grew up in a small town in the Piedmont country of the Carolinas. His family was part of the country club set, and he became a member of the high school basketball team, active in student government, and connected with his high school's "in crowd" in other ways. Still, as he later explained during an interview with Jim Sears, there was always a part of him that "felt different," and as early as the eighth grade,

his mind and interests began to wander beyond the town's boundaries: theater, performing arts, art decoration; Charleston, Atlanta, New York. "I desperately wanted out of town," Royce confesses. While his friends were reading *Hot Rod and Guns*, Royce's interests turned to *GQ* and *The New Yorker*. "I started discovering fashion," he recollects. "I was big on new styles. . . . I can remember the other guys wearing blue jeans and plaid shirts. They knew I was different. I was the first guy to wear a jump suit to school. The first guy to wear his jeans tucked in his boots. The first person to carry a back pack." (Sears 1991: 100-101)

Later in the interview, Royce said more about his growing desire to move away from his hometown:

Knowing what I wanted and what I wanted to be, I had to get out. There were those who had no further aspirations but to follow in their father's or mother's footsteps. It did not bother them to stay. But me and Rebecca [a childhood friend] knew we had to get out. Everybody was going to Clemson. She was going to Yale to be a doctor. I was looking for a good theater school. (Sears 1991: 106)

As it turned out, Royce actually enrolled in a small private college near his hometown, and after graduation, he moved to one of the region's larger cities

and found employment in a men's clothing store. He lost that job after a disagreement with his supervisor, and at the time of the interview with Sears, he
was planning to return to his hometown and open his own business. Royce
explains: "I got very frustrated because I knew my work was good. . . . I am
tired of playing politics. I want to have my own business, doing free-lance
home decorating, consulting, and weddings." (Sears 1991: 106)

What Royce is talking about in these paragraphs—being gay and leaving
home—are themes that frequently occur in stories that gay men tell about
their childhood. Often, as in Royce's case, the desire to move comes much
earlier than do opportunities to move, which explains why expressions of
this desire need not include an explicit agenda for action, and why, even
when it is stated, that agenda need not be maintained. Indeed, the particulars are never as important here as is the general theme: As Royce put it,
"knowing what [he] wanted and what [he] wanted to be" meant that he
"had to get out"—out of town, out of domains controlled by family and
friends, out of the limitations of "the closet" imposed by small-town living.
And get out he did, even if he ultimately decided to return to his childhood
home.

John Rechy's narrator in *City of Night* presents another form of this argument, when he explains to the reader why he decided to move from El
Paso (his childhood home) to New York City:

> After my separation from the army, I had come into my first contact with the al-
> luring anarchic world which promised such turbulence. On my way to El Paso, I
> had stopped in Dallas for about a week, to postpone facing my mother with my deci-
> sion to leave El Paso. In Dallas—suddenly!—with the excitement of someone dis-
> covering a new country, I discovered that world. As abruptly as that, it happened;
> that suddenly, that immediate: one day, nothing, and the next it was there as if a
> trapdoor had Opened.
>
> Those days in Dallas without entering it then, I explored the surface of that
> seething world; and from the isolation of my early years and the equally isolated
> time in the army—purposefully apart from everyone else—I resolved to free myself
> swiftly, to leave my place by the Window, uninvolved with life, and hurl myself into
> its boiling midst. But it had to be after I faced my mother again.
>
> I couldn't tell why I was determinedly taking that journey. Perhaps in part it was
> because of the obsessive ravenous narcissism craving attention. Whatever it was, it
> was a compulsion for which I didn't have clearcut reasons. I only knew that in the
> world I had discovered and not yet entered there was a desperation which somehow
> matched—and justified—my own. . . . And although now to you it sounds very un-
> clear, I'll clarify it very soon. This is only by way of saying that when I reached New
> York, that world was waiting for me. I required no slow initiation. (Rechy 1963: 21)

Rechy's narrator admits that he "couldn't tell why [he] was determinedly
taking that journey." Unlike Royce, Rechy's narrator does not yet know

what he wants or what he wants to be. He recognizes only that he is acting in terms of "a compulsion for which [he] didn't have clearcut reasons." Even so, Rechy's narrator is confident that "in the world [he] had discovered and not yet entered there was a desperation which somehow matched—and justified—[his] own." So, like Royce, he also wanted "to free [himself] swiftly, to leave [his] place by the Window, uninvolved with life, and hurl [himself] into its boiling midst." And this meant that he, too, "had to get out."

Finally, for a third version of this feeling, here is a passage from one of my interviews with Jonathan, a forty-seven-year-old community college instructor, born and raised in southeastern Georgia:

> I remember that, as a child, I had the same feelings. I'd sit listening to the radio late at night, listening to stations from far away—places like Atlanta, New Orleans, New York City (maybe I imagined that, but it fits with the memory, ok?), and I'd think, that's where I want to be. There'd be these television movies with, one I remember, a black guy playing saxophone on a rooftop, by himself, jazz on a rooftop, and the sound echoing in a lonely, melancholy way across the neighborhood, and I'd think, that's where I want to be. That's the place. Now if you asked me why, I don't know how I would've answered. There was something that was appealing, attractive—much more attractive than life in my hometown!
>
> (Q: Did you think about these far-off places in gay terms?) I didn't even know what "homosexual" meant, back then [in the 1950s—WLL]. I mean, I was attracted to boys, but I didn't know there were words for those feelings. I guess the city was the same thing. I didn't have a word for that, either, but the attraction was just as strong. (Leap 1992d: 8)

I identify strongly with Jonathan's comments, because I also remember, as a child, sitting in my room late at night, listening to the radio, dreaming about leaving home. Like Royce's, Rechy's narrator's, and Jonathan's, my hometown (Tallahassee, Florida) was a temporary way station in my life. It didn't matter that, like Rechy's narrator, Jonathan had no words for what he was looking for or for what he would find; I didn't either, as I recall. And even though Royce was more certain about what he wanted to be, all four of us began to realize that "the city" offered alternatives to home and family, even if the alternatives were, for three of us, still packaged in an undefined imaginary.

This vision of leaving home differs from that commonly championed in the mainstream, heterosexual discourse. The city is a much less ambiguous place in heterosexual discourse because—unlike in Royce's, Rechy's, or Jonathan's narratives—the benefits of urban living are fully detailed. The city is a terrain filled with opportunities in this discourse, and residents willing to make the commitment can be confident that they will be able to ap-

propriate those opportunities for their personal ends. Even the physical geography of the city is recast, with (for example) the mysterious, brooding
background landscapes found in Rechy's prose upstaged by more intimate
portrayals of residents and practices as they play out in specific locales.

One accessible, and I think influential, representation of this discourse
in U.S. society is popular music, particularly the music programmed to the
general public through radio broadcast. Songs like "(Goin' to) Kansas City,"
"On Broadway," "12:30" (also known as "Young Girls Are Comin' to the
Canyon"), and "New York, New York" are among the older examples of
what I have in mind here, and "Fast Car," "Into the Great Wide Open," and
"Big Time" are more recent examples. As presented in the lyrics of these
songs, leaving home is just the first step toward moving to the city, a place
where (according to the specific claims of the narrative) anything is possible. The message in these songs is similar to that presented in novels like
*Soft City* (Raban 1974), *Slaves of New York* (Janowitz 1986), and *Story of
My Life* (McInerney 1988), in which the city offers "a series of stages upon
which individuals [can] work their own distinctive magic while performing
a multiplicity of roles," and "marks of social distinction [become] broadly
conferred by possessions and appearances" (Harvey 1989: 3, 5) rather than
by occupation, ethnicity, and class alone.

Songs like these certainly heightened my interest in moving to the city
when I was a child and, as I have learned by collecting life-story narratives
from other gay men, these songs were equally influential for them. This
made it worthwhile to determine the techniques of representation that
these songs contain: How, exactly, does popular music convey to the listener the idea that the city is a site of explicit possibilities?

As an example in that regard, let me use the Peter Gabriel song, "Big
Time," an extended narrator commentary about his successful experiences
in the city, where success is defined (as in David Harvey's commentary) in
terms of acquired possessions and appearances.[2] Appropriately, this is a first
person narrative; the pronouns "I" and "my" appear in the text thirty-three
times, while "they" occurs in only three instances, and in all cases refers to
undefined persons whose presence provides contrast with the narrator's
more explicit successes. And the "you" pronoun appears nowhere at all.

"Big Time" is, in other words, a monologue, with the narrator as subject
and actor and with the listener as passive participant in the narration. The
narrator's voice is either accompanied by an echo or multiply reproduced,
so that the narrator sounds as if he is talking (and constantly agreeing) with
himself. A chorus joins the narrator to provide an antiphonal contrast to his
comments during the two presentations of the refrain, then as a back-

ground to his description of at-home, entertainment skills in verse three and as a background to his inventory of oversized accomplishment in the song's conclusion. At no point, however, does the chorus offer commentary on its own; instead, the chorus strengthens the narrator's position as the central figure in this text.

Accordingly, words—which are almost exclusively supplied by the narrator—provide the primary format for the presentation of text content. The narrator's articulation is clear and precise, and never obstructed by the overplay of instrumentation or musical effects. The album provides the listener with a written version of the lyrics, to further minimize the chance of misconveyed or misunderstood features of text detail.

The focus of the text content is displayed in its opening line: "I'm on my way, I'm makin' it." This is a song about *self*-styled achievement within an urban setting. The narrator came from a small town, where "the people think so small, they use small words." The narrator, in contrast, saw through those limitations: he was smarter than that, he says; he "worked it out and [has] been stretching [his] mouth to let those big words come right out." That is why he decided to come to the city: He wants to do big things, and he needs an environment that will let him meet these expectations.

Now he is eager to convince his listener that he has addressed (or surpassed) his original goals. "My parties have all the big names," he explains. And besides, "my car is getting bigger, and so is my house . . . , my eyes . . . , my mouth . . . , my belly . . . , my circumstance . . . , as well as [my] bulge." All the while, the chorus continues to chant "big time, big time" in the background. And, appropriately, the last words in the song are "big, big, big, big."

In sum, this text confirms the city as a site for opportunity and mobility. It offers an upbeat and optimistic description of a person in control, someone whose carefully crafted agenda for success not only leads him away from his hometown but blueprints ways to make full use of the city's resources once he arrives.

This is not, of course, the representation of leaving home found in gay men's life stories—nor is this the representation of this theme displayed in explicitly gay popular music.[3] And to suggest some of the points of contrast, I want to examine the treatment of the leaving home theme in Bronski Beat's "Smalltown Boy."

Bronski Beat was a rock band that was popular in the 1980s. (Their members subsequently separated to pursue independent interests.) Like Peter Gabriel, they are also British, and they wrote "Smalltown Boy" during the same period in English history (the budget tightening and economic recession of the Thatcher years) that Gabriel wrote "Big Time." Both of these songs were released on what became popular long-playing albums, and each song received additional play, as a single release, on the radio and in the dance clubs.

But here the similarities end. Peter Gabriel is not, to my knowledge, a publicly declared homosexual. Members of Bronski Beat are, however, openly proud gay men, and they display their gender politics in the topics of their songs, in their lyrics, and in the packaging of their records and tapes.

In the center of the cover of *Age of Consent* (the album on which "Smalltown Boy" was released), for example, there is a pink triangle imposed on top of a square and a circle of more ambiguous color; the subtitle of the album is *Forbidden Fruit*. (The cover of Peter Gabriel's album contains a photograph of the singer, onto which the album's title and the artist's name have been superimposed. There is no additional iconography.)

A close examination of the construction of this text reveals additional points of contrast with "Big Time." For one thing, the narrator in "Big Time" was both the subject of the text and the primary actor within it. The chorus provided backup for the narrator's statements but never spoke alone. In "Smalltown Boy," the narrator and subject are different individuals, and instead of a narrator-centered monologue, the narrator talks to the subject and about the subject throughout this text, and so does the chorus. Accordingly, the pronoun "you" appears eleven times in this text, while "they" appears only twice and "I" never occurs at all.

In "Big Time," the narrator was the primary voice, and the chorus spoke in accompaniment to the narrator, but never on its own. Comments to the text subject have a less consistent presentation in "Smalltown Boy." While the narrator speaks alone in twenty-three of the fifty-one lines of the text, the narrator and chorus jointly address the subject through various combinations of voices for twenty lines. In one of these segments, for example, the narrator joins with one member of the chorus to produce a statement ("bye-bye, trouble child") whose musical dissonance matches its derogatory content. In a second segment, the narrator and the full chorus exchange antiphonal messages. And in the remaining two segments, the chorus speaks independently of the narrator.

The constant shifting in textual voice parallels and reproduces the conditions in the subject's real-life experience that prompted his decision to leave home. The narrator notes that the subject has been "pushed around and kicked around, always a lonely boy" and was "the one they talked about around town, and they put [him] down." While their motives are certainly different, the narrator and chorus are acting in a similar fashion in this text.

One-third of the statements in the text consist of a repeated set of commands, which are directed at the subject: "run away, turn away, look away." The remaining statements contain the narrator's observations about the subject and about some important events in his life—information of which the subject is already aware.

So while these comments are directed at the subject (note the frequency of the "you" pronoun in these statements), they are really intended for some other party (such as the audience). The subject himself is silent through the presentation of the text, adding to his status as a person talked-about, in text construction as well as real life.

"Big Time" began with a verbal statement, and words were the primary format for presentation of text meaning. "Smalltown Boy" contains a different design. The song begins with a musical interlude, followed by the narrator's voice speaking quite softly, then a series of banshee-like wails, a quieter nonverbal comment, and a return to the musical interlude. Only then does the text shift into its verbal format.

At this point, without knowing much about the content of this song, the listener is aware that some issues to be explored in this text cannot be put into words. Appropriately, while the lyrics to "Big Time" were reprinted on the back of the album cover, Age of Consent provides no such inventory. And because the narrator sings some of his lines in falsetto, and the musical overlay and other factors obscure his pronunciation in key words in other lines, there is a persistent ambiguity in the presentation of the verbal text that parallels the ambiguity presented in the text content. When listeners find themselves saying, "I don't understand" or "I am not certain what he's saying here" while they listen to the song, their reactions intensify the presentation of ambiguous message.

Equally ambiguous is the outcome of the actions that the text describes. The small-town boy has decided to leave home, according to the narrator's opening lines. His reasons for leaving are personal and are also influenced by the treatment he has received from others. What the narrator and chorus are saying serves only to confirm and reinforce the course of action that the subject has already begun.

But where he is going, and what he will do once he arrives there, is another matter entirely. Unlike "Big Time," "Smalltown Boy" contains no brassy, self-serving agenda for success. All the narrator and chorus can suggest is "run away, turn away, look away." And if the subject has developed such an agenda on his own, the text offers no indication of its detail. Even the means of transportation that will take him away from home is unspecified; we know only that he is standing alone on a platform, in the wind and

rain, with all of his possessions in a single suitcase. This is the opening image of the song, and it is the image that closes the song, while the chorus
continues to echo its advice, "run away, turn away, look away," as the song
fades into silence.

"Smalltown Boy" is not the only gay-explicit popular song that explores a
leaving-home theme, but its treatment of this theme suggests the treatment
that I generally find in these sources. Consistently, the immediate concern
in these texts is getting away from life back home. What the subject will do
next is of secondary importance to text content; in fact, as is so vividly the
case in "Smalltown Boy," the act of leaving is usually the high point of these
narratives.

Usually, these texts describe the subject's *hometown* setting in less than
favorable terms, and while the world outside of the *hometown* may be more
favorably represented, the texts also describe that world as an unfamiliar
and largely undefined place, filled with practices that the subject does not
yet fully understand. For this reason, the narrative voice in these songs (and
often, the subject himself) relies on imagination and anticipation to make
the unfamiliar more accessible, and any blueprints for success in the outside world (if the narrative actually contains such comments) are filled with
irrealis (that is, contrary to fact) references and if–then constructions, and
have many fewer concretely worded declaratives.

Treatments of this leaving-home theme also show up in songs that may
not have been intended to have an explicitly gay appeal but that gay audiences have incorporated into gay repertoire, all the same. I have in mind
here songs like Judy Garland's "Over the Rainbow" and Frank Sinatra's
"New York, New York." Much has been written about Judy Garland's strategic position in gay–camp iconography (cf. Koestenbaum 1993: 33-34; Newton 1993: 176, 240), and I do not need to revisit that issue here. I simply invite the reader to listen once again to Ms. Garland singing "Over the
Rainbow" and to notice how greatly imagination, fantasy, and irrealis references contribute to the textual message.

"New York, New York" is another matter. The first time that I heard gay
men singing this song was during a summer trip to Key West, Florida, in
1980. I was spending a relaxing evening in a piano bar, watching the traffic
on Duval Street, listening to the piano player and the two men joining him
in an occasional song. Then the piano player played the introductory notes
to "New York, New York," and one of the men standing by the piano in-
toned the opening line "Start spreading the news, I'm leaving today." Suddenly, hundreds of voices (or so it seemed) surrounded the tenor to con-

tinue the narrative: "I'm going to be a part of it—New York, New York." By the time the tenor and chorus reached the closing lines—"If I can make it there, I'll make it anywhere"—almost everyone in the bar was singing out loud, humming along, or swaying back and forth in time with the music. The song ended, applause and cheers roared across the bar, the tenor took his bow and sat down, and the piano player moved to the next song on his play list.

I have heard crowds in other gay piano bars perform this song, and there has usually been a similar display of energy in each performance, almost as if "New York, New York" has become a theme song or gay national anthem, at least for the segment of gay America frequenting piano bars. The song's bouncy melody line, its equation of narrator and subject, and its use of harmony so that the chorus supports rather than competes with the lead singer and his message—all of these features suggest a presentation of an upbeat, optimistic message that is quite different from that in "Smalltown Boy" and similar gay texts. In fact, if anything, "New York, New York" appears to parallel the presentation of the message in "Big Time."

A closer look at text construction reveals a different way to interpret these contrasts. The opening line establishes the leaving-home theme on which the remainder of the text depends: "Start spreading the news, I'm leaving today." The next line locates the portion of the outside world that he plans to enter: "I'm going to be a part of it—New York, New York." The "it" pronoun in this statement could refer to New York, or to something else known to the narrator (and perhaps, to the audience as well) but not specified in this text. Either way, the antecedent of the "it" is ambiguous—a quality that is alien to the narrative in "Big Time" but integral to the depiction of life away from home in "Smalltown Boy."[4]

So is the use of if–then constructions and irrealis references, both of which occur frequently in the "New York, New York" text (for example, "If I can make it there, I'll make it anywhere"). So is the use of abstract imagery and anticipation (for example, "I want to be there where the city never sleeps") rather than a specific agenda for success, of the sort explicitly displayed by the narrator of "Big Time." And so is the narrator's willingness to believe that life outside his *hometown* will be better, somehow, than the life he leaves behind, even if he only understands the opportunities outside in imaginary terms.

### Contesting Space: "Queer" as Spatial Practice

During the period 1978–1989, I worked on several language and education projects on the Northern Ute reservation in northeastern Utah. Part of this work involved classroom observations at the on-reservation elementary school, formal interviews with school personnel, and simply "hanging out" with Ute students and staff on campus and at other locales. Part of it involved talking with Indian students and members of their families about their interests and concerns about the educational opportunities made available to the tribe.

One morning, during spring 1986, I was talking with a sixth-grade Ute student and with his sister, a third grader. They had known me for several years and had talked with me about many issues, serious and silly, so I expected that the conversation would shift at regular intervals between topics on my agenda and topics of greater interest to them. I was somewhat startled, however, when the sixth grader (whom I identify hereafter with the pseudonym Ben) interrupted our school-centered discussion to ask a rather pointed question about queers. Example 5.1 is my transcript of the conversation.

Ben concluded line 26 with a firmness in facial features that I had seen many times in Ute conversations: We have said enough on this topic, that gesture conveys, so let's move on to something else. We did move on, but as our conversation explored other items on the afternoon's research agenda I kept going over this exchange in my mind.

In one sense, I was not surprised by Ben's statement. I had heard other students (Ute and non-Indian) at the elementary school make similar derogatory comments about "queers," some of which were even more explicitly violent than Ben's. I knew that this is how children raised in heterosexist societies often talk about alternative sexualities. And, after almost ten years of work on this reservation, I knew that many factors—such as daily contact with non-Indian classmates, conflicting messages about gays and lesbians presented by the media, the influence of conservative, "pro-family," Christian missionization (particularly, in this case, from Roman Catholic, Mormon, and fundamentalist Protestant sources)—contextualize and reinforce these stereotypes within reservation-specific social discourse, as does a general fear of the AIDS pandemic, blame for which, here as elsewhere, is regularly traced to homosexual men.

At the same time, I knew Ben and his family were strong supporters of traditional Ute practices as they are understood and maintained in the contemporary reservation setting. Ben himself regularly attends sweat lodge ceremonies with his father and other family friends, and he has told me how he looks forward to being part of the late-summer Sun Dance, a general ceremony of renewal that benefits participants and the tribe as a whole. And more than once (I know this through his narratives and through comments from his teachers), Ben has reminded classmates of the need to maintain Mother Earth and the dangers of abusing the richness of her landscape, when the school's science and social studies curricula focused only on the appropriation of natural resources.

---

**Example 5.1** Kill the queers.

| 1 | Ben: | Bill, are there many queers in Washington, D.C.? |
|---|------|--------------------------------------------------|

1   Ben:   Bill, are there many queers in Washington, D.C.?
2   WLL:   [*Four beats of pause, as I try to submerge my shock and*
3          *surprise*] Yes, there are a lot of gay people in D.C.,
4          yes.
5   Ben:   I think they should kill all the queers.
6   WLL:   [*Two-beat pause*] How come you say that?
7   Ben:   Well [*Two-beat pause*] I don't know.
8          [*started on a high pitch (I), dropped into low*
9          *pitch (don-), and ended with movement from low*
10         *into mid range (-t know)*].
11  WLL:   Do you know any queers?
12  Ben:   There's this one kid in my class. All the kids pick
13         on him because he wears glasses and doesn't like to
14         play baseball.
15  WLL:   Does that mean he is queer?
16  Ben:   Well, he acts like it.
17  WLL:   What does he do?
18  Ben:   He doesn't like to play sports. He doesn't do anything.
19         He just hangs around with the girls or with
20         the teacher. [*Said with a slightly annoyed tone, as*
21         *if he has already explained this, and why am I not*
22         *catching on?*]
23  WLL:   So how come you want him killed? How come all the
24         queers should be killed?
25  Ben:   [*Same pitch contour as line 7*] I don't know. They
26         just should.

---

Central to the Ute philosophy at issue in these settings are notions of autonomy and responsibility, notions that allow individual Ute people great latitude in their personal behavior. Over and over again, I heard Ute people use the simple phrase "that's her way" or "that's his way" to explain why someone's actions are noticeably different from the actions of others in the same setting. Those alternatives may not agree with an observer's own pref-

erences for personal conduct, but each person's right to pursue an individualized course of action, whatever the topic or task, is rarely challenged in
Ute social space.[5]

For some Ute people, male homosexuality can be one of the challenge-
able topics.[6] Ute people who hold this position argue that homosexuality is
a distasteful abomination and definitely not part of traditional Ute culture,
and they speak stridently against it and against homosexuals whenever they
have the opportunity.[7] More commonly, however, Ute people respond to
instances of gender diversity within the tribe—ranging from effeminate behavior in men, short- or long-term cosexual partnerships, or berdache/two-
spirit (re)presentation of social self—in the same fashion as they respond to
encounters with other people's individualized alternatives: "That's his way,"
and no more discussion is required.

That is why I was perplexed by Ben's comment and with the exchange
that followed it. Given that Ben often spoke out against Anglo-American
values when they conflicted with Ute tradition, what prompted Ben to by-
pass Ute endorsements of personal autonomy and embrace such an explicitly derogatory perspective?

Ben knew that I was involved in a long-term relationship with another
man. Ben often heard me talking about our relationship with his parents,
and (Ben later told me) he and his brother regularly listened on the bedroom extension when I made my telephone calls to my partner from their
home. Ben knew that his parents were not troubled by my being gay, and
that other Ute adults with whom I worked were equally accepting in this regard.

At first, I thought that Ben might be teasing me; perhaps his comments
were a preadolescent form of the joke telling and joke playing commentary
that permeates all Ute conversations between good friends. But the somberness of his commentary dispelled this claim; Ben wasn't acting or playing
when he made these statements—not as I heard it, at least.

I next thought that he might be experimenting with the sounds of a
homosexual-centered conversation, perhaps as a first step toward a later discussion of these issues. Perhaps he was beginning to come to terms with his
own cosexual feelings. Perhaps, by using violence to frame his commentary,
he was trying to distract me from recognizing his internal exploration.

But taking a closer look at the transcript, I found another way, and I believe a more productive way, to interpret Ben's comments. I noticed that
Ben was somewhat unfamiliar with the content of the label he was using.
When I asked him if he knew any queers, he mentioned only a male class-
mate who preferred being with the girls to playing baseball. He did not refer

to any of the movie actors, recording artists, or other individuals whose homosexuality has become nationally prominent in recent years. He told me that queers have distinctive actions (lines 16, 18-20), but when asked to explain in greater detail, all he identified were a dependence on eyewear and a reluctance to play baseball. He said nothing about homosexuals as perverts, as immoral persons, as people condemned to hell—arguments that non-Indian children Ben's age who are familiar with Christian constructions of homophobia will repeat mechanically in response to similar questions. "Kill all the queers," he said, but he never told me why queers should be killed: "I don't know," he said early in the conversation (line 7). "I don't know. They just should," he repeats, at the conversation's end (lines 25-26).

Apparently, Ben is aware that "queer" is something "bad," but that awareness does not extend to any of the descriptive details that justify that assessment in Western, heterosexist logic. In other words, Ben had acquired the affect associated with the term, but he had not yet localized the affect within particular forms of gendered practice.

Ben's allegiance to traditional Ute philosophy helps explain the separation of affect and content in this case, since Ute respect for personal autonomy and tolerance for individual behavior are incompatible with the negative characterization of "queers" and "queer" behavior that occurs in vernacular English discourse. But equally relevant to his response are some of the linguistic properties of the term "queer" as an item in English lexicon, as well as the effects that those properties bring to the construction of meaning within English conversations.

"Queer" is one of a handful of terms in English that establish references by opposition and exclusion, not just by simple description. That is, instead of identifying properties that the object under discussion contains, calling something "queer" suggests that it is out of place in some sense, that it is excessive and overextended, that it disrupts and subverts an otherwise tranquil domain. The starting point for such references is always an established social order, allegiance to which is expected and appropriate behavior. Calling something "queer" locates the referent at distance from that order and signals a contrast with the expectations that that order maintains.

In other words, queer does not identify or describe as much as it provides a point of view in terms of which the participants in a conversation can explore the identified referent. This "framing" function of "queer" is well established throughout English linguistic history. Judy Grahn notes (1984: 276) that modern-day English "queer" derives from (Old English?) *cwer* 'crooked, not straight.' Wayne Dynes (1985: 119-20) adds that "the current slang meaning is probably rooted in the use of the word for counterfeit coin or banknotes (from the eighteenth century)" and cites "the modern slang expression 'queer as a three-dollar bill'" as a contemporary reflex of this older reference. And George Chauncey observes:

> By the 1910s and 1920s, the men who identified themselves as part of a distinct category of men primarily on the basis of their homosexual interest rather than their womanlike gender status usually called themselves *queer*. Essentially synonymous with "homosexual," *queer* presupposed the statistical normalcy—and normative character—of men's sexual interest in women; tellingly, queers referred to their counterparts as "normal men" (or "straight men") rather than "heterosexuals." (1994: 15-16)

In all three cases, "queer" identifies its referent in oppositional terms, specifying reference by drawing attention to characteristics that the referent does not possess and focusing the remainder of the discussion accordingly on the significance of that absence. Unavoidably, a negative tone always creeps into any discussion of something queer, even if negative comments are never explicitly stated, as such, during the exchange. Calling something "queer" assigns the referent to an out-of-place, irregular, and in-contrast position, vis-à-vis the established norms. Under such circumstances, further validation of the liminal status of the referent is not required.

Ben's comments in our conversation followed this blueprint quite closely. He called for "killing the queers," but he never gave an explicit justification for this position. Indeed, it is not clear that he actually had one—or even needed one. Knowing that queer was something "out of place," something that, by definition, conflicted with expectable practice, made it acceptable to propose steps to restore balance to the status quo. Ute toleration for personal autonomy only prolongs the conditions that are out of balance and offers no incentives for resolving them. On the other hand, homophobic rhetoric—exemplified in the phrase "kill the queers"—speaks directly to this condition and to its resolution.

This anecdote shows how the linguistic properties of the term "queer" help to frame the nonlinguistic references associated with it. Important in that framing are notions of position and the construction of social place. Equating queer with something "not straight," "counterfeit," or "in contrast to normalcy" locates "queer" in relationship to an assumed position of normalcy; that location becomes the base onto which additional attributes and characteristics of queer behavior can then be applied. As Ben's commentary suggests, location prefigures description for queer referencing in vernacular English discourse, and the same arrangement holds for the term "queer" and for queer-related references in Gay English.

As Chauncey's statement suggests, gay men have been aware for some time that "queer" implied a contrast against a more inclusive and more mainstream-oriented reference ideal. As he explains:

Before the [Second World] war, men had been content to call themselves "queer" because they regarded themselves as self-evidently different from the men they usually called "normal." Some of them were unhappy with this state of affairs,but others saw themselves as special—more sophisticated, more knowing—and took pleasure in being different from the mass. (1994: 19)

In order to accommodate this new identity, gay men did not attempt to diffuse the negative messages conveyed by "queer," or otherwise to reconstruct its meanings. Instead, they turned to a different item of English vocabulary— "gay"—and recast the meaning of this term to that end. "Gay began to catch on in the 1930s and its primacy was consolidated during the war. By the late 1940s, younger men were chastizing old men who still used queer, which the younger men now regarded as demeaning" (Chauncey 1994: 19). Gay men have also appropriated other terms from heterosexual discourse and used those terms to express positive imagery and pride. In some cases— "queen," "fairy," "faggot"—reclaiming these terms required a significant recasting of the antigay sentiments that the terms express elsewhere in vernacular discourse. Yet gay men have generally continued to exclude "queer" from their inventory of reclaimed vocabulary—at least, until recently.

For now, it seems, "queer" is everywhere: adorning coffee mugs, sweatshirts, and baseball caps; incorporated into political slogans, chants, and bumper stickers; displayed on book covers and record jackets; included in college courses and in public debates on gender and sexual politics. The source for much of this usage was the emergence of the Queer Nation movement, whose "outspoken promotion of a national sexuality" and "desire to reclaim the nation for pleasure, and specifically spectacular public self-entitlement" (Berlant and Freeman 1993: 195) was quite different from the more familiar and more conservative notions of gendered practice found in (gay and straight) America. As Queer Nation gained visibility through its members' carefully constructed, localized activities, so did queer theory—a collection of perspectives that challenges and destabilizes more conventional interpretations of popular culture by searching for "the ways in which texts—either literature or mass culture or language—shape sexuality" while assuming that "fantasy and other kinds of representation are inherently uncontrollable, queer by nature" (Warner 1993: 19). In effect, uncontrollable representations (or "messy representations," as Warner terms them later in that passage) are the primary concern of Queer Nation as well as queer theory. The difference in action, in that regard, lies primarily in the particular representation under scrutiny: The queer theorist confronts sexual assumptions displayed in episodes of *Laverne and Shirley* (Doty 1993: 39-62), the queer national confronts similar assumptions in the daily practices at a shopping mall (Browning 1993: 31-40). And, even then, differences in particulars often rapidly dissolve into evidence of underlying similarity (as they would in this case, since television programs and shopping malls are in some ways merely variants of the same cultural representation).[8]

Using queer as the anchor point for these new constructions of practice (Queer Nation) and theory (queer theory) is not entirely accidental. Notions of opposition, of contrast with established modes of thinking, and of distance from the conventions of the mainstream are central concerns in all of the written, oral, and visual texts created by queer nationals and queer theorists (see the sample texts in example 5.2). Under this formulation, "queer" is no longer a status of "the other," as defined by the conventions of the mainstream. Queer is now the starting point for a queer's own social critique, and the mainstream is now positioned, in spite of its objections, within the margin. No longer is the discussion of out-of-place, irregular places or the association of individuals to those spaces an activity initiated by high school bullies, jealous coworkers, or "straights" hoping to disguise their own insecurities about sexuality. *Queer is now a space identified and defined by its own practitioners.*

One interesting thing about queer (as) space is the flexible and fluid qualities of its boundaries. Just as queer identifies a distinct position at distance from dominant norms, queer also identifies a distinct position, at distance from dominant labels and categories. "At distance from" becomes underscored in this case by adopting a philosophy of plasticity; rather than enforcing allegiance to a predetermined definition, queer defines by contrast, by exclusion, by opposition. So anyone positioned at distance from the mainstream—either through contrast, exclusion, or opposition—falls within this category, and so does anyone who deliberately positions him- or herself in that regard. So describing the inhabitants of queer space becomes an open-ended and complex task, and that prompts many to resist doing so. After all, definitions had a lot to do with the marginalization of gay people to begin with, and the point of queer is to subvert, not reproduce, the social logic underlying the status quo.

These arguments have no appeal to persons who have no interest in positioning themselves at distance from and in contrast with the mainstream. These are not the only reasons why heterosexuals who may otherwise be

**Example 5.2** Sample texts: The queer logic of queer.

1 (Source: one passage from the Queer Nation Manifesto [n.d.] "I Hate Straights.")

I hate straight people who can't listen to queer anger without saying, "Hey, all straight people aren't like that. I'm straight, too, you know." As if their egos don't get enough stroking or protection in this arrogant, heterosexist world. Why must we take care of them, in the midst of our just anger brought on by their fucked up society? Why add the reassurance of "Of course I don't mean you. You don't act that way." Let them figure out for themselves whether they deserve to be included in our anger.

2 (Source: de Lauretis (1991: iii-iv), describing the goals of the 1990 Santa Cruz conference on theorizing lesbian and gay sexualities.)

The work of the conference was intended to articulate the terms in which lesbian and gay sexualities may be understood and imagined as forms of re-sistance to cultural homogenization, counteracting dominant discourses with other constructions of the subject in culture. We could, I hoped, be willing to examine, make explicit, compare or confront the respective histo-ries, assumptions, and conceptual frameworks that have characterized the self-representations of North American lesbians and gay men, of color and white, up until now; from there, we could go on to recast or reinvent the terms of our sexualities, then construct another discursive horizon, another way of thinking the sexual. . . . And hence, the title of the conference . . . : "Queer Theory" . . . The term queer juxtaposed to the lesbian and gay of the subtitle, is intended to mark a certain critical distance from the latter, by now established and often convenient, formula.

3 (Source: Warner [1993: xxvi-xxviii], explaining the issues at stake in the emergence of "queer" as a term for self- and group reference.)

The preference for queer represents, among other things, an aggressive im-pulse of generalization; it rejects a minoritizing logic of toleration or simple political interest-representation in favor of a more thorough resistance to regimes of the normal. For both academics and activists, "queer gets a criti-cal edge by defining itself against the normal rather than the heterosexual, and normal includes normal business in the academy. . . . The insistence on "queer"—a term initially generated in the context of terror—has the ef-fect of pointing out a wide field of normalization, rather than simple intol-erance, as the site of violence.

sympathetic to "lesbian and gay concerns" still voice dislike and distrust for self-identified queers, but certainly, queer claims to "our own space" contribute to such reactions. Similar factors help explain the widespread dislike and distrust of queer-positive philosophy and of self-identified queers within lesbian and gay circles. I use the term "lesbian and gay" generically here, though I find that gay men offer particularly vigorous objections in this regard, and disputes over position and space are consistently at the forefront of those objections. Example 5.3 contains some sample texts.

---

**Example 5.3** Sample texts: Gay resistance to "queer."

1 (Source: Souers 1992; by permission of the *Washington Blade*)

After reading the *Blade* Readers' Forum submissions [gives names and dates], I cannot help but express my concern over their free usage of the word "queer." I am angered and also confused at what appears to be an attempt at desensitizing people to a word that in actuality does not serve a purpose to the Gay community.

A check of three dictionary sources for the interpretation of "queer" found no differences except word order. Webster's II defines queer as "different from the normal or expected; strange; Eccentric; odd; Suspicious." I hardly think that the vast majority of gay people on this planet would want to be (forcibly) associated with such a word given its literal meaning. Is it not true that we have been trying for years to assure society that we aren't odd or strange and that we are normal? I sincerely doubt that being labelled "queer" is going to advance our cause significantly. . . .

The Gay rights movement and gay activism are supposed to move us forward into society with an ultimate goal of positive acceptance and equality. Using the word "queer" to represent ourselves not only degrades us individually but promotes the widespread use of prejudicial slurs and condones it.

2 (Source: Marcus 1993: 14-15; by permission of *Ten Percent Magazine*)

One of the claims I've heard made for queer is that it's an inclusive word, embracing all kinds of people. . . . As a gay man, I don't want to be grouped under the all-encompassing umbrella of queer. I am not even all that comfortable being grouped with bisexuals, let alone transsexuals, transvestites and queer straight . . . because we have different lives, face different challenges, and don't necessarily share the same aspirations.

Besides failing to define who I am, queer defines a set of values, beliefs, and goals that are not my own. In talking with men and women who identify themselves as queer and reading what self-described queers have written,

**Example 5.3** *continued*

I've learned that queer is about being different, setting oneself apart from the mainstream. To be queer is to be rebellious. It's about expressing anger toward and rejection of establishment values, whether they are the values of the straight majority or the gay and lesbian minority. For younger queers, who make up the bulk of those who consider themselves queer, being queer is a way to carve out a new path, different from the one created by an older generation of gays and lesbians.

I have no desire to set myself apart from the mainstream, or to carve a new path, and I believe that the majority of gay and lesbian people, both young and old, share that view. Of course, as a gay man, I am different from someone who grew up straight. . . . but I'd rather emphasize what I have in common with other people than focus on the differences. The last thing I want to do is institutionalize that difference by defining myself with a word and a political philosophy that set me outside of the mainstream.

3 (Source: Miles 1994: 96-97)

The New Gay Right is spearheaded by a very small number of intellectuals, almost all of them white men, who hope to bring together basic conservative ideas about government, liberty and rights with a "traditional values" social critique and a culturally conservative worldview. . . . Though they don't use the rallying cry of the "homosexual threat" in quite the same way as the straight Right, they do attack the same flamboyantly queer images to get the attention of Middle Gay America.

Liebman, after a few minutes of polite discussion, blurts out, "Tell me something, darling, are your nipples pierced?" Startled, I allow that they're not, and Liebman continues: "See? You're normal. Most of us are. We need new ideas and new organizations to overcome the stereotypes, both the ones our enemies have and the ones we make ourselves. The people in our community who cause the stereotypes—drag queens, pierced nipples, dykes on bikes—have a very valid place. I love them, but they're not us."

[Bruce] Bawer is less accepting, writing: "If the heterosexual majority ever comes to accept homosexuality, it will do so because it has seen homosexuals in suit and ties, not nipple clamps and bike pants; it will do so because it has seen homosexuals showing respect for civilization, not attempting to subvert it." He then makes the link between half-naked subculture queens and subversive politics. "From the minute that you timidly pick up your first copy of a gay newspaper or magazine," he writes, "you find yourself encouraged to look down upon the place you come from, to resent your

**Example 5.3** *continued*

parents and to mock the faith in which you were raised. In particular, you are expected to subscribe to the laundry list of leftist politics."

4 (Source: Barney Frank [D–Mass.] on the prominence of drag queens, leatherfolk, and fetishists in the Stonewall 25 parade, quoted in Gladwell 1994: A3)

I can't stop anyone from dressing bizarrely and parading around New York City. But do we have to put them at the head of our parade? We've been fighting to be in the mainstream, so why do we marginalize ourselves? . . . What I have been crusading for is for us to be more serious, to be more like the NAACP and the AARP. When you want political rights, it's not a good idea to go about trying to offend people.

---

As in Doty's, Warner's, and de Lauretis's discussions of "queer," the texts in example 5.3 are about normalcy and the positioning of the homosexual subject in relation to normalcy. Here, however, normalcy remains the starting point for mapping the sexual terrain; rather than challenging or subverting this arrangement, these authors seek to broaden the notion of normalcy, so that lesbians and gays can also have "a place at the table," to use Bawer's (1993) imagery.

The popularity of the term "queer" suggests, however, that not all lesbian or gay persons are interested in developing such an accommodation or interested in living under the restrictions (for example, the "don't ask, don't tell" requirement imposed on lesbians and gay men in the U.S. military) that such developments would require. There is more at issue here than disagreement over the "appropriateness" of a "label." "Queer," in its 1990s usage, reflects a uniquely positioned lesbian–gay experience. It identifies the (queer) subject's transformation of heterosexual place into personally gendered space, not an acceptance of a terrain that other parties have designed.

The issue is particularly problematic for Gay English discourse, since, as a male-oriented, gendered language, Gay English is already positioned in relation to, not at distance from, the discourse of the (heterosexual) mainstream. Perhaps this is why the construction of (gay) space figures prominently in so much of the risk taking associated with Gay English discourse as it unfolds inside heterosexually controlled social domains, and why miscommunications of message and meaning often overlap with spatial designations in other forms.

# 6

---

## Language, Risk, and Space in a
## Health Club Locker Room

---

Washington, D.C.–area health clubs have given me great opportunities for studying Gay English discourse in action.[1] While these are not always necessarily gay-identified or gay-oriented facilities, some male clients still find ways to express erotic interests in men in these settings, and the practices they use for this purpose show certain similarities across sites. Initially, I assumed that Gay English was the language of erotic negotiation in these instances and that studying contrasts between "gay" and "straight" text making at these sites would help me identify and interpret other components of on-site erotic practices. As it turned out, language use did not pattern so neatly along this gay–straight dichotomy; in fact, as a more detailed analysis of text making shows, *gay* and *straight* take on unexpected associations, as categories of personal identity, in these settings.

### Background

I did not originally intend to do fieldwork in health club settings. But, in the summer of 1988, I received a telephone call from one of my former students, and what she had to say started me thinking about the usefulness of these sites for gay language research.

Anita (not her real name) had become the daytime manager of a health club in a rapidly growing business and professional area in the D.C. suburbs. Since working at this club, she had become aware of client complaints about the frequency of male-oriented sexual activities in the men's locker room. She wanted to address the client concerns, but she had no interest in having her staff become an on-site "sex police." Did I have any suggestions for effective intervention, she wondered?

I asked for some details about the on-site practice. The list included subtle but sharply focused eye-glances and persistent, provocative verbal commentary, as well as instances of individuals, pairs of men, and occasionally men in groups engaging in what she termed "genital manipulation." According to the complaints, these activities usually took place in more-secluded areas of the locker room, but occasionally took place in areas where the actions could be visible to all. Some exchanges were conducted quietly and discreetly; others were noisy and raucous. Some involved spontaneous encounters between strangers; others appeared to be part of regular, recurring social relationships. Some instances of "genital manipulation" involved safe-sex practices, while others included obviously unguarded exchanges of bodily fluids.

In the past, Anita said, when the participants in these activities could be identified, the managers had tried to convince them to use greater restraint, particularly when they were in the public areas of the facility (such as the weight room floor and the changing areas of the locker room). These efforts led to an increase in the incidence of male erotic practices in the showers, the sauna, and the steam room, and brought a new round of complaints to the front desk.

Up to that point, acting on stereotype as much as anything else, I had assumed that "straight men" were registering these complaints with the management and that "gay men" were initiating and carrying out the on-site erotics.[2] Not so, Anita replied. Self-identified gay clients objected to these activities just as often as did heterosexual men, and while the gay clients were not in favor of an outright ban on on-site cosexual activity (the action usually demanded by offended straight clients), gay clients were concerned that others were making inappropriate use of the club's homoerotic environment and hoped that management would do something to regulate such exchanges. Some gay men were also concerned about the image of gay men as sexual predators that the visibility of these activities was confirming. And some were concerned about the health-related consequences of on-site, unsafe sex.

Anita wanted to post safe-sex advertisements in the locker rooms and place complimentary condoms in bowls at the front desk and in other strategic locations throughout the club. And she and I discussed other avenues of action, including holding some focus group discussions with clients and staff members, so that the different perspectives on these issues could be more richly assessed.

The health club's director also wanted to take action in some form but did not want to bring unnecessary attention to an already awkward situation. The regional management wanted the whole issue ignored. They were afraid of negative publicity, and they wanted to protect several nationally prominent club members who were aware of these exchanges and who, on occasion, were also participants.

The regional management's position terminated what could have become an interesting project in the applied anthropology of gender. However, my conversation with Anita had encouraged me to look more closely at the patterns of gendered communication at my own health club, a facility whose membership was almost exclusively heterosexual—or so it seemed when my partner and I first joined. Out of town travel gave me the chance to explore similar questions at health clubs in other parts of the country, including Miami and Tallahassee, Florida; Chicago, Illinois; Albuquerque, New Mexico; Salt Lake City and Vernal, Utah; and San Francisco, California. These were not gay-oriented health clubs, but gay men were certainly present at these sites, some openly so, others in familiar disguise. Without intending to do so, I found that my visits to health clubs were providing me with opportunities to draw comparisons between Gay English discourse and other language-based expressions of gendered identities.

### Research Procedures

My research at these sites required a use of participant observation and other forms of data gathering that were familiar to me from studies of American Indian languages in reservation and urban Indian settings. This time, however, I was no longer an outsider to the speech events I was studying, nor was I completely unfamiliar with the linguistic and cultural rules structuring the exchange of messages in these settings. And as I became more familiar with the language dynamics at these sites, I began to find (and to be party to) examples of gaydar-initiated conversations, negotiations of gender disclosure between suspect gays, and the shielding effects of turn taking and hedging strategies.

But besides confirming the claims about Gay English text making that I had developed at other speech settings, I was now able to explore the significance of Gay English text making in a controlled environment—that is, in a setting where Gay English usage and its messages could be compared to the messages that other speakers were conveying through other forms of text construction. To study significance, I needed to observe conversations and other forms of on-site communication, then talk to participants about their reactions to those message-making experiences.[3] I pursued both forms of data gathering, as opportunities arose, on the workout room floor, in aerobic and weight training classrooms, in the locker room changing areas, and in the steam room, whirlpool, sauna, and showers.

My discussions of language and about instances of message making that

I had just observed usually began by building on the topic of the moment from the previous exchange. Some of these discussions were difficult for me to negotiate. Usually, they were quite productive, particularly when I was talking to a self-identified gay man and I confirmed my own gender identity. Once common gender interests were established, these men became quite willing to talk about health club–related gay experiences (conversations, fantasies, erotic encounters), to introduce me to gay friends who also worked out at the club, and to explain the details of "gay practice" relevant to each site, such as which bank of lockers gay men regularly used or regularly avoided, what times of day gay men frequented the club, and which areas of the weight room were likely to be sites for male-centered flirtation or for erotic negotiation. All of this information helped clarify the context for my observations of on-site language use and helped me further appreciate the messages that those texts contained. And in some instances, these conversations led to friendships that have continued to develop outside of the health club context.

Initially, at least, men who were not willing to self-identify as gay proved to be somewhat less enthusiastic about participating in these discussions. My attempts to begin these conversations became frustrating (the conversation about the availability of clean towels, described in chapter 4, was one such example), but the effort has taught me much about the linguistic erasure of gay message and about other forms of gender resistance.

Still, I have been able to elicit more focused, personal comments about language and other forms of on-site communication from some of these men. Unlike the case for my conversations with self-identified gay men, most of these discussions took place in the privacy of the sauna and steam room, usually when we were the only persons present for the exchange. On some occasions, I tried to arrange for follow-up conversations outside of the club; usually, these efforts were not successful. In the main, what I have learned from talking with these men, I have learned through on-site conversations.

Finally, one-on-one conversations with these men (and, though less often for reasons I will explain below, with some of the self-identified gay men) led to invitations to participate in some form of erotic activity, and what I learned as I negotiated these expressions of intent has also contributed to my understanding of men's use of erotic discourse at health clubs.

What follows in this chapter is an interpretive summary of the findings from my observations and interviews. Since I carried out most of my interviews inside health club settings, opportunities for note taking and verbatim transcription were more limited than in other locales. Where possible, I have included respondent commentaries, in verbatim or paraphrased form, to suggest participants' perspectives on the issues I am discussing.

### The Gay Attraction to Health Clubs

Health clubs have long been important locales for gay men in U.S. society, but they assumed a particular importance during the 1970s when "the gay body [became] a body of compensation for everything it had been denied in adolescence" (Browning 1993: 72).[4] For many gay men growing up in the 1950s and 1960s, physique was one of those denied arenas, and well-formed musculature joined 501 jeans, construction boots, and sunglasses as defining elements of the "gay clone look," the "idealized" forms of gay male persona that emerged during the years after Stonewall (Levine 1991).

To obtain that physique, and the desirable erotic image that accompanied it, gay men turned to the body-building facilities formerly dominated by heterosexual men or sought out the newer facilities specifically designed for the needs of an all-gay clientele. The actors here, Paul Monette explains,

were the guys who had always been chosen last in the schoolyard, banished to the outermost outfield, and now they made up for lost time with murderous concentration, forming a sort of Little League of lost preadolescence. In the mindless banter and shorthand of the weightroom, they recovered the willful merriment of boys. (1990: 60)

The AIDS pandemic recast these interests in physical fitness. Now a well-developed body not only signaled that a gay man was a "hot" erotic property but also indicated his interest in maintaining physical health (or, a façade of health) in the face of the pandemic. Hence the phrase "working out" became a coded marker in gay men's personal classified advertisements, indicating that the writer was HIV-negative (or, at least, that he wanted readers to consider him in those terms).[5]

Also during this period, pressure from public health authorities and other sources led to the closing of the "gay baths" or to extensive curtailing of the opportunities for erotic action that gay men had formerly enjoyed at these sites. Health clubs quickly became an alternative source for some of the social and interpersonal experiences formerly provided by the baths.[6] Certainly, both sites shared a similarity of ambiance—the group showers, the locker room facilities, the encouragement of expressive masculinity— and while the structural opportunities for on-site erotics were in some sense more limited in health club settings (that is, health clubs usually did not rent individual dressing rooms to their clients, and there was no officially designated "orgy room"), certain features that preluded on-site erotic practice at the baths (such as men taking saunas together, showering together, or changing clothes together) could also be found in health club settings. The fact that men who were not openly gay, or did not self-identify as gay, were also likely to be present (and this was the case unless the health club explicitly catered to an all-gay clientele) intensified the erotic potential in these settings.

The emergence of other gay-oriented institutions during the 1980s—political action groups, religious organizations, community centers, clinics—broadened opportunities for gay socializing during the 1980s and continue to do so today. However, the discreet gay socializing in the presence of a heterogeneous clientele characteristic of health club settings contrasts pointedly with the "out and proud" discourse and the more uniform membership at these other institutions. This contrast helps explain why some men still prefer to use health clubs as a source for making gay friends, and as I will explain, why some men use health clubs as sites for erotic exchange.

### Health Clubs as Settings for Risk

"Discreet gay socializing in the presence of a heterogeneous clientele" reads like a description of the conditions calling for risk-related language use, in the sense explained in chapters 4 and 5. Granted, health clubs present all of their members with an environment filled with ambiguity and uncertainty, but the conditions there have particular significance for gay clientele.

To begin with the basics: A health club is by design and practice a location set apart from the ordinary domains of everyday life and from the established conventions relevant to those domains. Entering a health club, for example, becomes a carefully regulated process of transition.[7] There is a check-in desk, where the client must present the necessary identification for staff review. Nonmembers may be admitted if they are accompanied by a member or approved by the management, though payment of a fee or other conditions (a membership sales talk, for example) may first be required, but access to club facilities is always short-term under these circumstances and can rarely be extended.

Before the client can begin his workout, he must already have acquired a set of specialized skills. Free weights do not come with instructions, and weight-lifting machines can be difficult to set up even when instructions are provided. This information has to be learned on-site, either from staff members or from clients already proficient in these details. The learning process is continuous. Even an experienced client may carry out an exercise incorrectly, unknowingly risking muscle damage or some other accident.

Additional, site-specific requirements also mediate the transition from the outside world to the club facilities. Business attire and street clothes are usually not an acceptable wardrobe for the workout areas, and street shoes will damage the gym floor and the workout equipment. So the client must bring additional, specialized clothing and shoes to the club, and change into that clothing and shoes. If he plans to swim, he will be expected to take a shower to ensure that he does not bring outside impurities into the pool. The same restriction applies if the client intends to use the steam room or sauna.

Unavoidably, under this arrangement, the locker room becomes a pivotal locale at a health club. Here is where clients complete the transition into the special domain of the club setting. Both the gym's and the outside world's expectations about "dress code" are suspended in the locker room. Here, instead of gym clothes or business or street attire, clients wear towels or nothing at all, and areas of the body not usually exposed to outside scrutiny become open to inspection. In fact, prolonged periods of client nakedness are often the norm in the locker room, particularly once clients have completed their workout and are beginning the lengthy process of cleaning up, changing to business or street attire, storing their gym clothes, and returning to the outside world.

Gay men enter into this domain with particular agendas and goals, but there are common themes to their behavior. As Monette observed, by working out at a health club, gay men regain opportunities denied them during their youth and recover what he terms the "willful merriment of boys" (1990: 60). Monette's comments refer to gay men interested in serious body building or in other extensions of gay clone imagery, but they are not restricted to that group alone. As Armstead Maupin has observed, gay men generally enter a "second adolescence" after they come out, a time when they can experiment with different aspects of gay society and sexuality just as they experimented with the possibilities of heterosexual adulthood during their teenage years.[8] Going to a health club is one form of experimentation, and so is working out. In fact, working out is particularly important in that regard because it allows gay men to act out personal fantasies about an idealized, imagined physical development that they may never have verbalized even to their closest friends.

Even being inside a health club may call forth feelings of ambivalence for some gay men. Locker rooms and showers frequently serve as sites for representations of erotic practice in gay fiction and gay video and may already be a prime source for a client's imagination. Joining a health club actualizes and enhances his repertoire of images in that regard. At the same time, memories of grade school teasing and high school harassment may impose less pleasant associations on a client's visits and lead him to wonder which of the other clients will be the first person to make ill-intended remarks.

Complicating these personal constructions of ambivalence is the fact that a health club is filled with strangers, or people who act toward each other as if they had never been introduced. Some gay men decide to come to the club in small groups and to work out together. Just as often, gay men use health club facilities individually, moving from activity to activity at their own pace. Several individuals (gay or gay–straight combinations) may alternate the use of one of the exercise stations, but those groups rarely endure once each member moves to the next location on his workout plan. Polite exchanges of greetings and brief small-talk often occur between clients who recognize each other from previous visits or other locales. Prolonged conversation while on the workout floor is unusual, and most clients find it disruptive to their own attempts at concentration. Portable cassette players and radios minimize such disruptions, and earphones further ensure the maintenance of each client's privacy.

These conditions do not change once clients leave the exercise area and return to the locker room. Some clients may start conversations, or seek to maintain them, while others are preparing for their showers or putting on their business or street attire. But silence remains the predominate mode in the locker area and, likewise, in the showers. Anglo-American constraints on expressive communication between men already work against attempts at prolonged conversation in these settings, particularly when a bathroom (or bathroom function) provides the occasion for the speech event. While two men may speak together briefly while in the shower room, they are likely to suspend conversation once a third party enters the showers unless he is someone known to both of the speakers. Even then, three-way conversations in the showers are unusual, in my observation. The notable exception is the butt-grabbing, towel-snapping clowning around that a preestablished group of men may jointly initiate while in the showers together. The collective, corporate focus for the activity is the important detail here. Entirely different messages result (between participants as well as for observers) when there are only two men participating in these activities.

### Health Club Risk-Taking Strategies

Because health clubs are environments set apart from the outside world, clients need to have more than a mastery of everyday knowledge and skills in order to function effectively in those settings. Rules and restrictions guard the transition from outside into the clubs, and the locker room is an especially significant environment in that regard.

Gay men bring their own images and fantasies to health club sites, though these also come with ambivalent associations and memories. The presence of strangers and constraints on conversation, even among friends, further restricts opportunities to develop those images and resolve those conflicting associations.

This package of features make a Gay English–based *language of risk* an appropriate format for health club text making. Silence is certainly a popular strategy in that regard. Forms of silence that I have observed in health club settings include offering minimal responses to another's commentary, complying strictly with site-specific topic-avoidance rules, introducing hedges and pauses at the beginnings of conversation and throughout the exchange, and not saying anything at all.

All of these practices reproduce characteristics of male-to-male communication that are widely attested among Anglo-American heterosexual males (see, for example, the papers in Abbott 1990; Nardi 1992) and that may apply to communication between heterosexual males in U.S. society who come from other cultural backgrounds. Although gay men's avoidance of verbal communication also patterns along similar lines in these settings, gay men's compliance with the situated expectations of silence does not necessarily lead to an avoidance of communication in other forms. Instead, verbal silence provides a backdrop for a range of nonverbal practices through which gay men can still initiate gay self-disclosure and against which they can evaluate the suspect gay status of another health club client.

Particularly valuable in this regard are a set of gay-meaningful positional activities that take place in the showers. The expected practice is for a man to face the showerhead while taking a shower, which means that he will be facing away from the other clients who are also in the showers unless he deliberately turns away from the showerhead and looks in their direction. Gay men may begin their shower facing the showerhead, but quickly turn and face away from the showerhead, thereby obtaining a full view of the shower room and the other clients using it. Rotations toward, then away from, the shower continue throughout the time in the shower, so that it is difficult for a suspect gay to enter the shower room without noticing, and being noticed by, this individual.

Gay men may also extend their showers, by soaping themselves carefully all over, then gently removing the soap lather, then enjoying an additional, all-over rinse, then repeating the process one or more times; by washing their hair as well as their bodies; and/or by using a mirror and safety razor to shave while they are showering. Following one or more of these practices lets gay men remain in the shower room longer than other clients, who move quickly into the showers, soap themselves with the thinnest patina of lather, rinse, and towel themselves dry while returning to the locker room—if they even shower after their workout at all.

The locker room is also a setting where gay men can provide other men with glimpses of gay disclosure and assess the disclosures of others. Even the location of a locker can be strategic in that regard, if health club rules allow clients to select a locker each time they visit the club. Several considerations define an ideal locker location at a health club, according to my respondents. An ideal location gives the client a broad view of the locker room and does not force him to stare at the wall or into an empty cul-de-sac; it allows him to watch as people enter and leave the room and, perhaps, enter and leave the showers as well. At the same time, the locker's location should not be in the middle of the room or in any other highly visible location; more appropriate is a location to the side of the room, adjacent to but not inside the primary traffic flow.

Locker room attire may also display messages relevant to gay disclosure. Ordinarily, men wrap a towel around their waist when they go to the showers or the sauna or move across the locker room for any other reason. Likewise, they turn away from persons around them when they take off their undershorts, change out of their gym clothes, or remove their towel after returning from the showers. The intent here is to keep their genitalia concealed at all times. Some younger men favor an alternative strategy: Instead of wearing the towel, the individual holds the towel in front of his body while moving through the locker room. Persons choosing this strategy still turn away from their neighbors while they are completely undressed.

This commitment to disguise and self-protection is not something to which gay men regularly subscribe, according to my observations. Gay men are more likely to walk to and from the showers with their towel draped across their shoulders and to remain undressed while they complete their after-shower activities (brushing their hair, cleaning their teeth, applying deodorant or aftershave, and so on). Similarly, gay men walk into the sauna undressed, and use their towel only as something to sit on while in the enclosure, not as something to wrap around their waist.

There are occasions where gay men will use spoken language to negotiate gay disclosure at a health club. Such exchanges are somewhat more focused, and therefore carry a higher degree of risk than is the case when nonverbal strategies are employed. I have given examples of such efforts in previous chapters (compare, for instance, example 3.7 and example 4.5) and described how the targets of these verbal strategies use their responses to shape forms of resistance to such overtures. Gay men may also find it awkward to be confronted with such resistance, especially in a setting like a workout room or locker room where others have overheard preceding segments of the conversation and can draw their own conclusions about the respondent's pointed commentary. This makes guarded, coded questioning a more appropriate strategy for negotiating disclosure, and makes nonverbal communication an even more appropriate option.

### Constraints on Risk Taking

Once I became accustomed to the subtlety of the risk-taking strategies employed at these sites, I began to notice negotiations of gay disclosure in virtually every health club setting I observed. Were there any constraints on these negotiations, or was this, in fact, an unrestricted enterprise?

My observations confirmed several such restrictions. Gay men's efforts to solicit disclosure from a suspect gay could begin in nonverbal terms, but once sufficient indication of common interests had been exchanged, nonverbal communication was replaced by quiet, verbal conversation. That is, nonverbal strategies were the prelude but not the centerpiece of the negotiation process.

Second, if the suspect gay was disinterested in disclosure and communicated his disinterest to the actor initiating disclosure, the actor usually shifted his attention to some other, equally intriguing target. Gay men, in my observation, did not continue efforts at nonverbal engagement with men who were unwilling to receive them.

Gay men may communicate such interest in one of several forms, such as responding to the actor initiating disclosure with a terse reply (one of the types of terminal constructions discussed in chapter 3) and then turning the upper body away from that actor; initiating conversation with a third party and excluding the original actor from the exchange; or shifting the focus of communication away from disclosure by initiating conversation on some more neutral theme. However, saying nothing and ignoring the attempts to elicit disclosure and the presence of the actor initiating these negotiations is not at all a workable option under these circumstances. Silence serves a variety of communicative functions in Gay English text making, as I have already explained in chapter 3. But whether it encourages transition into the next phase of the speech event or intensifies the ambiguity already established in the preceding segments of the conversation, silence always invites a continuation of risk taking between suspect gays; it rarely signals for risk-taking practices to come to an end.

A third constraint on risk taking centers around gay men's characterization of health club environments as *public* space. "Public" has been the consistent term of choice from gay respondents in these discussions. As these men explain, persons from diverse backgrounds (in this case, particularly, from diverse gender and sexual backgrounds) claim position within these locales; these places are not dominated or controlled by gay interests alone, and gay men have to position their conduct accordingly.

Clearly, the weight rooms and other workout areas are also public places, under this definition, and so are the showers, the saunas, and the locker rooms. Gay clients cannot claim exclusive or permanent control over any of these locales, and while they may certainly initiate negotiations of disclosure and other gay-centered practices in those settings, gay men report that they turn to off-site locations in order to complete such transactions. And my own observations support the overall claims of this assessment.

Of course, there have been instances where gay men have initiated and completed erotic exchange within health club sites. But the particulars of these events, as the men describe them and as I have been able to observe them, are sharply defined. The steam room, sauna, or one of the side rooms used for massage therapy are the most likely locations for these exchanges, and they occur (by respondent report) when no one other than the participants themselves are present. But respondents agree that even then the possibility of discovery as well as the unpredictable reactions of club management made on-site erotic action a potentially dangerous enterprise. A safer and more sensible practice, they told me, was to arrange a meeting later in the evening, to exchange telephone numbers, or simply to agree to meet at the health club at some future time and talk again.

So, if both these self-reported comments are accurate statements—that is, if gay men as a group prefer to have sex off-site, not within a health club setting, and if only a handful of gay men have actually had on-site sex with other men—then who are the actors creating the erotic occasions being reported to health club management? And what features define and distinguish the members of this category?

Answering these questions has become a central theme in my health club research in recent years. I do not have a label that precisely identifies the men in this category. Importantly, neither do they. Most of those whom I have interviewed self-identify as heterosexual. A few—very few, in my assessment—claim to be bisexual. None self-identify as gay or homosexual, and my attempts to encourage them to use those terms for self-reference in conversation always elicit substantial resistance and, at times, explicit denial: "I'm not gay, I'm married," one respondent reported to me in the sauna, af-

IN A HEALTH CLUB LOCKER ROOM

ter I had watched him attempt to interest a third man in an erotic exchange, and started teasing him about being interested in men half his age.[9]

Similarly, my attempts to explore gay-related themes during conversations with these men have elicited only minimal verbal responses. And I get equal evidence of disinterest when I begin to describe erotic experiences observed during previous visits to the health club or discuss male-centered erotic opportunities at other health clubs in the neighborhood.

On the whole, men in this category are as silent about male-oriented erotic interests and practices as my self-identified gay informants are explicitly talkative.

This reluctance to talk about erotic activities may not be entirely accidental, since, for the most part, the erotic activities in which these men participate involve very little spoken language. There may be verbal exchange during the initial stages of the encounter, during the time when the possibility of mutual erotic interest is just beginning to be explored. Comments during this exchange tend to be neutral: for example, the weather, an item in that morning's *Washington Post* or *Wall Street Journal,* or some topic relevant to health club membership. Paralleling the discussion is a discreet display of one or more nonverbal cues that suggest the speaker's erotic interests, such as unbroken eye contact, stretching or flexing of arm or chest muscles, rearrangements of the bath towel wrapped around the waist, and self-manipulation to increase the visibility of the penis. So while the words maintain a heterosexual façade, other actions suggest additional intents.

The prospective partner may ignore these nonverbal messages, or he may begin to acknowledge them through similar coding. Once acknowledgment occurs, the exchange shifts almost entirely into a nonverbal format, with an increased use of gaze, more strategic self-manipulation, and the first attempts at touching the partner's body. If verbal statements occur during this exchange, the speaker is usually the person who initiated the exchange, and the comments themselves usually inventory (or exaggerate) attributes that the speaker finds appealing in his partner.

One of the more commonly used formulas to that end is "Your [specify an item of the partner's anatomy] is so [add a characteristic that underscores that item's erotic appeal]." These statements are not designed to elicit replies from the other participant. However, they may blueprint the particular erotic activities that the speaker intends to perform, or would like his partner to perform, before the exchange concludes.

Note, moreover, that these are also performative statements: By saying that the partner has a beautiful chest or a large penis, the speaker is establishing the subjective presence of those attributes—even if the descriptions are not completely accurate in an empirical sense. By commoditizing the partner's presence in the erotic moment, the speaker increases his own control over the exchange.

The activities that occur within the erotic moment at these health clubs are still constrained by the details of on-site location. If the negotiations take place in the sauna or steam room, masturbation or mutual masturbation are likely activities. Oral sex is also possible, if a third party is willing to act as a lookout and warn when some other person is about to enter the sauna. Anal sex is also possible, according to health club folklore, but anal sex is more likely to occur when the participants move into the massage room, the room with the tanning bed, or a storage closet.

I have no evidence that penetrative sex in these instances involves the use of condoms. In fact—and again, at odds with the gay men's treatment of this theme—men in this category who were willing to talk to me have been quite explicit about their reasons for avoiding condoms and other safe-sex practices in these settings, and some respondents actually appear to me to enjoy bragging about their experiences with unsafe sex.

The rationales that these men give for condom avoidance are several, but the following sampling of respondent comments suggests what I consider to be the primary themes:

- *Condoms are irrelevant.*
  "Condoms may be necessary when gay men have sex, but I am not gay and do not need to be concerned with using them" (a thirty-five-year-old, unmarried worker from a federal regulatory agency).
  In another variant of this statement, speakers suggest that on-site sex with other men is not "really" gay sex, and therefore need not be considered high-risk behavior at all.
- *Condoms signal intent.*
  "To bring a condom into the steam room implies that I expect to have sex. That is not how it works. Sex between men 'just happens.' You don't plan it and you certainly don't try to regulate it" (a forty-plus-year-old, married attorney in private practice).
- *Condoms are impractical.*
  "How do you carry a condom in your bath towel? And what do you do with the condom once it's been used?" (a forty-year-old director of a federal management agency, and a self-identified bisexual).

By offering these comments, speakers are verbalizing their thoughts regarding their male-centered erotic behavior, something that these men are not otherwise likely to do in a health club setting. This helps explain the tone of irritation and impatience that I hear throughout these men's comments about safe-sex avoidance. Probably the subtext of the discussion—the AIDS pandemic—also contributes, in part, to this tone.

Talking with these men about unsafe sex disclosed a final theme relevant to the men in this category: They consider health clubs to be a *private* domain, rather than a public place in the sense suggested by my gay informants and friends. They describe the health club as a place of retreat and escape, a locale that allows them to get away from the pressures of work, home, and family. To quote a forty-four-year-old administrator at a nearby federal agency (the same speaker who reported, "I'm not gay, I'm married"):

After a full day of in-your-face federal regulations, with the paperwork grind, and with a boss who wins national awards for being a jerk, I like to come to the club, do some exercises, work out for a while, have a leisurely sauna, see who walks through the door [*pause*], then take my shower and drive home to the kids.[10]

The point of view in this statement differs from that of the self-identified gay men whom I interviewed. As I have explained, these gay men describe health clubs as public space, governed, therefore, by the constraints regulating gay men's public behavior on the job, in department stores, and in other "outside" locales. Describing a health club as a *private* space, in contrast, positions the locale "away from" sites of ordinary, everyday practice, and from the expectations that govern behavior there. Hence, just as gay men report that they will initiate erotic negotiations at a health club but will move to an off-site (that is, private) location to conclude them, men in this unnamed category establish erotic interests on-site and vigorously pursue those interests to an on-site conclusion.

### Some Interpretations

Initially, I was attracted to the study of Gay English text making in health club settings because I wanted opportunities to observe gender-based differences in text making as texts were being formed and to assess the significance of those differences for other forms of on-site activity. The heterogeneous composition of clubs' membership, combined with the members' common use of the same settings and activities, seemed ideal in this regard.

What I have found are contrasting patterns of verbal and nonverbal communication that I am able to associate with other site-specific differences in presentations of gendered self. Erotic communication provides a particularly vivid set of contrasts in this regard, in that male-centered erotic interests provided a recurring focus for many of the forms of text making described in this chapter, and men were consistently the objects of speaker desire. Closer inspection shows, however, how erotic communication is itself shaped by additional constraints in this case—specifically, by conflicting notions of public place and private space and the obligations that those notions impose on individual behavior.

So it is misleading to assume that Gay English is the language of male-centered desire in such settings. That argument highlights only one portion of the erotic negotiations taking place in these sites. It also ignores the equally complex use of English by self-identified heterosexuals, whose erotic text making is equally male-oriented but is still quite different from that of self-identified gay men. It is much more appropriate, I think, to recognize that Gay English *can* be a language of male desire, but that the significance of such usage derives from site-specific communicative practices and not from more generic claims about male cosexual attraction.

# 7

---

## Gay English in a "Desert of Nothing": Language and Gay Socialization

---

I have assumed in the preceding chapters that Gay English is an accessible set of language skills and that learning Gay English does not present any particular problems to would-be speakers.[1] The time has come to look more carefully at the acquisition of Gay English grammar and discourse.

### Background

At issue in this chapter are questions about language socialization and about connections between language learning and gender socialization in U.S. society. Even with the growing visibility of lesbian and gay cultures in recent years, compulsory heterosexuality (Rich 1980) continues to frame expectations about gender in this society and to promote fragmentary and often conflicting messages about alternative forms of sexuality. Young people, who are already struggling to define themselves in terms of a limited inventory of gender categories, become especially vulnerable by these messages. As Richard Troidan explains:

Lesbians and gay males typically begin to personalize homosexuality during adolescence, when they begin to reflect upon the idea that their feelings, behaviors or both could be regarded as homosexual. The thought that they are potentially homosexual is dissonant with previously held self-images . . . [Their] sexual identities . . . are in limbo; they can no longer take their heterosexual identities as givens, but they have yet to develop perceptions of themselves as homosexuals. (1989: 52-53)

Understandably, under such conditions, adolescence becomes a period of gender-related "identity confusion" (Troidan 1989: 52), a time of isolation and of loneliness.

Gay men speak vividly and pointedly about identity confusion, isolation, and loneliness when they reflect on their teenage years while telling their life stories. Here is a selection of such statements, chosen from life-story interviews that I have conducted during my Gay English research and from other materials that I have located in published sources. Background profiles on these speakers presented in Example 7.1 and on the other individuals whose life-story comments are included in this chapter are as follows (age as cited indicates the respondent's age at the time he was interviewed):

Alston: Twenty-five, gay white male, raised in a rural South Carolina town, former female impersonator, now a computer specialist.

Barry: "Under forty," gay white male, pop music critic for the *San Francisco Examiner*, columnist for *The Advocate* and other national publications.

Billy: "Over fifty," gay white male, interior designer, born in Schenectady, New York, moved to New York City after being expelled from college because of a "homosexual incident," and has lived in New York City ever since.

Jim: Twenty-two, gay white male, university sophomore, born in Buffalo, New York, lived there until he started college in Washington, D.C., majoring in clinical psychology.

Joe: Twenty-four, gay white male, campus gay activist, born and raised in a small town in Indiana, resident of Washington, D.C., since 1985, currently completing requirements for a BA in political science and communication.

John: Forty-one, practicing business and taxation attorney, gay white male, born and raised in downstate Illinois, son of nationally prominent conservative activist whose political philosophy he publicly endorses.

Marc: Gay teenager, ethnic background unknown, frequent participant in activities at Horizons, the Lesbian–Gay youth center in Chicago.

Nick: Midforties, gay white male, minister of a gay Protestant congregation in Kentucky, currently lives near the small Kentucky town where he was born and raised.

Robert: Forty-seven, gay white male, born and raised in northern Florida, finished graduate school in North Carolina, now on the faculty at a community college in northern Virginia.

Sam: Twenty-one, gay white male, university senior, born and raised in central Ohio, moved to Washington, D.C., to attend college, now in graduate school in Rhode Island.

Vincent: Twenty-three, gay white male, born and raised in the Piedmont region of South Carolina, where he still resides; his struggle to reconcile gay sexuality and his loyalty to Southern Baptist tradition is the focus of his interview in Sears 1991: 27-46.

Wallace: Early thirties, gay white male, born and raised in the D.C. suburbs, now a professional actor associated with several acting companies in
the D.C. area.

---

**Example 7.1** "Identity confusion" in gay adolescents

[Nick] When you are gay and twelve years old in a small town in western Kentucky
like where I grew up, . . . you don't know anyone else who is gay. The only gay people you hear about or read about tend to be unsavory. The extent of gay life as you
know it are scribblings on a bathroom wall. (Miller 1981: 237)

[John] At the time I had no idea what being gay meant or what homosexuality was
because nobody talked about it. I didn't know anyone. The only thing I knew of homosexuality was people who hung out at bus stations. I can't say that I heard any
negative comments about it growing up either from my family or from school.
There was just silence. (Mosbacker 1993: 34)

[Billy] The first name I had for what I was, was "cocksucker." Must have been seven
or eight. It was years before I heard "homosexual," more years til I heard the word
"gay." "Cocksucker" was an awful word the way they used it, but it meant that my
condition was nameable. I knew I was awful, but I finally had a name for all those
odd feelings. I wasn't nothing. I was awful, but I wasn't nothing. (Reinhardt 1986: 25)

[Vincent (preceding comments describe his struggle to maintain a "straight" façade
in front of his friends)] I still had the wool pulled over their eyes. But inside I was
deeply depressed. There was nowhere I could go when I was in high school to get
information about what I was from people of my own. I didn't know anything about
rest areas. I couldn't have gotten to them if I wanted to 'cause I didn't have transportation. I couldn't go to a gay bar. Homosexual-oriented material just was not
within my grasp. (Sears 1991: 27)

[Sam] I started being aware of feelings and emotions in seventh grade. At first, I didn't
know what it was called. But by year's end, I worked it out: It was me against the
world, a kind of "defensive happiness." (Q: Did you talk to anyone about your feelings?) All this was entirely internal. I had no help at all. (Leap 1992b)

[Jim] I have this kind of theory. From 13 until my bar age which was 17, I kind of
was in touch with myself and I knew what was happening internally, but as far as it
relating to the rest of the world, there was this vast desert of [pause] nothing. No information, no individuals I could go to, really, I mean, I had two teachers [whom he
suspected were gay] and that was it, I think. (Leap 1992a)

[Marc] [At that time] there was an awareness that things aren't always the way you
are told they are. It's like being an expatriate in another country and you can view
your own country from that distance. The isolation I experienced in being gay and
feeling that there was no one to go to resulted in my mustering up my own resources. Mustering up that fiber once was important. (Boxer and Cohler 1989: 323)

But as these comments suggest, gay men's life-story narratives associate other emotions with this period of gender-identity development, and while adolescence was certainly a painful period in their lives, confusion, isolation, and loneliness did not render these speakers totally unresponsive in the face of an emergent gay sexuality. According to their recollections, they took notice of other people's comments about homosexual behavior and assimilated gay ideas displayed in graffiti and other public sources. They inventoried places where gay people were likely to be found and sought alliances with adults or other teenagers who were known to be gay or who, according to various criteria explained later in this chapter, were likely to be so. But most important, they sought out information about "homosexuality" and "gay experience," and they used that information to focus their gender-related self-reflection.

I recognize that life-story comments are reconstructions of life experience, and in the final section of this chapter, I assess the validity of such statements and explain why I consider them to be useful data for the study of gender socialization. For the moment, I want to focus in greater detail on four of the sources of information that, according to the gay men's narratives I have reviewed, proved to be particularly valuable for making sense out of life "in a desert of nothing" (as Jim so aptly phrased it). And I want to show how language skills—specifically, the development of familiarity and fluency in Gay English—were central to the construction of gay identity and to other components of gender socialization during this period.

### Source 1: Written Texts

[Jim] I was never sat down by my mom and dad and said the heterosexual version of the "birds and the bees." Um, and, you know, when you get to the time where you're twelve, thirteen, or fourteen, you begin to be sexually aware, you really look, strive for sources of information. . . . I started looking for information about homosexuality, what it means to be gay, what this all means. I did not know exactly how I did this or why, but I kind of separated myself from it, distanced myself from it. And I said: I have these feelings, emotional, sexual, right on down the line, but what does this mean, what does this translate into? . . .

And I think eventually I branched off into the *Encyclopaedia Britannica* [laughs] we had in the house. . . . I looked up in the index, as far as sexual goes: penis and phallus and every single adjective, uh synonym of that. And then I progressed off into homosexuality and then read into the history and what, whatever. I was striving for knowledge.

I eventually went to the public library, school library, and that wasn't as easy because it was public and you had to build up your confidence. . . . I had this feeling that if I take this book out, they are going to think I am, you know. . . .

I tried to do as much as possible, reading, whatever I thought might have gotten somewhere. For example, if I came across like a column, like for example Ann Landers might have mentioned it, and I'd like be her fan for a couple of months so maybe she'd bring it up again. And even in, I think my dad had one *Penthouse* magazine and I think they had their Q[uestion] and A[nswer] section, I think they had "I have fantasies about this or something and that was: "Whoa! You know, you know, like, connect!" (Leap 1992a: interview 1)

Jim's comments focus on his use of published resources—books, magazines, newspapers—to find information about gay experience and sexuality. Different people cite different resources in that regard, and they mention works of fiction—for example, *City and the Pillar, The Best Little Boy in the World, City of Night, The Catcher in the Rye, The Picture of Dorian Gray*— as frequently as they mention nonfiction sources, and the works of fiction do not have to be explicitly gay to be valuable here. Sam comments, regarding *The Catcher in the Rye*, "I had heard there is a homosexual character in the book. If not read too deeply, the lead character is gay" (Leap 1992b).

Nor do the nonfiction sources have to be explicitly gay-affirming to be useful. Jim, in a separate interview, recalls reading the section on homosexuality in a copy of David Rubin's *Everything You Wanted to Know about Sex (but Were Afraid to Ask)*, which he found hidden in the basement of their home. Sam explained his fascination with fundamentalist Christian tracts against homosexuality: "Who can resist a reference to homosexuality—any reference!" (Leap 1992a: interview 2, p. 2).

Jim mentioned a fear of disclosure if he looked for reference materials like these in the local library. Other people's narratives describe how they faced similar fears during their teenage years. Here are Vincent's comments on this theme:

[Vincent] There was one book in the school library but I never had the courage to check it out 'cause it had "GAY" written on it. But, I did sneak a few peaks at it. It was a prize-winning novel written by a man about how he felt about homosexuality. I wanted to check that book out so bad. But, I didn't. I just knew that whoever the librarian was who stamped my card would look at that book, see that it was about being gay, and automatically say, "Why Vince, you're a faggot, aren't you?" So I never got to read it—except for the cover. (Sears 1991: 33)

These fears help explain why teenagers seek information about gay sexuality from nonacademic reference materials and from sources (for example, Jim's reference to heterosexual "soft porn" and Sam's use of fundamentalist tracts) that are explicitly nonsupportive of gay lifestyles. Such materials are available to adolescent males; usually there are no questions asked and there is no threat of stigma if a teenage male is found with copies of these texts in his possession.

**Source 2: Entertainment and Media**

[Jim] I remember TV shows, HBO, where they had those very heterosexual movies, like cheer-leading movies and stuff like that, where sex is all it is about. I remember filtering all that out, looking at the guys. I realize that along with that you are absorbing a lot of negative, you know, how gay is treated on a football team.

Mentioning football team, there was this after-school special once, where there was Scott Baio and his friend on the football team, and his friend came out to him and said: "I am gay," you know. I remember just devouring that film, just flashes of "gay," "gay," "gay" and you really hold on to it. (Leap 1992a: interview 1)

[Sam]: *Brothers* [a cable TV sitcom] had an effeminate stereotyped gay man. That was a good example of how not to talk; I didn't believe gay people talked like that. *Consenting Adult* related a view which I knew was true and was looking for: A normal guy can be gay. *Deathtrap*—My mom was disgusted by the kissing scene [between Michael Caine and Christopher Reeves]. I was distracted. (Leap 1992b: 2)

[Wallace] I grew up in Maryland, right outside of D.C. too, and spent my childhood listening to *West Side Story* and *A Chorus Line* too. Those cast albums and movie musicals on TV were sort of secret messages from a world we didn't experience in our suburban, private school upbringing. That saved us. (Brown and Swisher 1994)

[Barry] Freddie Mercury [lead singer in the rock and roll group Queen] made me gay. I kid, but it is quite possible that [he] was the first pop star I thought about sexually. I was only 13 when Queen's *Sheer Heart Attack* came out . . . and had no idea I was a boy queer. But I do remember contemplating Mercury's furry chest on the [album cover] with the same curiosity with which I perused the underwear section of the J. C. Penney catalog. . . .

The man who put the *queen* in Queen played a starring role in that homo-bi-wanna-be rock circus of the early 70's. . . . Although I did get beat up for my junior high school attempts at glitter-rock drag, Mercury and the others suggested another world where you wouldn't be despised for being yourself, even if that meant donning gold-lamé frocks, six-inch platform heels, and black nail polish. You might even be adored by millions. (Walters 1992: 79)

As was the case for books and magazines, gay teenagers report using spoken and visual media as resources in the orientation to gay culture. This was the case even when the materials were not overtly gay in content or were not even intended to be interpreted in those terms. Jim describes working with these materials as a "filtering" process; that is, he excluded information not relevant to the learning of gay culture while he identified and retained material that he found relevant to those ends. Similarly, Sam assessed any new information he encountered in terms of the perspective on gay culture that he had already acquired: "I didn't believe gay people talked like that. . . . a view which I knew was true and was searching for."

It would be worthwhile learning more about the criteria underlying Jim's use of filtering or establishing Sam's "belief" and "knowledge." What both men are describing appears to be a drastic reconstruction (or what some now call "queering") of plotlines and images, compared to the intent of the original script. Alexander Doty suggests that the construction of the sexualities of such texts is just as much a "real thing" (1993: xi) as is the construction of sexual identities. If so, perhaps Jim's and Sam's enthusiastic reworking of media content during their teenage years was a form of experimentation; that is, it allowed them to become acquainted with gender alternatives and their consequences before they began focusing their own sexual identities along the same lines.

Barry describes his attraction to the rock group Queen in similar terms. Barry found the group's lead singer (Freddie Mercury) erotically appealing, but appealing in other ways was the range of gender alternatives packaged within their music, lyrics, clothing style, and on-stage behavior. By listening to Queen, Barry gained access to "a world where you wouldn't be despised for being yourself, even if that meant donning gold-lamé frocks, six-inch platform heels, and black nail polish," a world where "you might even be adored by millions." Such options did not exist in Barry's junior high school environment, and his attempts to create school experience along these lines were not well received by his classmates ("I did get beat up"). The physical violence did not weaken Queen's gay appeal; if anything, their promise of a gay imaginary, fantasy though it may have been, helped him appreciate the differences between where he was (an emerging "boy queer" in a homophobic junior high school) and where he wanted to be (bedecked in glitter and adored by millions) and helped him chart pathways that would lead him toward that goal.

### Source 3: Gay-Related Folk Knowledge

[Jim] Uh, junior high, I remember being teased once in a while. Not, I don't remember anything like "gay" or "queer," but I remember the same sort of thing as when I was checking out that book [*Everything You Wanted to Know about Sex*]: Now they are making fun of me because of this. I do also remember that at the time there was some sort of "wear green on Thursday, it means you are gay" and I had accidentally worn a green sweater and someone told me that, just jokingly. And I took it off right then and there and said: "I'm not going to wear this." (Leap 1992a)

Jim's comments about subtle (and not so subtle) labeling or the "wearing of green on Thursday" are examples of the extensive inventory of folk knowledge concerning gay experience that is maintained and shared by American teenagers and preteens.[2] Among other things, this material gives young people criteria for identifying violations of local norms governing gendered behavior and provides them with a vocabulary for public discussion of such violations when they talk with friends in the classroom and school locker room, at the shopping mall, or in the dance clubs. The "truth value" of statements inspired by this folk knowledge is never at issue in these discussions; in fact, any number of conditions, including the social status of the speaker vis-à-vis the persons under discussion, contribute to the authority of these claims. So even if individuals are not cited by name, circulating comments about activities remains a powerful form of social control.

Equally powerful are the contributions that these comments make to gay socialization. While the formal discourse of family, school, and community may silence any open discussion of gay themes, the informal discussion that unfolds through gay-related folk knowledge can be substantial. According to the life-story narratives, gay men often noted such comments when they heard them, even if they did not fully understand the significance of the message.

Describing one segment of his interview with Alston, Jim Sears writes:

In seventh grade Alston started being more of a teacher's pet, doing extra credit work in his classes and talking with the teachers in the library during recess. . . . He also became less introverted. During lunch he associated with two older female students, one of whom went to his church. Eating at a big round table off to the side of the cafeteria, Alston listened more than he talked. It is here that he remembers hearing his first "fag joke." [See item 1 in example 7.2—WLL.] Alston laughed along with everyone else. But "it didn't dawn on me that they were talking about a guy and

---

**Example 7.2** Jokes as insights into gay culture.

1 (Source: Sears 1991: 238)

A little boy finds two flies on top of one another. He asks his mother if there are boy flies. His mother says "Yes." Then he asks her if there are girl flies. His mother thinks, "Oh no. He is learning about the birds and the bees and he is much too young." So she says, "No son. There are no such things as girl flies." The boy goes back into the other room and swats the two flies. As they fall to the floor, he mutters: "Faggots."

2 (Source: Leap 1993c)

Driving into a small town, a tourist notes the name of the community—Queerville—and wonders how the town got its name. When he stops at a gas station to fill up the tank, he asks the attendant. "I don't know," the attendant replies, "let me ask my wife." He turns to the side door and shouts: "Hey, Ralph!"

---

a guy together. I was still pretty naive. When someone would say the word 'sex' I would blush." (Sears 1991: 238)

Robert brought a similar story to a different conclusion during one of my interviews. He told me the joke 2 in example 7.2, with these comments:

[Robert] I heard that joke in the locker room, after junior varsity basketball practice. Everybody was standing around, changing clothes, talking, trying to avoid having to go home and do the homework. And Charles—he was one of the stars of the team, Mr. Popularity, whatever he did was right, OK?—Charles starts to tell the joke. Everybody starts to laugh, and after that, all you had to do was shout "Hey Ralph," and team members would laugh. Even saying "Listen, Ralph . . . " when talking to someone else, or just calling someone Ralph instead of their real name, could get you a laugh.

I laughed too, but I kept thinking: Does this mean that two men can live together? I mean, OK, I knew this was a joke, but I kept wondering, where is this place and how can I get there? (Leap 1992c)

In a statement cited earlier in this chapter, Billy describes an extraction of personal knowledge out of gay-related folk knowledge. In this case, the folkloric practice was name calling, and the outcome was not intended to be positive. "The first name I had for what I was, was 'cocksucker'. . . . I wasn't nothing. I was awful, but I wasn't nothing." Robert, later in our interview, also discussed how being the object of name calling became an incentive for self-reflection:

[Robert] Later in high school, my junior year, I guess, people started calling me "faggot." I don't know if it was a joke or what, but they called me that. A lot. Even my teammates, they'd toss me a towel and say, "Hey faggot, catch this," or someone'd say "Hey faggot, the coach needs to talk to you."

(Q: Did you get angry? Did this upset you? How did you react?) You know, it's funny. I did not get mad at all. I was uncomfortable, but I wasn't mad. See, I knew by then that I was gay, so—without even knowing it, they were right. I was a faggot. They were telling the truth. I could not get angry at them telling the truth.

(Q: In today's term, you were being "outed.") Yeah. I guess so. But what really bothered me was not just being outed, being exposed. I couldn't understand how they found out: What had I done, how had I slipped? What gave away my secret?

And you know what else? They were saying something about me that I had never said. And if they knew this about me, what else did they know? That's what really made me uncomfortable. (Leap 1992c)

#### Source 4: Best Friends

[Joe] I have been gay since the womb. I started experimenting with sex when I was very young, and when I found others doing the same thing, I knew there was something to all this—but I didn't exactly know what it was. (Q: So when did you come out?) You mean, telling anybody about all this experimentation? Not 'til I was a teenager. I met an older woman, middle-aged, who had lots of gay friends. She introduced me to some other, older, gay men, and they took me under their wing. That is how I learned about the rest of it, the social thing, the networks. (Leap 1991b)

[Sam] (Q: Did you know or know about gay people in [hometown] when you were in high school?) Not at first, but by the time I ended ninth grade I had learned about five people: one, aged thirty-five, three older than that, and one my own age. He became my best friend in high school.

(Q: How did you meet these people?) Pure luck. The first one, an older man, was someone I had seen who was feminine enough to be gay. So I arranged to be in situations where I could meet him. I put out feelers. He knew what to do and how to act. (Q: Did he come on to you?) If he did, I'd not have known. Besides, he was in a relationship. He had a thirty-five-year-old lover. Also his sponsor. So I was not interested.

I wanted to find someone like me. Found him by pure luck. Met him in the eighth grade. I told him in the ninth grade. He told me he was bisexual in the tenth grade. Both of us were scared. Having been friends, we did not want to jeopardize each other's secret. We talked a lot; no topic was safe. Though really, it was me doing the talking. He was the novice, someone for me to talk to. (Leap 1992b)

[Jim] I first began to acknowledge [being gay] to a teacher of mine. I must have been sixteen or seventeen at the time. There was a couple of gay teachers, gay male teachers at my school, my high school. And I thought, God, I had become old enough where we weren't just student-and-teacher, but we were friends.

And we sat down, and you know, I said: Can we talk? And my primary concerns at the time, I remember, were with the family: how I feel about telling my father, how I feel about this, about that?

(Q: How did you know that the teacher was gay?) That is interesting too because I never heard directly someone say, "That teacher is gay." Though I guess there was rumor. This one particular teacher, Mr. Johnson, for some reason, . . . I just knew, for some reason I just knew.

I later, in my senior year, when I was seventeen or eighteen, I had an English teacher, too. It was real interesting, our relationship, because he was very, very "pull student aside and get into their lives" kind of thing. I do not know for what reason, but he did that with me. He was very helpful in that he knew I was gay and kind of brought me out a little more. I remember that, for some reason, he approached me, and said: How does your mother feel about this? And I said: Wow! And I told him, and the dam was lifted, and all the information I needed in my life was there, me seeking advice from him, that sort of thing. (Leap 1992a)

Ethan Mordden (many of whose short stories also explore this theme) observes that "the need for friendship, for nonerotic affection, for buddies" is one thing shared equally by members of both gay and straight worlds (1986: xii). Still, as his short stories demonstrate, buddies serve important functions in gay life: They provide examples of appropriate behavior, answer questions, and give advice. And while buddies are not intended to be sex partners, they can certainly "soothe the less permanent relationships of one's love life" (Mordden 1986: xii) in many ways.

The information giving and sharing functions, not the erotic ones, seem to be most important to gay teenagers, as far as life-story commentary is concerned. Some respondents' narratives equate buddies with sex partners. Most distinguish carefully between the two, confirming the statistical pattern that Boxer and colleagues found during the Horizons study (Herdt and Boxer 1993). Respondents also suggest reasons for making these distinctions: the age difference between teenager and intended confidant (as in Joe's, Sam's, and Jim's discussions of this theme), and the complications that one or both parties feared would emerge once friendship and erotic ties were combined.

Given the limitations placed on other areas of gay adolescent sexuality, I am not surprised that respondents report finding a buddy during their teenage years through "luck" or by "accident." The same restrictions also explain why persons believed to be gay (by the respondent, and often by his peer group as a whole) were reported to play critical roles in this regard. In chapter 5 of this volume, I used the term "suspect gay" to identify persons within this category, and I described the process of mutual recognition and identification that confirms gay identity under these circumstances. Some of the stages in that process are displayed in comments in Sam's and Jim's life stories: "The first one, an older man, was someone I had seen who was feminine enough to be gay. So I arranged to be in situations where I could meet him. I put out feelers. He knew what to do and how to act"; and "In my senior year, when I was seventeen or eighteen, I had an English teacher, too. . . . he was very, very 'pull student aside and get into their lives' kind of thing. I do not know for what reason, but he did that with me. He was very helpful in that he knew I was gay and kind of brought me out a little more." In both accounts (and elsewhere in my collection of narratives), respondents describe how they sought out more-experienced gay individuals, but let those individuals take the initiative and make the first concrete gesture toward gay friendship. As Jim adds, later in the interview: "I don't think I would have been quite that comfortable myself, as identifying, if he hadn't already identified" (Leap 1992a).

I consider Joe's use of a middle-aged, heterosexual female as an intermediary in this regard to be a variation on the general pattern just described. I wish I had more data on the roles that women can play in such negotiations. Also unclear at this time are the factors prompting gay teenagers to look for buddies among their own peer group or among persons who are older than they. Here, however, I suspect that persons seeking a buddy use whatever opportunities are available to them, and that the age of one's confidant may be a by-product of opportunity as much as the result of any other single constraint.

What I want to stress is the contributions to gay socialization and the learning of gay culture that buddies provide. Certainly older individuals are especially valuable in this regard, given their (presumably) broader experience and greater familiarity with these themes. As Jim put it: "I remember that, for some reason, he approached me, and said: How does your mother feel about this? And I said: Wow! And I told him, and the dam was lifted, and all the information I needed in my life was there, me seeking advice from him, that sort of thing."

Conversations with persons one's own age can also be worthwhile here. They give gay teenagers someone with whom they can share ideas, often ideas they have not expressed before. These verbal constructions, like the fantasies inspired by rock-and-roll imagery or derived from the plotlines of motion pictures and television programs, are important to culture learning in two ways: as experimentation (as I have already explained) and as opportunities to inventory knowledge already acquired on some theme.

These conversations also assure gay teenagers that someone is listening to what they have to say—whatever the content or the topic at hand. As Sam explained: "We talked a lot; no topic was safe. Though really, it was me doing the talking. He was the novice, someone for me to talk to."

### Language and Gender Socialization

If identity confusion creates "a desert of nothing" for gay adolescents, then language is a critical feature within that terrain. Notice how often these life stories traced the sources of gender-related dissonance to some form of oral or written text making: comments from classmates, teachers, librarians, and other authority figures (as well as comments that respondents feared those parties might convey); endorsements of heterosexual living contained in television programs, motion pictures, and music; the negative depictions of gay society, culture, and behavior that those sources also convey. But notice, also, how often oral or written text making provided the means through which respondents constructed gay-positive alternatives to these negative messages: acquiring words and phrases to identify new interests and activities, asking questions about sexuality during conversations with older authority figures, finding sympathetic age mates with whom they could talk about gay ideas, locating materials relevant to life experience within print media resources, identifying gay messages within visual media. Indeed, the buddies and adult role models who figure so prominently throughout these narratives are always described as coparticipants in cooperative conversation or in terms of some other type of linguistic exchange.

To talk with others about gay issues, to listen to gay-oriented texts, or to extract information about gay culture from sources in the popular media — all these assume the availability of a language suitable for such discussion, and they assume familiarity with that language, as well. "Suitable," in this sense, means that the terminology, metaphor, and imagery provided by the language specify gay-relevant ideas in an explicit and unambiguous fashion, and that texts constructed through this language will mesh closely and consistently with other components of gay experience. In other words, "suitable" means *authentic*. But how do (nascent) gay adolescents acquire authentic gay language without already being familiar (to some degree, at least) with the culture that surrounds and informs it? And how do they acquire familiarity with gay culture, without first knowing something about gay language?

The circularity presented by those questions is not unique to gay experience; rather, it is part of the process of language and culture acquisition that learners have to address in *all* social domains. When gay respondents used heterosexually oriented discourse and text as their initial sources of information about gay language and culture, they were following the strategy that second-language learners often employ in such settings: they used what they already knew as their bridge to new knowledge and skills. Successful learning depends on effective translation — in this case, the translation of information across gender boundaries and between gendered categories which may not themselves be fully defined; and translation, too, is a language-related skill.

Translation is a central theme in the gay men's life stories that I have collected in my research and gathered from other sources. And it resembles some of the responses to conditions of *risk* that I explored in chapter 4, conditions that take on particularly powerful meanings within adolescent social settings. Learning how to locate and retrieve gay messages in heterosexual texts shows gay adolescents how to disguise gay messages in heterosexual formats. Negotiating between display and disguise — a central theme in conversations with suspect gays, as I have explained — has its antecedents, for example, in Vincent's selection of books in the school library, in Jim's removal of the green sweater accidentally worn on "queer Thursday," and in Alston's and Robert's restrained responses to their friends' exchange of "faggot" jokes.

Finally, I realize that this description of an open-ended, fluid, and individualized process of gay-identity formation differs from the more tightly structured sequencing suggested in Troidan's work and in other accounts of adolescent sexuality. As Troidan explains, sequences of ideal types, like those he proposes in his research, are "abstractions, based on concrete observations of the phenomena under investigation" and are intended to serve as "heuristic devices, ways of organizing materials for analytical and comparative purposes" (1989: 47). He adds, citing Theodorson and Theodorson (1969), that ideal types can be used "as benchmarks, against which to describe, compare and test hypotheses relating to empirical reality." Language-oriented studies of gender socialization are focused somewhat differently: not on ideal types, but on the details of text construction that unfold through the speakers' lived experiences. Troidan's ideal types helped me locate evidence of gender socialization contained within those texts; and what I learned through this analysis certainly elaborates on his claims about gendered identity confusion during early adolescence.

### Using Life Story Narratives to Study Gender Socialization

Having examined gay socialization in the light of gay men's life-story narratives, I now want to shift the focus of this discussion and consider the appropriateness of life-story narratives as a database for such a project.

Boxer and Cohler's review of research from developmental psychology argues strongly against this practice. They explain:

The bulk of the developmental research on homosexuality is retrospective and based on adults' reconstructions of their childhoods. Causal inferences made from retrospective data are highly problematic, because adults' self-representations and understandings are infused with current cultural constructions and ideologies. (1989: 328-29)

Ellen Lewin, a cultural anthropologist, reached a similar conclusion in her study of lesbian motherhood. Because lesbians and heterosexual women "use narratives to construct their experiences as mothers, and by extension as women, from shared cultural elements," Lewin writes, their accounts of their experiences as single mothers "would be best interpreted as having cultural, rather than descriptive significance" (1993: 10-11). Arthur Kleinman uses the term "retrospective narratization" (1988: 50—see discussion in chapter 8) to highlight the descriptions of personal illness that some elderly patients provide to their younger kin.

All of these positions remind us that speakers regularly use present-day practices and interests to frame their accounts of earlier events and that narratives reconstruct original action more than they actually reproduce it. While these observations caution against treating narratives as verbatim truth, they also suggest ways in which narrative recollections can be productively included in historically oriented ethnographic inquiry. If it is true that respondents are likely to frame narratives about their past in terms of their concerns in the here-and-now, then we can use narrative data to identify those frames and use those frames as the focal point for the interpretation of the narratives. In other words, rather than attempting a literal reconstruction of history in textual terms, narratives allow us to explore how narrators themselves interpret their own history and to assess the significance that the narrators assign to such details.

This argument assumes that life-story narratives are intentional documents and not arbitrary, irrational constructions. Certainly, narrator intentions may change, from one narrative setting to the next, and the texts they produce will change accordingly. But one thing remains constant, as Henry Louis Gates has observed: "Our social identities represent the way we participate in a historical narrative" (1993: 231). And, in that sense, the narrative process itself contributes directly to the speaker's gender socialization.

By concluding, as I have in this chapter, that language was an important resource in the formation of these respondents' gay identities during adolescence, I am really underscoring the importance that the respondents place on language and on information gleaned through conversation, media presentation, and other textual formats. If they choose to organize their recollections in communicative terms, then communication needs to be the starting point for my analysis of those recollections. By doing so, I learn that gay teenagers may not automatically be rendered powerless by the discovery of their sexual interests, and I am reminded that gay teenagers *become* powerless in that regard when the surrounding social system denies them access to information about who they are, as sexual beings and as gendered persons, and otherwise limits their efforts at self-discovery.

# 8

## *Gay English and the Language of AIDS*

*All* speakers of English use language in special ways when they talk about the AIDS pandemic and its effects on their lives.[1] They draw on code words and phrases when identifying HIV illnesses, describing symptoms, and assessing treatment strategies. They adjust word order, disguise references to subjects and agents, and make other changes in sentence and paragraph form when discussing high-risk activities or commenting on the social conditions that encourage risk taking. Sometimes, when AIDS is the topic under discussion, people explore their thoughts and feelings in great verbal detail; other times, people make their thoughts and feelings known by saying nothing at all.

This language of AIDS is a recent construction for speakers of English, as it is for speakers of all languages.[2] In the United States, sources for this language include conventions of reference that already describe other sexually transmitted diseases (Leap 1990: 144-47), and characteristics commonly associated with any "dangerous and anti-social 'other'" (Clatts and Mutchler 1989: 14). Moreover, like other instances of health and illness text making, the language of AIDS is not a unified or a uniform construction. Speakers use this language in various ways, and the linguistic variability also contributes heavily to the messages that this language displays.

For some time, I have been interested in how gay men talk about AIDS and in the perspectives on AIDS (and related themes) that their talk displays, and I review some of the findings from these studies in this chapter. While my primary research concern has been to describe the representations of AIDS that gay men incorporate into Gay English text making, I have also discovered certain discontinuities between Gay English texts about AIDS and Gay English texts addressing other themes. The examples that I have included in this chapter address both of these themes.[3]

## AIDS in Gay Men's Life-Story Narratives

Arthur Kleinman has used the term "retrospective narratization" to describe a narrative style that allows the elderly ill to "establish . . . a kind of final expertise[,] to authorize the giving of advice and to reaffirm bonds with the young and with those survivors who will carry on the account after a person's death" (1988: 50). Kleinman continues:

Retrospective narratization is also frequent in situations where an illness had a catastrophic end, or when such an end has narrowly been avoided. In these cases, the narrative may hold a moral purpose; it acts something like the recitation of myth in a ritual that reaffirms core cultural values under siege and reintegrates social relations whose structural tensions have been intensified (Turner, 1967). The story of a sickness may even function as a political commentary, pointing a finger of condemnation at perceived injustice and the personal experience of oppression (Taussig, 1980). (Kleinman 1988: 50-51)

Retrospective narratization, as defined in these terms, is not just the property of the elderly. Similar narrative forms are prominent in the life stories told by gay men who are living with HIV illnesses (and, probably, by others who are HIV-positive and symptomatic). In fact, affirming one's loyalty to certain "cultural values under siege" while attacking the failure of other parties to maintain similar commitments is a particular form of text-internal dialogue (Bakhtin 1981: 268), against which gay narrators then interpret (or, just as frequently, reposition) specific events and episodes from their lives.

In the spring of 1986 (the date is important: popular discussions of AIDS were still not extensive, and neither was personal familiarity with a language suitable for such discussion), one of the doctors on staff at a D.C. hospital gave me a tape recording of a set of life-story interviews that he had conducted with a group of PWAs (persons with AIDS) admitted to the hospital for treatment of HIV-related illnesses. While the doctor was not directly supervising their care, he had gotten to know each of the respondents and members of their families in the course of his other duties on their floor. And when he explained that he wanted to conduct some open-ended interviews to help him learn more about people's thoughts on AIDS, all of the PWAs he approached agreed to participate, and so did members of their families.

I examined the texts of four of these interviews (three respondents were gay men, the fourth was a heterosexual female) in Leap 1991a, and I have reproduced the texts of the gay men's interviews in example 8.1. I analyze the first of these interviews (interview B) in some detail in the following paragraphs, and I use those findings to point out characteristics shared by other texts.[4]

**Example 8.1**   Representations of AIDS in three gay men's life stories. (Note: this example retains the format used in the original publication [Leap 1991a: 278-81] of these interviews.)

Interview B (Respondent: middle-aged white male)

B1   I:   Where do you think you got the HIV?
B2   R:   The person I was living with.
B3   I:   Where did he get it?
B4   R:   His travels.
B5   I:   Was he, did he have many partners?
B6   R:   I really couldn't say; I believe so.
B7   I:   Did you have many partners?
B8   R:   No. Uh, none.
B9   I:   Do you have any friends with HIV?
B10  R:   Not to my knowledge.
B11  I:   Do you know people with AIDS?
B12  R:   No, not that I know of.
B13  I:   How about friends, do they treat you . . .
B14  R:   I have not told my friends.
B15  I:   You've kept this secret?
B16  R:   Yes.
B17  R:   . . . as far as the disease itself, it is not worth what I
B18       have to go through.
B19  I:   Say that again.
B20  R:   The severity of the illness. If I knew this was what it
B21       was all about, I would not have gotten involved.
B22  I:   . . . When you say if you knew what you had to go through you
B23       wouldn't have done this, what would you have done? What
B24       could you have done to protect yourself?
B25  R:   I would not have gotten involved in the gay lifestyle.
B26  I:   Do you feel that people have a choice between a gay life-
B27       style and a straight lifestyle?
B28  R:   I did, since I was primarily a bisexual.
B29  I:   Were you ever married?
B30  R:   Yeah, seven years.
B31  I:   Can you tell me about your ideas when you switched from
B32       primarily heterosexual to primarily homosexual?
B33  R:   Oh, this is a new experience, let me try this out, let me
B34       try this also . . .

**Example 8.1** *continued*

Interview C (Respondents: two middle-aged white males, one assigned
to the ward, the other a visitor and his partner of several years)

C1  I:  . . . What is the most common topic of conversation within
C2       the gay community? . . .
C3  R2: I guess at dinner parties AIDS always comes up. . . .
C4  R1: And people talk, about change in life . . .
C5  R2: More, long-term relationships, staying, more
C6       relationships.
C7  R1: Less promiscuity, which is nothing wrong with that.
C8  I:  . . . Do you think it has made a big difference in
C9       protection, in style, you think there is more . . .
C10 R2: Oh yes, it has changed social lifestyle, at least for
C11      middle-aged gay men I know.
C12 R1: I think the younger men . . .
C13 R2: We have some contact with the younger ones. They go to
C14      bars, but not the promiscuity that we saw back . . .
C15 R1: What we see is change, they see as just the way things
C16      is, things are. . . . Now I am talking about the gay, the
C17      gay white community. I do not know about the ghetto.
C18 I:  What do you think about it ?
C19 R1: I cannot tell you for sure . . . I understand that Blacks
C20      are very [reluctant] to admit to the fact that a lot of
C21      this exists. They are not as aware, they are not as openly
C22      aware, they do not talk about this as much.
C23 R2: I think it is perceived as a white disease.
C24 R1: The white gays have come forth and been the ones willing
C25      to do something . . . the gay community has done as much or
C26      more than anything to combat, they've done all they can
C27      do . . .

Interview D (Respondent: middle-aged white male)

D1  I:  Tell me your perceptions on controlling HIV.
D2  R:  We, I haven't really thought about controlling HIV. A
D3       lot of people have it. I think a lot of people that get
D4       stressed out about having it are the ones who come down
D5       with the actual disease itself. A lot of it is mental.
D6  I:  . . . Do you have friends who have HIV-positive infections?

**Example 8.1** *continued*

D7    R:   I have one, yes, and he is scared to death that he is
D8          going to come down with the disease and I told him not
D9          to worry about it, that if he leaves well enough alone
D10        everything will come out just fine.
D11        . . . And I have a friend who is retired, can't figure out
D12        why in the world he would be a candidate for AIDS, but
D13        he's got it. But he is taking it very lightheartedly and
D14        making the best of everything.
D15   I:    He doesn't know where he got it?
D16   R:   No.
D17   I:    What is his sexual preference?
D18   R:   He is gay.
D19   I:    And is he, does he have a lot of contacts?
D20   R:   He has lived with the same guy for the last ten years . . .
D21   I:    . . . Do you think that people in the gay community are
D22        doing enough to protect themselves?
D23   R:   The majority are. There is still a few people that need
D24        to have their hands spanked . . .
D25   I:    Is there a way to predict people who won't protect them-
D26        selves?
D27   R:   Well, mostly the ones who won't protect themselves are
D28        the ones who go to the bars, and they are pretty obvious.
D29   I:    Young? Old?
D30   R:   Mostly young.

For the record, the doctor who conducted these interviews was in his midforties, of Eastern European Jewish background, heterosexual, and married with children. He has treated gay men for AIDS and other health problems and considers himself accustomed to talking with gay men and their partners and friends in professional contexts. I think this accounts for the abrupt, to-the-point style of his interviewing; that is, I suspect that he is equally direct when he asks questions of his patients in his office.

The first interview in example 8.1 displays the text of the doctor's bedside interview with a fifty-year-old HIV-positive, symptomatic gay Caucasian man. The topics discussed during this interview fall into three sections: how he contracted HIV (lines B1-B16), how he assesses his illness (lines B17-B21), and how he describes his own gender career (lines B22-B34); the middle, briefest segment provides a transition between the material in the longer segments at the opening and closing of the interview.

Let me begin by describing the doctor's questions and the respondent's comments in each of these sections.

At the beginning of this discussion, the doctor asked the respondent to explain how he contracted his illness. His reply cited another, specifically, the person he was living with (line B2), who, the respondent believed, had many sex partners during his travels (lines B4, B6). In contrast, the respondent claims that he had not had many sex partners (line B8). Moreover, he claims that he did not know anyone with AIDS and had not told any of his friends about his own illness (lines B9-B16).

In the middle segment of the discussion (lines B17-B21), the respondent looks critically at his own illness—"it is not worth what I have to go through" (lines B17-B18)—and then recasts that statement into a reflection on his life as a gay man: "If I knew this was what it was all about, I would not have gotten involved" (lines B20-B21). Contextually, the referent of the "it" pronoun in line B20 could be either the disease (as was the case for "it" in line B17) or the gay lifestyle, the implied object of the verb in line B21 and the focus for discussion in the end (lines B26-B34) of this text. The dual reading of this pronoun grounds its transition function in the syntax and pragmatics of text form and underscores the importance of this comment within the broader structuring of text meaning, as I will explain.

The respondent's comments in the third segment assess a range of gendered experiences across the life course (what I will call his "gender career"). He explains that he was primarily a bisexual (line B28), that he was married for a period of time (line B30), and that he *chose* to switch from a heterosexual to a gay lifestyle (lines B33-B34). He claims to have responded enthusiastically to opportunities that became available to him once he began to define himself as primarily homosexual: "Oh, this is a new experience, let me try this out, let me try this also" (lines B33-B34).

Several features characterize the respondent's use of language in this exchange. First of all, AIDS is clearly the central theme in this discussion, and concerns about AIDS are implicit in both the speakers' statements; however, the term "AIDS" never occurs in the respondent's comments. It occurs only once in the doctor's questions, which could be one reason why the respondent avoids the term.

But other, and more informative reasons, can be found in the respondent's use of language in those instances in the text where direct reference to AIDS was unavoidable (for example, lines B17 and B20). Here, instead of direct naming, he turned to more neutral, highly context-dependent synonyms ("illness," "disease"). Otherwise, in those instances, he let the wording of the physician's questions establish the frame of reference for a concise and usually unelaborated reply.

Concise, unelaborated responses were especially evident in the opening segment of the exchange. Here, building directly on the doctor's questions, the respondent's statements contain noun constructions, with verbs qualifying the truth value of the respondent's statements but not elaborating directly on the content of the response. In effect, while the respondent is willing to identify persons or states of activity as appropriate to the discussion, he leaves the details of the action undescribed. He notes that his roommate traveled, though he does not explain why he traveled and denies knowing anything about the roommate's sexual activity while he was away from home. He indicates that he has friends, though he says nothing about them nor does he explain why, if they are his friends, he has not told them about his illness. Line B14, which speaks to this point, is the one syntactically "complete" statement in this segment, and the formal use of "have not" instead of the more colloquial "haven't" further distinguishes the message conveyed through this sentence.

Even when the doctor probed for greater detail during this segment, the respondent continued to be succinct and cryptic, obliging the doctor—and the reader—to interpret sentence meanings through inference rather than in terms of referential meanings, exclusively. For example, the respondent's expression "the person I was living with" (line B2) could refer to several types of domestic relationships, even within the context of gay culture. The linkage between the respondent's illness and the roommate's adventurousness while away from home provides the only clue that the living arrangement was personal and sexually intimate, yet this linkage has to be pieced together from multiple comments of physician and respondent. The respondent included no explicit statement on this arrangement in his commentary.

The respondent's comments continued to be tersely constructed during the third segment of the interview, and as before, the comments offer only glimpses into the issue under discussion (his gender career). This time, however, the glimpses are much more richly detailed. Instead of presenting himself as a shadow figure with only vaguely detailed social connections to those around him, the respondent positions himself as the central actor in the events he identifies in this final segment. That is, he made the choice to become predominantly homosexual (line B28) and to be involved in the gay lifestyle (line B25). And he was the person eager to explore everything that this lifestyle had to offer.

Once again, the respondent's use of syntax and pragmatic structures supports and confirms these meanings. Sentence subjects in this segment contain first person, singular references, and the indicated subject is always the agent, not the recipient, of verb action. Actions carried out by the subject are specified precisely, not left undefined. And sentence-initial negative constructions, which occurred three times in lines B1-B16, do not show up in these statements.

There is a shift from vague to concrete commentary, and from speaker-as-object to speaker-as-actor, as the discussion in the interview moves from segment one into segment three. The middle section of the interview (lines B17-B21), and specifically the ambiguity of the "it" pronoun in lines B20-B21, provides the setting for this transition. Importantly, line B17, the opening statement in this segment, did not come in response to one of the doctor's questions. The respondent volunteered this reflexive comment and, by rephrasing it (lines B20-B21), he was then able to identify the connections between AIDS and gay lifestyle and to comment on the significance of those connections within his own life.

The respondent's comments in the remainder of this third segment display a rather different perspective on gay life. According to his statements, being gay was something he chose, something he enjoyed, and something he found exciting. He did not make such comments when AIDS was the topic of the discussion. There, his roommate was the adventurous risk taker, the man with the multiple sex partners; he, however, was the lonely victim of circumstances over which he had no control. But once the topic changed, the respondent, who initially had nothing to say about his own erotic activity, began to speak quite directly about his enthusiasm for new sexual experiences. He never connects those experiences with his HIV illness, though the time frame of these events (as later described to me by the doctor-interviewer) was certainly relevant to the narrative: Respondent B "switched from primarily heterosexual to primarily homosexual" in 1981, well before safe-sex practices had become widely accepted within the D.C. gay community, and he certainly gives no indication in this segment of the text that AIDS was an issue that needed to be addressed in any of those encounters.

My point here is not to condemn respondent B's enjoyment of this "second adolescence" but to draw attention to certain differences between his comments on his participation in erotic experience as displayed in the closing segment of this exchange and his comments on the same theme in the opening segment. There, the respondent claimed to have adopted an aloof, at-distance posture in the face of the AIDS pandemic, unlike the enthusiasm for gay sexuality displayed in lines B33-B34. Not only did he not have sex partners, but he did not even acknowledge having any friends with AIDS, and now that he was symptomatic, he was keeping his illness a secret from his friends. Accordingly, he located the source of his illness in the actions of others—"the person I was living with" and the sex partners his roommate had while traveling—all of whom were persons over whose behavior he had no control.

How can this respondent maintain these contradictory positions—innocent victim (lines B1-B16) versus active adventurer (lines B26-B34)— within the same text? First, let me point out that respondent B is not alone in his use of this narrative practice. Similar contradictory statements show up in the life-story narratives of other gay men, particularly when AIDS is one of the topics addressed in their narration. For example, the respondents in interview C in example 8.1 discuss the responsible changes in lifestyle (lines C10-C17) now undertaken by "the gay white community" (to which they belong), but (lines C17-C22) cite reluctance of persons in "the ghetto" even to admit "that a lot of this exists." As respondent R1 concludes, the white gay community have "been the ones willing to do something" (lines C24-C25), while black gays, in his assessment, "are not as aware . . . not as openly aware, they do not talk about this as much" (lines C21-C22).

And likewise, in interview D in example 8.1, the respondent contrasts his friend who "can't figure out why in the world he would be a candidate for AIDS, but he's got it" (lines D11-D14) with the people who "need to have their hands spanked" because they "won't protect themselves" (lines D23-D24, D27). Respondent D's friend has "lived with the same guy for the last ten years" (line D20) and is recently retired; those he places in the other category are persons "who go to the bars, and they are pretty obvious" (line D28).

As respondent B did in his narrative, these respondents are also using their construction of text to identify a generalized category of *irresponsible others*, persons who refuse to act appropriately even when confronted with the realities of the pandemic. Identifying that category allows respondents to establish a second category, *responsible, innocent victim*, which always includes the respondent himself and may include others close to him. The respondent describes himself and his colleagues as persons who, unlike those in the first category, do their best to follow the conventions appropriate to the given circumstances, regardless of personal inconvenience. In other words, these are the persons maintaining "cultural values under siege," according to the respondent's retrospective narratization (to return to Kleinman's phrasing).

The moral position that the respondent assumes (and assigns to his colleagues) through membership in this category of innocent victim is more than a descriptive convention. Adopting this position allows the respondent to disregard similarities between events in his life experience and behaviors associated with the "others" and their irresponsibility. Indeed, by concentrating on the contrasts between innocent victim and irresponsible others—which is what each of the narrators do in these passages (see lines B1-B8, lines C17-C27, and lines D21-D30)—the respondent increases the moral authority of his own self-description (that is, the more irresponsible "they" are, the more responsible the narrator becomes), and strengthens his own narrative goals.

Selective "repackaging" of truth is not restricted solely to AIDS narratives. As I explained in chapter 7, the same practices occur when respondents tell life stories, regardless of theme, and the effect on the narrative process always makes it unwise to attempt a literal interpretation of such texts. But other features of text design also occur with these reconstructions in AIDS narratives, and the combination yields a distinctive narrative style, especially when viewed in terms of Gay English grammar and discourse.

Particularly influential in this regard is the appeal to ambiguity and inference that permeate these texts. I pointed out that AIDS is never directly identified or labeled in respondent B's commentary and that he used several alternatives when reference to AIDS could not otherwise be avoided: for example, "it," "the illness," "the disease," each of which makes its own demands on the listener's ability to recognize the respondent's intended meaning from the minimal clues. Respondent B did the same thing when he identified his lover as "the person I was living with" (line B2), when he assigned a potentially multiple meaning to "it" (line B20), and when he described his sexual experimentation during his second adolescence as "a new experience" (line B33).

Speakers of Gay English regularly use ambiguous references and appeal to listener inference skills in conversations that take place within and outside of gay-friendly, gay-controlled speech settings. Indeed, ambiguity and inference are key themes in gay men's language of risk. The point of risk taking in these settings is to *conceal* reference, not to obscure references or to avoid reference making altogether. But obscuring references in some cases and avoiding reference making in others are major tactics in respondent B's text making. Indeed, much of the success of his narrative depends on his willingness to overlook his own at-risk behavior and his success in convincing the listener to do the same.

The presence of obscured references and reference avoidance in AIDS-related narrative texts is not surprising, given the nonneutral, and often quite frightening, position that AIDS now commands in U.S. society. Nor is it surprising that constructing texts about AIDS introduces such sentiments into the text making. But as far as Gay English is concerned, the introduction of those sentiments preempts certain features of text design and, in effect, changes the quality of the text. Principles of cooperative discourse and risk taking that are widely attested in other Gay English speech settings now give way to a more cautious and self-serving narrative style, and opportunities for the listener's creative involvement in the coconstruction of text messages, equally integral to Gay English discourse, is now secondary to a speaker-controlled disclosure of meaning.

### AIDS in the Gay Erotic Imaginary

Besides being very much a disease "of the other," AIDS is also a disease that is closely tied to sexual activity. And this means that negotiating commitments to safe-sex practices has now become a part of a generalized erotic discourse in U.S. society, even though individuals may or may not include those negotiations within their own erotic practices.

Ralph Bolton, a prominent anthropologist and AIDS activist, has observed (1992; Leap forthcoming a) that we know very little about the ways in which gay men talk about sex, either in the abstract or in the erotic moment. Participant-observation is one research strategy that will yield useful data in this regard, he recommends, and so will an analysis of gay-oriented, sexually explicit literature.

In this section I report on my analysis of an additional type of data, and describe the connections between AIDS and erotic negotiation that this analysis revealed.

The data in question came from a set of letters sent by self-identified gay men in response to two advertisements placed in a New York City gay men's magazine.[5] Both of these advertisements expressed a similar interest: A young, blond "hunk" (the author of the ad) sought sex partners willing to be the recipient in anal sex. Both ads specified that age, weight, and physical features would not be important points in Blond Hunk's selection of his partners. However, condom use would be important in that regard. In one advertisement, the text specified that Blond Hunk did not want condoms to be included in the erotic transaction. In the second advertisement, Blond Hunk specified that condom use was obligatory.

The advertisements appeared in the gay men's magazine in September (condoms required) and November (no condoms) 1987.[6] There were fifty replies to the "no condoms" advertisement and forty-six replies to the "condoms required" advertisement. After comparing home addresses to see if anyone had responded to both advertisements (they didn't) or responded more than once to the same advertisement (one respondent did, but I retained both of his letters), I sorted the text content according to a coding system that made unnecessary any further references to the respondents' specific identities.

On first review, I found many features in these letters that resembled the uses of metaphor, imagery, cooperative discourse, and other linguistic features commonly found in Gay English texts. Those similarities, plus the fact that all of the respondents identified themselves as gay men, led me to conclude that these letters are examples of written Gay English, a conclusion that subsequent analysis continues to confirm.

This did not mean that the letters were completely homogeneous. In fact, I suspected that the difference in each advertisement's position on condom use would elicit differently structured replies. And comparison of the content and design of these texts confirmed those suspicions. Example 8.2 displays primary points of contrast, and I elaborate on each point briefly below.

### Focus of the Respondents' Comments

Replies to the no condoms advertisement highlighted the physical attributes and interests of the respondent and said very little about the author of the ad. Replies to the condoms required advertisement centered on Blond Hunk's attributes and interests and minimized discussion of the respondent's personal details. A comparison of the sample letters in example 8.3 indicates some of the tactics that individual respondents employed to these ends.

As I read it, this difference in text content speaks to the widely held belief that using a condom greatly decreases a man's sexual pleasure. If condom use is a required component in the erotic exchange, a prospective partner will be especially appealing if he can guarantee pleasure to the condom wearer. As the letters in example 8.3 will confirm, some respondents were quite explicit in their guarantees.

### Explicitness in References to Erotics

The treatment of this issue in each set of letters patterns along the same lines as in the preceding point. Replies to the no condoms advertisement contain vivid discussions of the pleasure that the respondent will receive from the proposed liaison: for example, "like the feel and warmth of man juice in me" (example 8.3, letter 1); "I figure if you're living your fantasy you're having hot sex and that's what I want" (example 8.3, letter 3).

**Example 8.2** Differences between replies to Blond Hunk's personal advertisements.

| | | No Condoms | Condoms Required |
|---|---|---|---|
| 1. | Focus of the comments | Respondent-centered | Blond Hunk–centered |
| 2. | References to erotics | Describes pleasure respondent will receive | Describes pleasures respondent will provide |
| 3. | References to health | Respondent's health affirmed through direct reference as well as metaphor or imagery | Health alluded to in self-description, if discussed at all |
| 4. | References to physical attributes | Reinforce respondent's other comments about health | Reinforce respondent's promises to provide pleasure |
| 5. | References to safe sex | Occasional cautions re proposed at-risk erotic practices | Treated as self-evident comments, if mentioned at all |
| 6. | References to AIDS | Few indirect references to AIDS or HIV status, even fewer direct references | Few indirect references to AIDS or HIV status; even fewer direct references |

Replies to the condoms only advertisement play up the pleasure that Blond Hunk will receive, and that the respondent guarantees he can provide: for example, "I'm a total bottom. I don't even like to get sucked. But I love giving good head for hours and I love getting fucked" (example 8.3, letter 7).

### References to Health

Sex without condoms raises questions about HIV transmission, whether or not the questions are explicitly stated. Accordingly, some replies to the no condoms advertisement contain direct assurances that the respondent is healthy, supplemented by a range of metaphors—"I am clean and ready" (example 8.3, letter 2); "I haven't had sex in over three years" (example 8.3,

**Example 8.3**   Selected replies to Blond Hunk's advertisements.

### A. Selected Replies to the No Condoms Advertisement

*Letter 1*

Hey Blond Hunk

You want G/P you got it. GWM 35, slim 135# goodlooking, with shaved equipment. Hate condoms, like the feel and warmth of man juice in me. Enjoy long sessions, some kink and 3somes also. Give me phone # and where to reach you.

Write. Lets meet & give it to me.

[name, street address, hometown]

*Letter 2*

Hey Hunk

Saw your ad in the [newspaper] I really can satisfy a guy who's looking for a good skin to skin sensual, hot fuck I'm 33, 6′ 1″ 185 masculine brown hair blue eyed hunk, Italian, hairy chest and firm butt really handsome, a real Tom Selleck look-alike.

If interested I am clean and ready

[telephone number, first name]

*Letter 3*

I am very hot, horny sex looking to connect for a good time.

I'm 32, very healthy, strong, 6′ 1″, 180 lbs.

I've got blue eyes blond hair handsome masculine good looks. My chest is shaved. I've got horny sensitive nipples. I'm a fabulous kisser, big full lips, big tongue. I've got a solid thick 6″ and a real fuck-me ass with a tight, sweet hole.

I'm into hot, horny sweaty sex. I'm very versatile. I figure if you're living your fantasy you're having hot sex and that's what I want. I can give you what you want.

Call me at my job I work alone pretty much at night. Around 12 mid is good. [phone].

You will not be disappointed.

[first name]

**Example 8.3**   *continued*

*Letter 4*

Hi. Your ad in the [magazine] caught my eye.

I'm a GWM, 32, 5'7", 150 lbs. brown hair/eyes, Italian. Nice average looks.

I like to get fucked. I don't like condoms, either. I haven't had sex in over three years. I miss the weight of someone on me, inside me. I've been told I have a nice tight ass.

The idea of unsafe sex bothers me, but maybe it'll be all right. I've always wanted to do it with a blond. Never have.

If you think you might be interested, drop me a photo and a letter so I can see how your sexual thoughts form. I doubt you'll be disappointed.

[name, PO box, hometown]

### B. Selected Replies to the Condoms Only Advertisement

*Letter 5*

Dear 'Hunk':

What kind of person am I? Older, wiser, well-educated as well, restless for satisfactions both mental and physical and perhaps, above all, an excellent sense of humor—in sum, both intense and laid back.

Physically I am between handsome and goodlooking. The picture [photo enclosed] is about a year old. I am 5' 9", 144 lbs., dk brown hair, work out regularly and keep myself well toned. I also like to play the passive role (especially to good looking blonds). I have hot tits and a tight ass and love to be made submissive and gradually let myself go by giving way to the right person. You can reach me at [telephone number] if you are interested—and I hope you are.

Best Wishes,

[name]

*Letter 6*

Dear Blond Hunk

My name is [first name]. I am [age]. Have dark hair and brown eyes. I'm very attractive and have a nice body

I have never answered an ad before but after reading yours I just had to. I like the fact that you use condoms, very smart. I would like to meet you. I

**Example 8.3**   *continued*

think I'm right for you. Let's get together. You won't be sorry. I hope to hear from you soon. I rather talk to you personally. You can write to [address] or machine answers, please leave a message.

[first name]

*Letter 7*

Hi

I'm a [age] construction worker/med student. I'm 6′ tall with a good build (I work out 4 times a week). I'm Italian with a hairy chest black hair brown eyes.

I'm a total bottom. I don't even like to get sucked. But I love giving good head for hours and I love getting fucked. I practice safe sex and have been doing so since 1981.

I'm into being totally passive. If you'd like to get together you can call me at [telephone number] or you can write.

[name, address]

*Letter 8*

Dear Hunk:

Sounds great.

I'm WM, 6ft., 165 lbs. Brn/Grn, 28 yrs with a muscular body (aerobics/ free weights) with an ass many compliment me for. So if you love to fuck I love to get fucked in all sorts of positions, particularly when you drive it in hard and deep. Also love to suck.

If you care to discuss it call [telephone number]. Later is best, as I work 9-5 and then work out. But with you in mind [strikeover] can be very flexible for a rendez-vous.

Love to get fucked by a really hot guy. Call!

[name]

---

letter 4)—that underscore those assurances. And some replies also provide rationales that minimize any sense of risk: "I've always wanted to do it with a blond" (example 8.3, letter 4).

Respondents to the condoms required advertisement do not address health questions directly; they do, however, include the image of a healthy person as part of their promises of pleasure: for example, "I . . . work out regularly and keep myself well toned" (example 8.3, letter 5); "I'm very attractive and have a nice body" (example 8.3, letter 6); "I practice safe sex and have been doing so since 1981" (example 8.3, letter 7); "I work 9-5 and then work out" (example 8.3, letter 8).

### References to Respondents' Physical Attributes

Once again, the responses pattern along the lines of the overall text focus, with replies to the no condom advertisements providing detailed commentary about the respondent's appearance—"masculine brown hair blue eyed hunk, Italian, hairy chest and firm butt really handsome, a real Tom Selleck look-alike" (example 8.3, letter 2)—whereas replies to the condoms only advertisement position all descriptions of the respondent's physical features in terms of the feature's potential to give Blond Hunk pleasure: "I also like to play the passive role. . . . I have hot tits and a tight ass and love to be made submissive" (example 8.4, letter 5).

### References to Safe Sex

Respondents to the no condom advertisement occasionally included cautionary statements about unsafe sex in their replies: for example, "The idea of unsafe sex bothers me, but maybe it'll be all right" (example 8.3, letter 4). And in two instances (not included in the data presented here), respondents require that Blond Hunk agree to take an "AIDS test" to ensure that he is not already HIV-positive; importantly, the respondents also agreed to be tested at the same time.

Otherwise, respondents to this advertisement did not make an issue out of safe-sex practices in their replies—presumably because Blond Hunk's advertisement had already made his expectations in this area explicitly clear.

There are occasional comments in the condom only replies that reinforce the safe-sex preferences in the advertisement: for example, "I like the fact that you use condoms, very smart" (example 8.3, letter 6). Otherwise, since the condoms only advertisement assumes safe-sex practices, safe sex is not an issue discussed in the replies to this advertisement.

### References to AIDS

AIDS, like safe sex, is a prominent theme in the issues being negotiated in these letters. Condom avoidance is synonymous with high-risk erotic practices; condom use is synonymous with safe-sex practices and with the prevention of HIV transmission between participants. Given the other differences in the respondents' comments about health, physical attributes, intended beneficiary of the erotic exchange, and related topics, I expected to find that references to AIDS were also presented differently within each set of replies.

My review of these texts did not confirm that expectation, however. Other than in the replies of the two respondents who insisted that Blond Hunk take an AIDS test, respondents treated reference to AIDS in a similar fashion: Respondents did not mention AIDS, as such, in these texts, and neither did they mention HIV illnesses, disease, or any of the other AIDS-related synonyms and code words found in life-story narratives or in other textual settings.

### Discussion: Gay English and the Language of AIDS
### as Competing Linguistic Codes

That references to AIDS did not occur in these texts did not surprise me at first. While AIDS is certainly relevant to these negotiations, neither advertisement created a context that invited respondents to comment on this theme. The wording of the no condoms advertisement already prohibited condom use during the intended exchange, and a potential sex partner disagreeing with this posture would be unlikely to reply to this advertisement in the first place. And, other than paraphrasing a statement like "I like the fact that you use condoms" (example 8.3, letter 6), there is little about AIDS that a respondent needs to say to the author of the condoms only advertisement.

Moreover, the nonneutral sentiments associated with even an indirectly worded comment about AIDS would easily weaken the appeal of a respondent as a partner in erotic exchange. In that sense, both advertisements actually discouraged the respondent from making such comments.

So although AIDS was a prominent topic of discourse and a viable feature within the discourse context, AIDS still remained unnamed throughout the construction of the individual texts. The silencing was not because of any feature of Gay English grammar or discourse, but was a consequence of constraints widely attested in U.S. society that have nothing to do with cosexual genders (or gendered languages) at all.

I cannot continue to claim, as I did initially in my analysis, that Gay English is the language that these respondents used for text construction. That claim masks the tension between erotic negotiation and representations of AIDS that is at the center of the text message in each reply. While erotic negotiation takes on diverse forms in these texts, representations of AIDS impose a more unified cast to their detail. To argue this position is to claim that the language of AIDS is in some sense independent of Gay English grammar and discourse, and that raises questions about what a Gay English commentary on AIDS might contain, if the more generally occurring language of AIDS were not influencing the construction of the text. I suspect that answers to those questions can be found through a careful analysis of Tony Kushner's *Angels in America*, Terrence McNally's *Love! Valor! Compassion!*, and other works by gay authors that consciously and imaginatively seek to undermine mainstream expectations about appropriate AIDS-related discourse.

# CONCLUSION

## Gay English, Authenticity, and Performative Effect

I began this book by describing how I discovered Gay English, first as a young man coming to terms with my own gendered identity, and later as a middle-aged, tenured academician looking for ways to bring my personal and professional lives into close connection. Accordingly, each of these chapters combined ideas gained through a more formalized linguistic analysis of gay grammar and discourse with insights gained from my own experiences with gay text making.

I am certain that some gay men will not agree with some of my subjective claims or will find fault with the technical analysis of my data. Such disagreements will reflect, in part, the diversity that permeates gay communities in the United States, and in that sense, they are unavoidable.

So let me conclude by reviewing what I have said about Gay English in this volume, particularly as it relates to questions of authenticity in Gay English text.

I indicated in the introduction that it was misleading to refer to my subject matter as "gay men's English"—even though this was the subtitle selected for the book. Some gay men know nothing about Gay English and deny the existence of this code, and some persons who are in no sense gay (and may not even be queer, for that matter) are proficient Gay English users. The gendered identities of the speakers do not define or determine the distinctive properties of this code, and neither does a list of the structural features that can be associated with its presentation of coded messages (such as the cooperative turn taking, the strategically positioned terminals, the use of silence, the constructions of metaphors, and other forms of coded meaning). Instead, as I have shown by analyzing conversations and narratives from a number of settings and sources, the distinctiveness of this code and the authenticity of Gay English text as a whole derives from the performative effects that Gay English discourse has on context, topic, and participants relevant to these moments of text making.

I mean by "performative" something similar to John Austin's claims (1962, 1970) about sentences like

- I now pronounce you husband and wife.
- I dub thee Sir Lancelot; arise Sir Knight.
- We find the defendant not guilty as charged.
- What you have said does not answer my question.

These sentences are forms of action themselves, not merely descriptions of actions initiated elsewhere, and assuming that certain conditions are met (for example, that the person uttering the sentence has the authority to initiate the indicated action), speaking is the same as doing.

The conversations and narratives that have been the subject matter for this book have displayed such equations of speaking and doing. Recall, for example, the verbal formula that I heard men using as a prelude to erotic exchange in health club settings: "Your [specify an item of the partner's anatomy] is so [add a characteristic that underscores that item's erotic appeal]." This statement has nothing to do with truth value, but it has everything to do with the erotic negotiation of the moment. By offering this statement, the speaker helps create or maintain that erotic milieu.

Or, turning to some nonerotic examples, recall how, by using risk-taking strategies when talking to strangers, speakers allow strangers to confirm or deny their own suspect gay status without formally challenging their gender status at all. And, similarly, recall how being called "queer" in a high school locker room ensured that one was at distance from the speaker's sense of appropriate behavior, but how calling oneself queer reversed the location of normativity and established a claim to gendered space.

The speakers themselves become the site for the equation of speaking and doing in these examples, but in none of them are the speakers the sole participants in text construction. Performative effect requires listener, as well as speaker, involvement—what I have called *coconstruction* and *cooperative discourse* in this book, and what Eve Sedgwick has termed "the interpellation of witnesses" in her writing about queer performativity (1993: 4).

Sedgwick notes, for example, that the speaker considers a sentence like "Shame on you!" to be filled with performative meaning since, by saying "shame on you," the speaker imposes an attribution of shame onto the listener.[1] How the listener reacts to this performative act is another matter entirely, Sedgwick suggests. The listener may not recognize the speaker's authority to make such assessments, or the listener may be too preoccupied with other matters (or too thick skinned) to be made vulnerable by such a statement. The utterance itself cannot account completely for the performative experience of the exchange, and neither can the fact that the speaker constructed the utterance; listener involvement is equally relevant to this outcome.

Judith Butler's discussion of performativity (1990: 139; 1993) also underscores the importance of performative coparticipation. Because "the body" is socially constructed, physical properties alone cannot "determine" gender in any society. Rather, gender is a by-product of a particular kind of dramatic, presentational style. Building on claims suggested in Newton 1972, Butler considers *drag* to be one of the more accessible embodiments of this style; bodily form poses no barrier to the drag artist's assumption of a gendered identity, and that identity may have nothing (or everything) to do with the gendered identity assumed by that performer once the drag show has ended.

Butler's discussion of performativity also underscores the importance of witness appellation. Clearly, if a drag performance does not satisfy the audience's expectations about gendered characterization, the audience's rejection of that performance also rejects the performer's claims to a successful presentation of performed identity within that setting. On the other hand, like the recipient in Sedgwick's "Shame on you!," the drag artist's personal satisfaction with a particular performance may outweigh audience criticism and neutralize their rejection.

So, in addition to the cooperative discourse that flows from the appellation of witnesses, performativity is also linked to notions of vulnerability, situated politics, and ultimately, authority and power. Austin never addressed political themes or used the word "power" in his linguistic analysis, but he filled his discussion of performativity with examples of situated negotiations between sovereign and squire, minister and layperson, and other actors with unequal social rankings. Moreover, as Butler (1993) has observed, the performative force that Austin's examples display is either heterosexually sanctioned, or it offers its own sanction to compulsory heterosexuality in other forms.

This is why, as Butler and Sedgwick both conclude, a *queer* performativity always disrupts ties to heterosexual sanction and displaces the expectations about gender that people otherwise accept on face value. And by doing so, queer performativity unavoidably disrupts connections between power and performance that are otherwise implicit in each gendered setting.

Certainly, *displacement of expectations* and *disruption of the ordinary* are recurring themes in Gay English text making. Whether the speech setting is private or public, whether the participants are all gay or mixed-gender, and whether the text content is cordial or combative, restrained or outrageous, gay text design packages gay meanings within an impression of "familiar" language, and retrieving gay message involves a rejection of self-evident assumptions about text and a disruption of the familiar.

Even the presence of gay text can be disruptive in some instances. Recall how the comment "That's Mr. Faggot to you, punk!" refocused the bathroom-wall dialogue in figure 5.7; how speaker S1's repeated attempts to take charge of S2's weight-lifting routine (example 4.5, lines 1, 6, 8, and 12) prompted S2 to terminate his workout and leave the weight room floor; and how the queering of the Klan (example 2.3, lines 13-20) rearranged and solidified previously separate social alliances during an all-gay Sunday brunch. At issue in these instances is not the meaning of the statements but the fact of performance, the speaker's strategic placement of gay-oriented commentary within the text, and the listeners' acceptance of the commentary and the other listener-based responses that it elicited.

That the outcomes of Gay English textual performativity are different in each of these examples speaks directly to the situated nature of Gay English text making. And they are reminders (contrary to mainstream assumptions) that displacive, disruptive performance does not always have negative consequences.

The performative effect of Gay English text making also helps explain the attractiveness of Gay English as a gendered code—to gay men and to persons claiming other gendered identities. The creative metaphor, the clever turn taking, the strategics of pausing and silence, the exaggeration— all of these characteristics make speaking and listening to Gay English enjoyable activities, even for persons who are not as familiar with this language or as fluent in its grammar and rules of discourse as they might prefer. Some indications of this enjoyment may show up directly in text content (and even in text form), but on the whole, enjoyment is a product of the action of speaking and listening and not merely an attribute of the text itself. So Gay English enjoyment, too, is a performative construction.

But so are all components of gay experience. Gay is not a rigidly bounded, harshly defined social category; gay references an aggregate of flexible, polyvocal arrangements connecting self, sexuality, and power. Social practices impose definitions on these arrangements, and we live with the consequences of that imposition, or in spite of them. This is why, as I have argued throughout this book, language—specifically, gay language—occupies such an important place in gay experience. Through language use, and specifically through Gay English text-making, we are able to define ourselves and establish the conditions of our existence on our own terms.

# Notes

## Introduction: Studying Gay Men's English

1. Although I have included signed text making in this paragraph, I have not studied Deaf Gay English or Deaf American Sign Language (ASL) at firsthand, and I will not be discussing either of these languages in this book.

2. I refer to speakers of Indian English in this paragraph, but clearly grammar and discourse are equally important to Indian English listeners and to readers of Indian English as well as to writers. Similarly, text can be spoken or written, and may be presented in additional formats as well.

3. How closely linguistic discourse (in the sense just defined) parallels or overlaps with the institutionally centered social discourse of interest to, for example, Michel Foucault, Pierre Bordieu or Michel de Certeau requires further discussion. In some cases, it may be possible to study social discourse independently of its linguistic representations. But categorically equating language use with nondiscursive practice—which is the position these scholars recommend—raises particular problems for Gay English research, as I explain in chapter 1.

4. I offer a more detailed discussion of the issues in this section in Leap forthcoming b.

5. The extent to which there are equivalent issues for gay men is itself problematic, given that gay men, because they are men, have more opportunities to position themselves comfortably within patriarchal political structure than do lesbians, whose status as women automatically places them at a disadvantage in that regard even when they successfully disguise their lesbian identity. I have more to say on this issue in chapter 1 and in the conclusion.

6. These conditions explain, in part, why I became interested in the language use of Indian students in classroom settings and in Indian varieties of English in general. But the outsider status remained, even when pursuing those interests, and that did not make my fieldwork very pleasant. Indeed, without the support given me by individual tribal members (often those who had invited me to work in their community in the first place), it is likely that I would have moved away from Indian language studies much earlier than I did.

7. Especially important studies of gay culture and collections of life narratives were sections of Browning 1993; Chauncey 1994; Herdt 1991; Herdt and Boxer 1993; Newton 1993; Pronger 1990; Sears 1991; and Weston 1991. Especially important fictional accounts of gay life included Monette 1990; Leavitt 1986, 1990; Mordden 1986, 1987a, 1988; Feinberg 1989, 1991; and Rechy 1963, 1979.

### Chapter 1: Can There Be Gay Discourse without Gay Language?

1. I developed ideas in this chapter for an invited presentation at the 1994 Berkeley Women and Language Conference (now in print in Leap forthcoming a), and for presentations on Gay English research at the American University during the 1993-1994 academic year.

2. Gilbert Herdt and Andrew Boxer derive their notion of authenticity and their distinction between genuine and spurious in cultural experience from a classic essay by Edward Sapir ([1924] 1949: 308-31). For example, Sapir defined *genuine culture* as "inherently harmonious, balanced, self-satisfactory. It is the expression of a richly varied and yet somehow unified and consistent attitude toward life, . . . a culture in which nothing is spiritually meaningless, in which no important part of the general functioning brings with it a sense of frustration, of misdirected or unsympathetic effort" ([1924] 1949: 314-15).

3. Of course, discussing gay experience in terms of its authenticity and genuineness appeals directly to assumptions about gay normativity and value that may make some readers uncomfortable or be open to challenge on other grounds. Herdt and Boxer's research (1993: 27-36), for example, led them to question whether there was an authentic gay culture in Chicago prior to the Stonewall rebellion and its aftermath. Esther Newton (1993: 39, and see also her footnote 5 on that page) observes that such research draws an artificial distinction between homosexual (the more secretive, closeted identities from the pre-Stonewall era) and gay (the open, proud and defiantly erotic identities that have emerged since that time) and erases the creativity and fulfilling sophistication that characterized life during the earlier "homosexual period." Elizabeth Kennedy agrees: "To encapsulate the lives of gays and lesbians before Stonewall as furtive, rather than to value the ways in which they built culture and community in bars, in homophile organizations, and in resorts such as Cherry Grove, is to let the perspectives of the present overpower the past" (1994: 699). I hope to avoid such difficulties here by developing criteria for Gay English authenticity out of the actual conditions of the linguistic moment and in the language of the participants themselves, as I observe, record, and report those details. Ellen Lewin found such site-specific descriptions of text to be invaluable for her studies of lesbian motherhood; as she explains: "Women say what they do, or what they did, as a way of constructing key notions of self, and in the process go on to construct gender. More than hopelessly unmeasurable indicators of gender (or race, or class, or sexuality) as it affects opportunities or interactions, personal narratives offer us a chance to see how women *account for themselves*, make sense out of their situations, and designate themselves in relation to others—how they, in fact, negotiate their identities in collaboration with or in opposition to prevailing cultural expectations" (1993: 14, emphasis in original). I take the same position regarding the connections between text, personal representation, and social experience in Gay English discourse.

## Chapter 2: Gay English as Cooperative Discourse

1. I first used this term in Leap 1993, and segments of the following arguments build directly on material from that essay.

2. Still being new to gay language ethnography at the time, I did not attempt to make note of the nonverbal dimension of this exchange. Including the nonverbal cues would certainly have extended the richness of this example, but the give-and-take displayed through the spoken detail is more than sufficient for my purposes here.

3. This observation may appear to be overly mechanical in description of turn taking, but even the most spontaneous and informal of conversations contain such highly structured alternations of speaker–listener roles. See, for example, Goodwin's descriptions (1990: esp. 63-140, 229-80) of the rules governing participation structures in the recreational speech of urban black children and Tannen's discussions (1994: 53-84) of interruptions in adult male–female speech.

4. I will have more to say about the multiple meanings of "queering," and about the designation "queer," in chapter 5.

## Chapter 3: Ensuring Cooperative Discourse

1. I was close enough to the passenger to be able to observe the exchange first-hand. I made notes during the exchange, and I discussed the event with the passenger once the conversation had ended, using its openly gay content and the friendliness of the flight attendant as my opening themes for this discussion. Regrettably, I did not take detailed notes on my own linguistic risk taking in this setting.

2. After FA had moved his drink cart to another station, I talked with P about this conversation and asked him about his restrained reply. As I explained in my earlier analysis, "[P] expected that FA would give a particular response to his 'safe before six' statement, and was caught off guard when FA did not respond as planned. FA's use of such a blatantly erotic reference also surprised him. The exchange was taking place in a heterosexually controlled social domain. According to P's notions of appropriate speech, explicitly gay sexual references should always be avoided in those settings—at least, as far as the initial stages of the dialogue. Complicating matters even further, P said, he found himself unable to come up with a reply that would equal or surpass FA's remark. Under these circumstances, a noncommittal hedge seemed to be an appropriate reply, since it would shift the responsibility for structuring the exchange back to the co-participant" (1993: 63-64).

3. Tallulah Bankhead, star of film (*Lifeboat*) and the Broadway stage (*The Little Foxes*, a revival of *A Streetcar Named Desire*), was a popular performer for gay audiences, particularly upper-class urban gay men. According to Lee Israel's biography, Ms. Bankhead offered them "a kind of atrophy, a kind of triumph of form over content, that makes a drag ball terribly, terribly funny. They wanted sham, and Tallulah gave it to them. She was configurational rather than substantive. Her lip-line had ceased, for instance, to have anything to do with the shape of her mouth. Her clothes were almost but never quite right; they were about glamour rather than glamourous. . . . One of Tallulah's secretaries analyzed her fetishistic appeal to them this way: 'She was doing on-stage what they all did when they played dress-ups

with their friends. Hers was their kind of talk, their gestures. She was a highly identifiable character. They identified'" (1972: 306). John Herrick agrees, without tying gay interest specifically to drag and dress-up: "In her public behavior, she was what we all were in our cocktail parties behind closed doors" (cited in Joseph Goodwin 1989: 40). Moreover, as Goodwin explains, Ms. Bankhead was one of several female entertainers continually involved in confrontations with authority (1989: 40-42). Telling stories about her personal life, like repeating lines from her performances on the Broadway stage or in film, becomes a way to honor the courage of a brave woman who refused to conform to the expectations of a heterosexist society.

4. Friends who are active in Integrity, Dignity, and the Metropolitan Community Church remind me that church is not always a negative institution, or a negative reference for lesbians and gay men. I agree, but I also realize that these congregations would not need to exist if establishment churches were not so resistant to lesbian and gay interests and so blatantly homophobic in their theological practices. This ensures that church has negative connotations for gay men, even if particular churches are welcoming, affirming congregations.

### Chapter 4: The Risk Outside

1. The discussion of example 4.3 restates ideas originally presented in Leap 1993.

2. I started taking notes on this conversation, transcribing statements on the back of a shopping bag, as soon as I realized the interesting gaydar negotiation that it contained. My verbal participation in the exchange was more limited than my partner's—but that is usually the case and not a consequence of my ethnographic research.

3. Although I made notes during this conversation, I did not attempt verbatim description; hence the narrative form in the following paragraphs.

4. I reconstructed the events in the sauna from memory after this exchange came to an end. I took notes during the follow-up conversation with the younger man, and I quote his responses verbatim.

5. Some gay men use "chicken" to identify "any boy under the age of consent, heterosexual, fair of face, and unfamiliar with homosexuality," or any male who is "juvenile, youthful, young-looking" (Rogers 1972: 44). Chicken stories, besides being jokes told at the Centers for Disease Control conference, can therefore also refer to gay men's narratives focused in terms of this theme.

6. By contrast, "uncertainty" denotes instances of unmeasurable loss, conditions that cannot be offset by carefully anticipated, negotiated planning.

### Chapter 5: Claiming Gay Space

1. I presented a variant of the analysis in this section at the second Lavender Languages and Linguistics Conference (American University, September 1994) and included that analysis in Leap forthcoming d.

2. Readers unfamiliar with Peter Gabriel's "Big Time" (So, Warner Brothers Records, 1986) or Bronski Beat's "Smalltown Boy" (The Age of Consent, London

Records, 1984) may want to listen to performances of those songs before going further with the analysis in this section.

3. By explicitly gay, I mean songs that are (1) written by gay composers, (2) designed to explore gay themes, and (3) intended for gay as well as heterosexual audiences. This category is admittedly artificial, given that gay themes may appear in any modern-day English literary text. At the same time, the category anticipates the differences in text construction displayed in the following paragraphs. At issue here, once again, are questions of authenticity in gay text, questions I will revisit in the conclusion of this book.

4. Indeed, in a standard English reading of this sentence, "it" has no antecedent, because neither of the nouns preceding "it" in the sentence (news, today) can function as its referent.

5. Cuch (1987), the former education director for the Northern Ute Tribe, examines these notions of autonomy and personal responsibility from an insider's perspective.

6. I did not "study" Ute theories of gender and sexuality, as such, during my fieldwork on this reservation. Comments made during informal conversations have provided the database for this discussion. I restrict my focus here to male homosexuality because I became more familiar with Ute discourse on this theme. How Ute people think about female homosexuality is not clear to me; I cannot recall being part of a discussion on that topic while working and visiting on the reservation.

7. I find it difficult to categorize precisely the mix of people who hold this position. Some are members of conservative Christian congregations on the reservation. Others base their objections on personal rather than religious grounds. The only person ever to challenge me on these grounds was a woman from another tribe whose daughter had married an enrolled Ute and who was concerned that I was going to disrupt her daughter's marriage by seducing her son-in-law. But even then, this woman voiced her concerns in an appropriate Ute fashion—indirectly, to third parties, and never to my face.

8. Teresa de Lauretis comments somewhat differently on this point in her introduction to a collection of essays on lesbian and gay sexualities: "The term queer was suggested to me by a conference in which I had participated and whose proceedings will be published in the forthcoming volume edited by Douglas Crimp and the Bad Object Choices, 'How do I look? Queer film and video.' My 'queer' had no relation to the Queer Nation group, of whose existence I was ignorant at that time. As the essays (in this collection) will show, there is very little in common between Queer Nation and queer theory" (1991: xvii). To me, the essays in that collection are very much concerned with displaying and subverting assumptions about gender and power that limit exploration and expression of alternative sexualities. The same theme informed the "queering" of the shopping mall described in Browning's essay, and likewise the disruption of Sunday mass at St. Patrick's Cathedral in spring 1993, and the spectacular visual imagery of the Stonewall 25 parade in summer 1994. Perhaps the authors in de Lauretis's collection did not intend to address Queer Nation–like goals, but the fact is, queer theory is concerned with destabilization, even if its practitioners act on that concern in the relative safety of the classroom, the conference session, and scholarly publication rather than "in-the-streets." De Lauretis's comments, reproduced in example 5.2, speak directly to this point.

### Chapter 6: Language, Risk, and Space in a Health Club Locker Room

1. I have presented material in this chapter at several conferences, and acknowledge the helpful comments on the argument given by Ralph Bolton, Norris Lang, Michael Clatts, Ellen Lewin, Liz Goodman, Gil Herdt, Han ten Brummelhuis, Lesley Gill, and Sam Collins.

2. I also assumed that women, as a group, would have no opinion on this issue because the men's actions did not involve them directly. Anita confirmed that women had not complained about expressions of male cosexual erotic interests, but noted that women could only observe these events in public areas of the gym, such as the weight room, the areas adjacent to the fitness machines, and the aerobic classroom, where (in her opinion) erotic expressions were more likely to be more subdued. My observations suggest that erotic preluding between men occurs quite frequently in those settings. Whether women also noticed these events, or noticed but chose to ignore them, is an issue that I have not explored.

3. My partner, who also became a member of these clubs and usually joins me in my trips to local health clubs, has helped tremendously in the initial negotiations of many of these conversations.

4. I have removed the parentheses that Browning placed around "for everything it had been denied in adolescence."

5. I have more to say about the language of gay personal advertising in chapter 8.

6. In order to continue operations during this period, managers in some cities increased their inventory of workout equipment, added fitness trainers to their staff, restricted client access to the orgy rooms and other unsupervised areas of the site, and began to advertise as health clubs rather than as steambaths. By this time (mid-1980s), "health club" had already become a widely used alternative to the older term "gym" in mainstream advertising, particularly as a way of drawing attention to the range of comfort services that these facilities provided their clients. It is not coincidental, given widespread concerns about HIV illnesses, that "health" became the head word in this alternative label, or that "fitness center" (with its headword "fitness") became another reference alternative during this period.

7. A conversation with David Bergman (in the summer of 1994) helped clarify these thoughts about entrance and transition.

8. Clearly "second adolescence" does not apply to young men who come out during their teenage years and for whom adolescence becomes a predominantly gay experience.

9. The third man in this event was a self-identified gay man, someone I had met in the weight room several months before. He had already become the target of this "married man's" negotiations by the time I entered the sauna. When later I asked him about this event, he told me he did not want anyone to give him a hand-job while he was in the sauna, that he has never had sex with anyone at the club, and that he did not ever want to use his time at the gym to pick up men.

"That's why I go to the bars," he told me.

So why did he remain in the sauna, even though the "married man" was becoming persistent in his use of erotically explicit gaze and gesture? "I like to take a sauna after my workout, and I know how to fend off the creeps."

10. Each time I review this statement, I am intrigued by the speaker's pause in the final sentence. The pause could draw the listener's attention to the coded message contained in the preceding clause, or, as friends have pointed out to me when I discussed this statement, it could also have been the first (nonverbal) step in his come-on to me. At the time of the conversation, I was listening for his logic in his commentary, and I paid no attention to the alternative reading. Now, being more familiar with the multilayered messages about male-oriented erotic desire expressed through health club text making, I suspect that the second interpretation, or perhaps both interpretations, should apply.

### Chapter 7: Gay English in a "Desert of Nothing"

1. This chapter is a revised and expanded version of Leap 1994, used by permission of the editor of the *High School Journal*. My thanks to Brett Williams and Sam Collins, who gave a critical read to earlier versions of this text.

2. I am using the term "folk knowledge" here to avoid confusion with *gay folklore*, by which I mean information about local gay practices that is acquired, exchanged, and maintained by gay men and for gay men. Joseph Goodwin 1989 and the essays in Blincoe and Forrest 1993 provide examples of materials in this second category.

### Chapter 8: Gay English and the Language of AIDS

1. This chapter restates and expands on material that previously appeared in Leap 1990 and 1991a and that I have discussed in papers at several professional meetings. Leap forthcoming c offers another version of the life-story analysis presented in detail here. My thanks to Ralph Bolton, Norris Lang, Doug Feldman, Gil Herdt, Michael Clatts, Janet McGrath, and other colleagues who have encouraged my analysis of this material.

2. There were no conventions in place for describing or discussing HIV-related illnesses when these conditions were first noticed in the Western world (1981). Even basic vocabulary had to be invented, and it was only after a lengthy and heavily gendered struggle that "AIDS" (acquired immune deficiency syndrome), rather than expressions like "GRID" (gay related immune deficiency), "CAIDS" (community acquired immune deficiency syndrome), or "gay bowel syndrome," became the term of choice for researchers and health care practitioners. Clatts and Mutchler 1989, McCombie 1990, Murray and Payne 1989, and Shilts 1987 offer useful reviews of this history.

3. In the main, the literature on language and AIDS (cf. Goldstein 1991; Sontag 1988; Treichler 1987, 1992) has been broadly focused, exploring the "epidemic of signification" (Treichler's term) unleashed by the sudden appearance of AIDS in contemporary society and the various representations that those signifiers have assumed. These studies offer fascinating insights into the dynamics of popular culture, writ large, but they reveal very little about the representations of AIDS-related messages as they occur in daily conversations, in life-story narratives, and in other forms of site-specific text construction. This is the focus for linguistic research that interests me personally, but more important, this is the research focus that will show how

language use creates barriers to safe-sex practices and, thereby, hinders effective AIDS education.

4. Leap (1990: 151-55) gives two more examples of AIDS-related retrospective narratization in gay life-story narrative. These examples are narrative reconstructions of needle-sharing experiences. The first narrator (speaker A in that analysis), who both sold drugs and used them at after-hours parties, suggests that "they [a largely undefined category] were taking their chances" when they used his points (that is, needles) to shoot up (passage A1, p. 151), but he says nothing about the same at-risk consequences that he and his friends faced when they shared each other's points in those settings (passage A2, p. 153). It is important to note that a second narrator (speaker B, a heterosexual female) did not use such an opposition when relating her needle-sharing experiences. Accordingly, one of the outcomes of AIDS-related life-story research must be the identification of circumstances prompting narrators to incorporate this convention into their life stories, or to avoid doing so. In these instances, male versus female and/or gay versus straight narrative styles are especially significant influences.

5. My thanks to Douglas Feldman (Hollywood, Florida) for collecting these letters and providing me with copies of the texts.

6. Since that time, the editor of the magazine has decided not to print advertisements seeking partners for unsafe, high-risk sexual experiences. This is now common practice among the gay men's publications that include personal advertising.

### Conclusion

1. Note that the syntax of "Shame on you!" is quite different from that in "I now pronounce you husband and wife" or the other examples of performative constructions that I listed. Sedgwick's use of a second person, imperative construction is deliberate, and connected to Judith Butler's observation that first person performatives (like the example just cited) are forms of heterosexist privilege. However, Austin himself considered imperatives as a separate category of performatives, and he argued that such constructions have different performative consequences (for speakers or for the speech event) than do first person constructions. Ignoring those distinctions may not weaken Sedgwick's claims about gendered performativity, but keeping the linguistic facts in clear focus helps to embellish it, as my comments will suggest.

# Bibliography

Abbott, Franklin, ed. 1990. *Men and Intimacy: Personal Accounts Exploring the Dilemmas of Modern Male Sexuality*. Freedom, Calif.: Crossing Press.

Austin, John. 1962. *How to Do Things with Words*. Oxford: Clarendon Press.

———. 1970. "Performative Utterances." In *Philosophical Papers*, 232-52. Oxford: Oxford University Press.

Bakhtin, Mikhail. 1981. *The Dialogic Imagination*. Austin: University of Texas Press.

Baugh, John. 1983. *Black Street Speech: Its History, Structure, and Survival*. Austin: University of Texas Press.

Bawer, Bruce. 1993. *A Place at the Table: The Gay Individual in American Society*. New York: Touchstone Books.

Belenky, Mary Field. 1986. *Women's Ways of Knowing*. New York: Basic Books.

Bergman, David. 1993. Personal communication.

Berlant, Lauren, and Elizabeth Freeman. 1993. "Queer Nationality." In *Fear of a Queer Planet: Queer Politics and Social Theory*, Michael Warner, ed., 193-229. Minneapolis: University of Minnesota Press.

Biemiller, Lawrence. 1993. "Adventure in Rural America." *Washington Blade* 24, no. 30: 39.

Blincoe, Deborah, and John Forrest, eds. 1993. "Prejudice and Pride: Lesbian and Gay Traditions in America." *New York Folklore*. Special issue. 19, nos. 1-2.

Bolton, Ralph. 1992. "Mapping Terra Incognita: Sex Research for AIDS Prevention—An Urgent Agenda for the 1990s." In *The Time of AIDS: Social Analysis, Theory and Method*, Gilbert Herdt and Shirley Lindenbaum, eds., 124-58. San Francisco: Sage.

———. Forthcoming. "Sex Talk: Bodies and Behaviors in Gay Erotica." In *Beyond the Lavender Lexicon: Authenticity, Imagination and Appropriation in Lesbian and Gay Languages*, William L. Leap, ed. Newark, N.J.: Gordon and Breach Press.

Boxer, Andrew M., and Bertram J. Cohler. 1989. "The Life Course of Gay and Lesbian Youth: An Immodest Proposal for the Study of Lives." In *Gay and Lesbian Youth*, Gilbert Herdt, ed., 317-55. Binghamton, N.Y.: Harrington Park Press.

Brealey, Richard, and Stewart Myers. 1984. *Principles of Corporate Finance*. 2d. ed. New York: McGraw-Hill.

Bright, Susie. 1993. "Gaydar: Or, It Takes One to Know One." *Out* 12 (October/November): 121-23.

Brown, Joe, and Kara Swisher. 1994. "Backstage: The One Who Fit the Bill." *Washington Post*, 6 August, C2.

Browning, Frank. 1993. *The Culture of Desire.* New York: Crown.

Butler, Judith. 1990. *Gender Trouble: Feminism and the Subversion of Identity.* New York: Routledge.

———. 1991. "Imitation and Gender Insubordination." In *Inside Out: Lesbian Theories, Gay Theories*, Diana Fuss, ed., 13-31. New York: Routledge.

———. 1993. "Critically Queer." *GLQ* 1, no. 1: 17-32.

Chauncey, George. 1994. *Gay New York: Gender, Urban Culture, and the Making of the Gay World, 1890-1940.* New York: Basic Books.

Chesebro, James W., ed. 1981. *Gayspeak: Gay Male and Lesbian Communication.* New York: Pilgrim Press.

Clatts, Michael, and Kevin M. Mutchler. 1989. "AIDS and the Dangerous Other: Metaphors of Sex and Deviance in the Representation of Disease." *Medical Anthropology* 10: 105-14.

Cosgrove, D. E. 1985. "Prospect, Perspective, and the Evolution of the Landscape Idea." *Transactions.* New series, Institute of British Geographers. 10: 45-62.

Cuch, Forrest. 1987. "Cultural Perspectives on Indian Education: A Comparative Analysis of the Ute and Anglo Cultures." *Equity and Education* 23, nos. 1, 2: 65-76.

de Certeau, Michel. 1984. *The Practice of Everyday Life.* Berkeley: University of California Press.

de Lauretis, Teresa. 1991. "Queer Theory: Lesbian and Gay Sexualities." *Differences* 5: iii-xviii.

Delph, Edward William. 1978. *The Silent Community: Public Homosexual Encounters.* Beverly Hills, Calif.: Sage.

Dilallo, Kevin, and Jack Krumholtz. 1994. "Pork Is a Verb: A Gay Lexicon." In *The Unofficial Gay Manual*, 215-23. New York: Doubleday.

Doty, Alexander. 1993. *Making Things Perfectly Queer: Interpreting Mass Culture.* Minneapolis: University of Minnesota Press.

Downes, John, and Jordan Elliot Goodman. 1987. *Dictionary of Finance and Investment Terms.* New York: Barron's.

Duberman, Martin. 1991. *Cures: A Gay Man's Odyssey.* New York: Dutton.

Dynes, Wayne. 1985. *Homolexis.* New York: Monograph 5, Gai Saber Press.

Ephron, Nora. 1983. *Heartburn.* New York: Knopf.

Farrell. Ronald A. 1972. "The Argot of the Homosexual Subculture." *Anthropological Linguistics* 14: 97-109.

Feinberg, David B. 1989. *Eighty-sixed.* New York: Penguin Books.

———. 1991. *Spontaneous Combustion.* New York: Penguin Books.

Fordham, Signithia. 1992. "'Those Loud Black Girls': (Black) Women, Silence, and Gender 'Passing.'" *Anthropology and Education Quarterly* 24: 3-32.

Fuss, Diana. 1989. *Essentially Speaking: Feminism, Nature, and Difference.* New York: Routledge.

Gates, Henry Louis, Jr. 1993. "The Black Man's Burden." In *Fear of a Queer Planet: Queer Politics and Social Theory*, Michael Warner, ed., 230-38. Minneapolis: University of Minnesota Press.

Gladwell, Malcolm. 1994. "Message Confronts Image in March for Gay Rights." *Washington Post*, 26 June, A3.

Goldstein, Diane, ed. 1991. *Talking AIDS: Interdisciplinary Perspectives on Acquired Immune Deficiency Syndrome*. St. Johns: Memorial University of Newfoundland, Institute of Social and Economic Research. Research and Policy Paper no. 12.

Goodwin, Joseph P. 1989. *More Man Than You'll Ever Be: Gay Folklore and Acculturation in Middle America*. Bloomington: Indiana University Press.

Goodwin, Marjorie Harness. 1990. *He-Said-She-Said: Talk as Social Organization among Black Children*. Bloomington: Indiana University Press.

Grahn, Judy. 1984. *Another Mother Tongue: Gay Words, Gay Worlds*. Boston: Beacon Press.

Halliday, M. A. K. 1978. "Language as Social Semiotic." In *Language as Social Semiotic*, 108-26. Baltimore, Md.: Edward Arnold.

Harvey, David. 1989. *The Condition of Postmodernity*. Cambridge, U.K.: Blackwell.

Hawkins, David F. 1986. *Corporate Financial Reporting and Analysis: Text and Cases*. 3rd ed. Homewood, Ill.: Irwin.

Herdt, Gilbert, ed. 1991. *Gay Culture in America: Essays from the Field*. Boston: Beacon Press.

Herdt, Gilbert, and Andrew Boxer. 1991. "Introduction: Culture, History, and Life Course of Gay Men." In *Gay Culture in America: Essays from the Field*, Gilbert Herdt, ed., 1-28. Boston: Beacon Press.

———. 1993. *Children of Horizons: How Gay and Lesbian Teens Are Leading a New Way out of the Closet*. Boston: Beacon Press.

Hersker, Alan. 1993. Unpublished notes, interview with Ben, Washington, D.C.

Hoagland, Sarah. 1988. *Lesbian Ethics: Toward New Value*. Palo Alto: Institute of Lesbian Studies.

Irigaray, Luce. 1985. *This Sex Which Is Not One*. Translated by Catherine Porter with Carolyn Burke (original title: *Ce sexe qui n'est pas un*, 1977). Ithaca, N.Y.: Cornell University Press.

Israel, Lee. 1972. *Miss Tallulah Bankhead*. New York: Putnam.

Jackson, Peter. 1989. *Maps of Meaning: An Introduction to Cultural Geography*. London: Unwin Hyman.

Janowitz, Tama. 1986. *Slaves of New York*. New York: Washington Square Books.

Kennedy, Elizabeth Lapovsky. 1994. "Living with Gay and Lesbian Identity and Community, Dreaming of Utopia." *American Anthropologist* 96: 697-700.

Kleinman, Arthur. 1988. *The Illness Narratives: Suffering, Healing, and the Human Condition*. New York: Basic Books.

Koestenbaum, Wayne. 1993. *The Queen's Throat: Opera, Homosexuality, and the Mystery of Desire*. New York: Poseidon Press.

Kushner, Tony. 1993. *Angels in America: A Gay Fantasia on National Themes*. New York: Theater Communication Group.

Lakoff, Robin. 1975. *Language and Woman's Place*. New York: Harper and Row.

Leap, William L. 1990. "Language and AIDS." In *Culture and AIDS*, Douglas Feldman, ed., 137-58. New York: Praeger Press.

———. 1991a. "AIDS, Linguistics and the Study of Non-Neutral Discourse." In

*Anthropology, Sexuality, and AIDS*, Gilbert Herdt, William L. Leap, and Melanie Sovine, eds. *Journal of Sex Research*. Special issue. 28, no. 2: 275-88.

——. 1991b. Unpublished notes, interview with Joe, Washington, D.C.

——. 1992a. Unpublished notes, interview with Jim, Washington, D.C.

——. 1992b. Unpublished notes, interview with Sam, Washington, D.C.

——. 1992c. Unpublished notes, interview with Robert, Washington, D.C.

——. 1992d. Unpublished notes, interview with Jonathan, Washington, D.C.

——. 1993. "Gay Men's English: Cooperative Discourse in a Language of Risk. In *Prejudice and Pride: Lesbian and Gay Traditions in America*, Deborah Blincoe and John Forrest, eds. *New York Folklore*. Special issue. 19, nos.1-2: 45-70.

——. 1994. "Learning Gay Culture in a 'Desert of Nothing': Language as a Resource in Gender Socialization." In *The Gay Teenager: The High School Journal*. Special issue. 77, nos. 1-2: 122-31.

——. Forthcoming a. "On Authenticity in Gay Men's English." In *Proceedings of the Third Berkeley Women and Language Conference*, Mary Bucholtz, Kira Hall, and Anita Liang, eds. Berkeley, Calif.: Berkeley Women and Language Group.

——. Forthcoming b. "Studying Gay English: How I Got Here from There." In *Lesbian and Gay Ethnography: Fieldwork, Writing, and Interpretation*, Ellen Lewin and William L. Leap, eds. Urbana: University of Illinois Press.

——. Forthcoming c. "Talking about AIDS: Linguistic Perspectives on Non-Neutral Discourse." In *Culture and AIDS*, Han ten Brummelhuis and Gilbert Herdt, eds. Newark, N.J.: Gordon and Breach.

——. Forthcoming d. "Performative Effect in Three Gay English Texts." In *Queerly Phrased*, Anna Livia and Kira Hall, eds. New York: New York University Press.

Leavitt, David. 1986. *The Lost Language of Cranes*. New York: Bantam Books.

——. 1990. *A Place I've Never Been*. New York: Penguin Books.

Levine, Martin. 1991. "The Life and Death of Gay Clones." In *Gay Culture in America: Essays from the Field*, Gilbert Herdt, ed., 68-86. Boston: Beacon Press.

Lewin, Ellen. 1993. *Lesbian Mothers: Accounts of Gender in American Culture*. Ithaca, N.Y.: Cornell University Press.

Marcus, Eric. 1993. "Opinion: What's in a Name?" *10 Percent* 5: 14-15.

McCombie, Susan. 1990. "AIDS in Cultural, Historic, and Epidemiologic Context." In *Culture and AIDS*, Douglas Feldman, ed., 9-28. New York: Praeger Press.

McInerney, Jay. 1988. *Story of My Life*. Baltimore, Md.: Penguin Books.

McNally, Terrence. 1995. *Love! Valor! Compassion!* New York: Dramatists Play Service.

Miles, Sara. 1994. "Do the Right Thing." *Out* 14 (February/March): 94-99, 151-54, 157, 159.

Miller, Neil. 1981. *In Search of Gay America*. New York: Atlantic Monthly Press.

Mohr, Richard D. 1992. *Gay Ideas: Outing and Other Controversies*. Boston: Beacon Press.

Monette, Paul. 1990. *Afterlife*. New York: Avon Books.

Moonwomon, Birch. 1992. "Rape, Race, and Responsibility: A Graffiti Text Political Discourse." In *Locating Power: Proceedings of the Second Berkeley Women and Language Conference*, Kira Hall, Mary Bucholz, and Birch Moonwomon, eds., 420-29. Berkeley, Calif.: Berkeley Women and Language Group.

Mordden, Ethan. 1986. *Buddies*. New York: St. Martin's Press.

———. 1987a. *I've a Feeling We're Not in Kansas Any More*. New York: NAL Penguin.

———. 1987b. "The Precarious Ontology of the Buddy System." In *I've a Feeling We're Not in Kansas Any More*, 50-63. New York: NAL Penguin.

———. 1988. *Everybody Loves You*. New York: St. Martin's Press.

Mosbacker, Dee. 1993. "Right Answers: Dee Mosbacker Interviews John Schlafly." *10 Percent* 1, no. 2: 33-35, 66-69.

Murray, Stephen O. 1979. "The Art of Gay Insulting." *Anthropological Linguistics* 21: 211-23.

Murray, Stephen O., and Kenneth Payne. 1989. "The Social Classification of AIDS in American Epidemiology." *Medical Anthropology* 10: 23-36.

Musto, Michael. 1993. "Gaydar: Using That Intuitive Sixth Sense." *Out* 12 (October/November): 120, 124.

Nardi, Peter. 1992. "Seamless Souls: An Introduction to Men's Friendships." In *Men's Friendships*, Peter Nardi, ed., 1-14. Newbury Park, Calif.: Sage.

Newton, Esther. 1972. *Mother Camp: Female Impersonators in America*. Chicago: University of Chicago Press.

———. 1993. *Cherry Grove: Fifty Years in America's First Gay and Lesbian Town*. Boston: Beacon Press.

Ortner, Sherry, and Harriet Whitehead. 1981. "Introduction: Accounting for Sexual Meanings." In *Sexual Meanings: The Cultural Construction of Gender and Sexuality*, Sherry Ortner and Harriet Whitehead, eds., 1-27. Cambridge, U.K.: Cambridge University Press.

Penelope, Julia. 1990. *Speaking Freely: Unlearning the Lies of the Fathers' Tongues*. New York: Pergamon Press.

———. 1992. *Call Me Lesbian: Lesbian Lives, Lesbian Theory*. Freedom, Calif.: Crossing Press.

Petrow, Steven. 1993. "Being Brave." *Advocate* 644 (14 December): 58-61.

Plummer, Ken. 1975. *Sexual Stigma: An Interactionist Account*. London: Routledge and Kegan Paul.

Pronger, Brian. 1990. *The Arena of Masculinity: Sports, Homosexuality, and the Meaning of Sex*. New York: St. Martin's Press.

Queer Nation Manifesto. N.D. *I Hate Straights*. Multilithed.

Raban, Jonathan. 1974. *Soft City*. New York: Dutton.

Read, John. 1980. *Other Voices: The Style of a Male Homosexual Tavern*. Novato, Calif.: Chandler and Sharp.

Rechy, John. 1963. *City of Night*. New York: Grove Press.

———. 1979. *Rushes*. New York: Grove Press.

Rich, Adrienne. 1980. "Compulsory Heterosexuality and Lesbian Existence." *Signs* 5: 631-60.

Reinhardt, Robert C. 1986. *A History of Shadows*. Boston: Alyson Press.

Ringer, R. Jeffrey, ed. 1994. *Queer Words, Queer Images*. New York: New York University Press.

Rogers, Bruce. 1972. *The Queens' Vernacular: A Gay Lexicon*. San Francisco: Straight Arrow Books.

Russell, Ina, ed. 1993. *Jeb and Dash: A Diary of Gay Life, 1918-1945*. Boston: Faber and Faber Press.

Sapir, Edward. 1949 [1924]. "Culture, Genuine and Spurious." in *Selected Writings of Edward Sapir*, David Mandelbaum, ed., 308-31. Berkeley: University of California Press.

Sears, James. 1991. *Growing Up Gay in the South: Race, Gender, and Journeys of the Spirit*. Binghamton, N.Y.: Harrington Park Press.

Sedgwick, Eve Sokofsky. 1993. "Queer Performativity: Henry James' *The Art of the Novel*." *GLQ* 1, no. 1: 1-16.

Shilts, Randy. 1987. *And the Band Played On*. New York: Viking Penguin Press.

Smitherman, Geneva. 1977. *Talkin and Testifyin: The Language of Black America*. Detroit: Wayne State University Press.

Sontag, Susan. 1988. *AIDS and Metaphor*. New York: Simon and Schuster.

Souers, Millard B. 1992. "Degrading Word." *Washington Blade* 25 (3 April): 33, 35.

Spender, Dale. 1987 [1980]. *Man Made Language*. London: Pandora Books.

Tannen, Deborah. 1990. *You Just Don't Understand: Women and Men in Conversation*. New York: Ballantine Books.

———. 1994. *Gender and Discourse*. Oxford: Oxford University Press.

Taussig, Michael. 1980. *The Devil and Commodity Fetishism in South America*. Chapel Hill: University of North Carolina Press.

Theodorson, G. A., and A. G. Theodorson. 1969. *A Dictionary of Modern Sociology*. New York: Thomas Y. Crowell.

Tierney, William. 1993. "Self and Identity in a Post-Modern World: A Life Story." In *Naming Silenced Lives*, Dan McLaughlin and William G. Tierney, eds., 119-34. New York: Routledge.

Treichler, Paula. 1987. "AIDS, Homophobia and Biomedical Discourse: An Epidemic of Signification." *Cultural Studies* 1: 263-305.

———. 1992. "AIDS, HIV, and the Cultural Construction of Reality." In *The Time of AIDS: Social Analysis, Theory, and Method*, Gilbert Herdt and Shirley Lindenbaum, eds. 65-100. San Francisco: Sage.

Troidan, Richard R. 1989. "The Formation of Homosexual Identities." In *Gay and Lesbian Youth*, Gilbert Herdt, ed., 43-74. Binghamton, N.Y.: Harrington Park Press.

Turner, Victor. 1967. *The Ritual Process: Structure and Anti-Structure*. Chicago: Aldine.

Tyler, Carol-Anne. 1991. "Boys Will Be Girls: The Politics of Drag." In *Inside Out: Lesbian Theories, Gay Theories*, Diana Fuss, ed., 32-70. New York: Routledge.

Walters, Barry. 1992. "Freddie Mercury: Hot and Sexy." *Advocate* 607 (14 July): 79.

Warner, Michael. 1993. "Introduction." In *Fear of a Queer Planet: Queer Politics and Social Theory*, vii-xxxi. Minneapolis: University of Minnesota Press.

Warren, Carol A. B. 1974. *Identity and Community in the Gay World*. New York: John Wiley.

Weston, Kath. 1991. *Families We Choose: Lesbians, Gays, Kinship*. New York: Columbia University Press.

# Index

adolescence, 89–92, 125–36
AIDS, language of, xiii–xiv, xv, 29, 110, 113, 120–23, 140–58, 171ch8n2, 170–71n3
airplanes, as site for Gay English text, 24–26, 57–60
American Indian English, xvi
authenticity, 5–11, 13, 23, 124, 137, 157–58, 166n3, 169n3

Bankhead, Tallulah, 27, 167–68n3
bathrooms, as sites for Gay English text, 46–47, 74–89, 116
Bolton, Ralph, 150
*Boys in the Band* (Crowley), 12
Bronski Beat, 94–96
Butler, Judith, xii, 161, 172n1

cities, gay migration to, 89–97
cooperative discourse, xii, 1–4, 9–11, 13–16, 18–20, 21–23, 24–48, 50–53, 53–57, 57–60, 160

de Certeau, Michel, 74, 165n3
department stores, as sites for Gay English text, 13, 42–44, 53–57
discourse, defined, xvii
double subjectivity, 13–15

entertainment media, as sites for Gay English text, 26–27, 92–97, 130–31, 158

Feldman, Douglas, 172n5

Garland, Judy, 96
gaydar, xxi, 49–66, 168ch4n2
Gay English: AIDS and (see AIDS, language of); authenticity in (*see* authenticity); "city," descriptions in, 89–97; cooperative discourse in (*see* cooperative discourse); defined, xii; defusing tension through, 9, 15, 32–35, 38–39, 41–42, 45, 65; desire, as language of, xii, 124, 150–57; erotic referencing in, 1–2, 28–30, 89, 121–22, 124, 150–57, 160; exaggeration in, 20, 38, 68, 162; gay culture and, 4, 21, 75, 89, 132, 163, 166n7; gay space and, 74–108; graffiti and, 74–89; heterosexual discourse, contrasts with, 29, 66–69, 69–70, 70–72, 89–97, 104, 108, 109–24, 166n2; homophobia and, 10, 69–70; inferencing in, 3, 25–26, 51–53, 55–56, 59–60, 95, 96–97, 117–19, 121–22, 130–34, 137, 149–50; jokes in, 132–33; life stories in, 128, 138–39, 141–50, 166n7; metaphor in, 15, 21–22, 26–30, 51–52, 56, 71–72, 95, 152, 154, 162; minstrelsy in, 9, 21–23, 38–39, 162; nonverbal communication in, 3, 26, 41, 59, 62, 65,

179

WILLIAM L. LEAP is professor (and former chair) of anthropology at American University in Washington, D.C. He is the author of *American Indian English* (1993), coeditor of *Language Renewal among American Indian Tribes* (1982), and numerous articles on American Indian languages, language education, and applied linguistics. Recent articles on Gay English have appeared in *New York Folklore, High School Journal,* and in his edited collection *Beyond the Lavender Lexicon* (1995). With Ellen Lewin, he has coedited the first in-depth analysis of issues surrounding fieldwork, interpretation, and writing in lesbian and gay anthropology (1996). Leap was cochair of the Society of Lesbian and Gay Anthropologists (1989-91), is a member of the executive committee of the Anthropology and AIDS Research Group, and is the cochair of the American Anthropological Association's Commission on Lesbian and Gay Issues in Anthropology. Leap lives in Washington, D.C., where he continues his research on the language of the gay city.